A Led Zep Scrapbook

Volume One

Edited by Jonathan Downes
Typeset by Jonathan Downes
Cover and Internal Layout by Jon Downes for CFZ Communications
Using Microsoft Word 2000, Microsoft , Publisher 2000, Adobe Photoshop.

First edition published 2010 by CFZ Publications

**CFZ PRESS
Myrtle Cottage
Woolfardisworthy
Bideford
North Devon
EX39 5QR**

© CFZ MMXVIII

All rights reserved. Without limiting the rights under copyright reserved above, no part of this publication may be reproduced, stored in or introduced into a retrieval system, or transmitted, in any form of by any means (electronic, mechanical, photocopying, recording or otherwise), without the prior written permission of both the copyright owners and the publishers of this book.

ISBN: 978-1-908728-79-1

Over the Hills and.....

Let me take you back to the early summer of 1989. It is early evening, and we are outside a slightly ramshackle village hall in rural South Devon. The honeysuckle is blooming, and the air is sweet with its intoxicating scent. Two cock blackbirds are shouting obscenities at each other as they have a glorious Mexican stand off at the side of the dusty car park.

A battered long-wheelbase Ford Transit van is parked unobtrusively in the corner, and sitting on the tailgate are two men. You will recognise one of them immediately, but the other – with shorter hair and a smaller stomach, but still with a messy beard and wild, staring eyes – is me. A much younger me, a few weeks short of my 30th birthday. The other man is dressed in impeccable rock star good taste. Not for him, snakeskin boots and a studded leather jacket; but one can tell that the simple linen shirt that he is wearing probably cost as much as the van on whose tailgate we are sitting. Who is it?

Bloody hell! It's John Paul Jones!

What is the bass player of Led Zeppelin doing sitting on the tailgate of a knackered transit van with yours truly? Well, it's a long story.

At the time, I was running a small and generally unsuccessful music magazine, and I had been contacted by a folk music of polish extraction. His name was basil, and it turned out that he was playing a gig in a village hall on the outskirts of Totnes. Would we like to come and cover it?

Well, I didn't have any more gainful employment at the time, and I was minded to go out for a jolly in Totnes. But I don't think I sounded very enthusiastic on the telephone, and Basil – thinking that his journalistic fish was going to escape from the hook – dropped the big one. Was I interested in the fact that his bass player that night, on what was probably the only contra-based balalaika in South Devon, an enormous triangular instrument that looked like something out of a science fiction movie, was none other than John Paul Jones.

Now, was I interested? Well, what do *you* think?

We drove to Totnes in a state of high excitement, and I wasn't sure how the hell I was going to play this. Here was one quarter of the greatest rock band in the world, and I was a mentally ill wannabe journalist on the dole with a magazine that sold approximately 100 copies. What on earth was I going to do?

Furtively, we entered the village hall in time to watch the sound check. After the sound check we introduced each other to Basil and then did what every journalist has done ever since journalists were invented, and went up the road for a beer. The Gods of journalism were on our sides that night, because sat in the beer garden with a bunch of equally looking rock and roll group of friends, was Mr Jones. We sat at the next table staring at him in awe and wondering what the hell we were going to do. Eventually, my friend gingerly walked up to him, explained who we were, and asked if we could have an interview. Much to our great delight, Jones said yes, but only after he and his friends had had their evening meal. So, we retired back to our table, drank beer, and watched the rock star elite having their dinner. After about half an hour they went back down the hill and we followed them, cornering John Paul Jones for a memorable chat that will live in my memory as probably the most impressive interview I have done. The only other contender for that title being when I met Dave Brubeck a few weeks later. But that is another story.

At the beginning of the interview, John said, in a jocular manner that we could ask him anything except about Jimmy Page and Black Magic, or some of the then current legal problems, which the band were going through. He said it as if he was joking, but there was a steely glint in his eye which told me that he most certainly wasn't.

That was nearly three decades ago, and in the intervening time the greatest band in the world has only played two gigs, but they are still probably the most iconic members of the pantheon of rock royalty.

It is difficult to analyse quite why this is. They only released 8 studio albums, and at least one of them which is not as high quality as its predecessors. In the years since they originally split, legal challenges have been mounted against quite a few of their most iconic songs, claiming – and more than that, *proving* – that several of these songs, which had been credited to the band, were actually ripped of from other, less well known, musicians and songwriters. Jimmy Page has struggled with drug problems, and his highly publicized interest in the work of master magician Aleister Crowley has led to all sorts of unpleasant speculation about deaths and other misfortunes associated with the band. Several high-profile books have "exposed" alleged activities on tour involving drugs, groupies, and a dead fish, and in many ways, Led Zeppelin's reputation has been tarnished by this.

But they are still the greatest rock and roll band that has ever existed. Megalithic riffs, arcane lyrics and some of the classiest and most elegantly brutal arrangements ever put on tape mean that we forget all the nonsense; Led Zeppelin's standing as the über-rockers is secure, well beyond the projected life span of any of the band, and probably of any of the people reading this book.

Here, collected for the first time is the first volume of a fascinating collection of press releases and other memorabilia, which give a unique insight into how the band and its various alumni operated.

Enjoy!

Jon Downes
Gonzo Multimedia
December 2017

March 5, 1975

LED ZEPPELIN "PHYSICAL GRAFFITI" ALBUM SHIPS "GOLD" AND "PLATINUM"
SIXTH CONSECUTIVE SUCH TRIUMPH FOR GROUP;
MORE THAN TEN MILLION DOLLARS RETAIL BUSINESS ASSURED

Led Zeppelin's new album, "Physical Graffiti," a two-record set on Zeppelin's Swan Song label was immediately certified by the RIAA as a gold album upon its first shipments, it was announced today by Swan Song Vice-President Danny Goldberg.

"Physical Graffiti," the first Zeppelin album on Swan Song thus became the first certified "gold" album on an Atlantic Records distributed label since the inauguration of the new RIAA standards for "gold": in excess of 500,000 units. Since advance shipments were actually in excess of 1,000,000 units, the album immediately earns the catagoriztion of "platinum". "Physical Graffiti," thus becomes the sixth consecutive Led Zeppelin album to go "gold" and "platinum".

With a retail price of $11.98, the initial orders alone indicate a total retail gross sale of more than ten million dollars. Jerry Greenberg, President of Atlantic Records said, "No album in Atlantic history has ever generated so many immediate sales." Atlantic distributes Swan Song.

"Physical Graffiti" is the second gold and platinum album

-more-

444 MADISON AVENUE • NEW YORK, N.Y. 10022 • (212) 752-1330 • CABLE: SONGBIRD

-2-

for Swan Song in its ten months of operations. The first was Bad Company's "Bad Co.". Swan Song's other album, "Silk Torpedo," by the Pretty Things, has gotten bullets from the trades four weeks in a row. Forthcoming albums are "Suicide Sal," by Maggie Bell and "Straight Shooter," by Bad Company.

* * * * * *

November 11, 1975

From: Fran Fiman
       Janine Safer

<u>MIDNIGHT SPECIAL "TRIBUTE TO LED ZEPPELIN" AIRS NATIONWIDE NOV. 14</u>
<u>INCLUDES INTERVIEW WITH ROBERT PLANT;</u>
<u>FIRST U.S. TV APPEARANCE EVER BY A MEMBER OF ZEPPELIN</u>

The NBC-TV Network show "Midnight Special" being broadcast nationwide on Friday, November 14, includes a "Tribute to Led Zeppelin". This tribute includes an interview with Zeppelin lead singer Robert Plant -- the first TV appearance ever in the United States by a member of the English supergroup who hold record sales and attendance records around the world.

The interview was conducted at the Los Angeles NBC studios last March at the end of Led Zeppelin's last tour, with disc jockey J.J. Jackson, who currently works for radio station KLOS in L.A. Plant originally did the interview along with Pretty Things lead singer Phil May, in conjunction with a musical performance by the Pretty Things, who record for Zeppelin's Swan Song label. Procedural complications made it impossible for the Pretties segment to be broadcast, but Plant recently consented to allow the segment of the interview with him alone to be used as part of the Midnight Special "Tribute".

The interview is particularly timely in light of the recent car crash Plant and his family were involved in in Greece, which

-more-

444 MADISON AVENUE • NEW YORK, N.Y. 10022 • (212) 752-1330 • CABLE: SONGBIRD

-2-

caused the indefinite postponement of Zeppelin tours. Plant's ankle was fractured in the accident -- and while he has been seen a lot recently around L.A. and is known to be in good spirits -- and working hard on writing material for the next Led Zeppelin album -- he still cannot put any weight on his right foot, and no Zeppelin tour is currently scheduled.

J.J. Jackson was selected to do the interview because of his long friendship with Led Zeppelin, dating back to 1969 when J.J. was a disc jockey on Boston F.M. station WBCN, and was the first there to play the group's debut album.

Led Zeppelin consists of Plant, lead guitarist and producer Jimmy Page, drummer John Bonham, and bassist and keyboard man John Paul Jones. All six of their albums have been certified as "platinum" meaning more than one million copies sold in the U.S. alone. World wide they have sold more than 15 million albums. The song "Stairway To Heaven" from their fourth album has been voted by fans at FM stations across the country as the most popular song of the decade -- and they still hold the record for the largest paid attendance ever for one act: 56,800 on May 5, 1973 in Tampa Stadium, Florida. Their most recent LP, a two record set called "Physical Graffiti," was number one around the world. The members of Zeppelin and their manager Peter Grant own their own label, Swan Song, which has earned three "gold" albums in its first year of existance.

* * * * * * * *

Enc.

FROM THE LED ZEPPELIN FILM

"THE SONG REMAINS THE SAME"

From: Janine Safer
     Sam Aizer

October 8, 1976

SWAN SONG RELEASES LED ZEPPELIN FEATURE FILM

STARRING JIMMY PAGE, ROBERT PLANT, JOHN PAUL JONES, AND JOHN BONHAM

DISTRIBUTED BY WARNER BROTHERS

TWO RECORD SET SOUNDTRACK RELEASED ON SWAN SONG

CHARITY PREMIERES TO BENEFIT THE SAVE THE CHILDREN FEDERATION

    The long wait is over -- Led Zeppelin comes to the cinema in THE SONG REMAINS THE SAME. A motion picure record of the group's explosive 1973 Madison Square Garden performances, THE SONG REMAINS THE SAME captures the being and essence of the four people who make Led Zeppelin the most exciting and durable of rock groups.

    A film directed by Peter Clifton and Joe Massot, produced by Swan Song, Inc., with Peter Grant executive producer, the Warner Brothers movie has taken three painstakingly precise years of work to reach the cinema.

    Incorporating live concert footage, fantasy sequences, backstage glimpses of the band, and a personal view of them at ease at home, THE SONG REMAINS THE SAME is a rare and human look at four rock musicians: Jimmy Page, Robert Plant, John Paul Jones, and John "Bonzo" Bonham. The film was their idea, their project totally, and it is their special way of giving their millions of friends what they have been clamoring for -- a personal and private tour of Led Zeppelin.

444 MADISON AVENUE • NEW YORK, N.Y. 10022 • (212) 752-1330 • CABLE: SONGBIRD

Page has been at work on the soundtrack for three years, refining and honing, matching film and sound to perfection. Released as a Swan Song album, the two record set ships platinum the second week of October.

The movie opens October 20 in New York (Cinema 1) and October 22 in Los Angeles (Fox Wilshire), San Fransisco (Metro 1), Chicago (McClurg Court), Dallas (North Park 2), Toronto (Varsity 2), Boston (Cheri 1), and Atlanta (Loew's 12 Oaks 1). A limited number of tickets will be available to the public for the premieres -- October 19 in New York and October 21 nationwide. All proceeds will go to the Save The Children Federation. Premiere tickets go on sale at 9:00 AM, October 16, at the respective Box Offices.

THE SONG REMAINS THE SAME reveals the members of Led Zeppelin as they really are and, for the first time, the world has a front row seat on Led Zeppelin.

From: Janine Safer
Sam Aizer
Mitchell Fox

January 9, 1978

LED ZEPPELIN SWEEP MUSIC POLLS FOR FIFTH CONSECUTIVE YEAR

FIVE FIRST PLACES IN CIRCUS-----FOUR FIRST PLACES IN MELODY MAKER

JIMMY PAGE BEST GUITARIST IN NEW MUSICAL EXPRESS AND GUITAR PLAYER POLLS

For the fifth consecutive year, Led Zeppelin swept the top honors in the major U.S. and U.K. music polls. In Circus Magazine's Shure Music Awards Poll, Zeppelin took five first places including best group. In Britain's Melody Maker four top prizes were garnered. Completing the sweep, Jimmy Page seized top honors for his guitar artistry in the New Musical Express and Guitar Play polls.

The readers of Circus voted Robert Plant best male vocalist by a margin of over two to one topping Queen's Freddie Mercury. Jimmy Page took the honors as top guitarist and producer, and Page/Plant were again named best songwriters. In addition, John "Bonzo" Bonham was voted third best drummer and John Paul Jones placed third in the bass division.

In Britain's prestigious Melody Maker poll the sweep was repeated as Led Zeppelin were voted best group; Page and Plant best guitarist, producer and vocalist, respectively.

With eight, million selling albums behind them, Led Zeppelin's popularity continues to grow. This year they established themselves as the world's biggest concert draw setting the world's number one and two box office gross records. At the Oakland Stadium

444 MADISON AVENUE • NEW YORK, N.Y. 10022 • (212) 752-1330 • CABLE: SONGBIRD

pg. 2

(July 23&24), they played before 115,000 people, grossing $1,322,500 and for their six nights at Madison Square Garden (June 7,8,10,11,13,14) they grossed $1,146,367.50.

    LED ZEPPELIN are currently planning a new studio album.

From: Janine Safer
Sam Aizer

October 15, 1976

<u>LED ZEPPELIN ON NATIONAL TELEVISION</u>

<u>SEGMENT FROM FEATURE FILM "THE SONG REMAINS THE SAME" ON
DON KIRSHNER'S ROCK CONCERT</u>

<u>FIRST ZEPPELIN PERFORMANCE EVER ON T.V.</u>

A segment from Led Zeppelin's long awaited feature film, THE SONG REMAINS THE SAME will be aired on Don Kirshner's nationally syndicated televison show "Rock Concert". The segment will include a concert performance of "Black Dog" and a portion of "Dazed and Confused", incorporating Jimmy Page's fantasy sequence. This is the first Zeppelin performance ever on television.

Three years in the making, THE SONG REMAINS THE SAME is a personal and private tour of Led Zeppelin, in concert and beyond. The concert footage was filmed at Madison Square Garden during their record breaking 1973 tour. The fantasy sequences of each member of the band - Jimmy Page, Robert Plant, John Paul Jones, John Bonham, and their manager Peter Grant -, for the first time delve into the imagery and symbolism of these men and their music.

The broadcast times of Don Kirshner's Rock Concert are as follows: New York - Saturday, October 23 (1:00 AM); Los Angeles - Sat., Oct. 23 (1:00 AM); Chicago - Fri.,Oct.29 (midnight); Philadelphia - Sat.,November 11 (1:00 AM); Detroit - Fri. Nov.19 (11:00PM) Pittsburgh - Sun., Oct. 24 (1:30 AM); Dallas - Sat., Nov. 11 (12:30 AM); St. Louis - Sat., Oct. 23 (midnight); Houston - Sat., Nov. 6 (6:00 PM);

444 MADISON AVENUE • NEW YORK, N.Y. 10022 • (212) 752-1330 • CABLE: SONGBIRD -cont.-

-2-

Atlanta - Sat., Oct. 23 (11:30 PM); Miami - Sat., Nov. 6 (1:00 AM); Tampa - Sat., Nov. 12 (1:00 AM); and Balitimore - Fri., Nov. 12 (2:00 AM). For the air dates and times in other cities, please consult local listings.

The film will open October 20 in New York and October 21 in Los Angeles, Dallas, Chicago, Toronto, Boston, San Fransisco, and Atlanta.

A two record soundtrack live LP will be released on Swan Song, Led Zeppelin's record label on October 18. The record is shipping platinum.

Led Zeppelin

ATLANTIC 82144

- A definitive four CD/four cassette/six LP boxed set.
- Contains 54 tracks personally selected and sequenced by Jimmy Page, Robert Plant & John Paul Jones, and digitally remastered this year under Jimmy Page's supervision.
- Contains the single b-side "Hey Hey What Can I Do," available here for the first time on album.

SONGS *Whole Lotta Love ◆ Heartbreaker ◆ Communication Breakdown ◆ Babe I'm Gonna Leave You ◆ What Is And What Should Never Be ◆ Thank You ◆ I Can't Quit You Baby ◆ Dazed And Confused ◆ Your Time Is Gonna Come ◆ Ramble On ◆ Travelling Riverside Blues ◆ Friends ◆ Celebration Day ◆ Hey Hey What Can I Do ◆ White Summer/Black Mountain Side ◆ Black Dog ◆ Over The Hills And Far Away ◆ Immigrant Song ◆ The Battle Of Evermore ◆ Bron-Y-Aur Stomp ◆ Tangerine ◆ Going To California ◆ Since I've Been Loving You ◆ D'yer Mak'er ◆ Gallows Pole ◆ Custard Pie ◆ Misty Mountain Hop ◆ Rock'n'Roll ◆ The Rain Song ◆ Stairway To Heaven ◆ Kashmir ◆ Trampled Underfoot ◆ For Your Life ◆ No Quarter ◆ Dancing Days ◆ When The Levee Breaks ◆ Achilles Last Stand ◆ The Song Remains The Same ◆ Ten Years Gone ◆ In My Time Of Dying ◆ In The Evening ◆ Candy Store Rock ◆ The Ocean ◆ Ozone Baby ◆ Houses Of The Holy ◆ Wearing And Tearing ◆ Poor Tom ◆ Nobody's Fault But Mine ◆ Fool In The Rain ◆ In The Light ◆ The Wanton Song ◆ Moby Dick/Bonzo's Montreux ◆ I'm Gonna Crawl ◆ All My Love*

	LP	CASSETTE	CD
LED ZEPPELIN ATLANTIC 82144	82144-1-SB 0 7567-82144-1 7	82144-4-SB 0 7567-82144-4 8	82144-2-WC 0 7567-82144-2 4

PRICE CODES: SB = $54.98/WC = $69.98

Complete catalog information is available in Atlantic's Release #10 Sales Book.

CUSTOMER ORDER DUE DATE: AUGUST 31st
TENTATIVE STREET DATE: OCTOBER 23rd

LED ZEPPELIN BRICHT ALLE REKORDE

"1974 - hat das überhaupt stattgefunden ?" fragte Led Zeppelins Wundergitarrist Jimmy Page ironisch in einem Interview, und er fügte hinzu : "1975 wird besser !" In der Tat es geht schon mächtig los : Nach zwei ausverkauften Konzerten in Rotterdam und Brüssel, wo die Rückkehr der von manchen totgesagten britischen Band besiegelt wurde, gingen sie gleich anschließend auf eine 60-Tage-Tour nach Amerika. Alle Konzerte wurden innerhalb weniger Stunden ausverkauft. Im legendären "Madison Square Garden" in New York spielten die Hardrocker (mit neuer modernster Anlage) drei Tage. Schon vier Tage vor Schalteröffnung hatten sich Schlangen von Fans gebildet, die sich mit Schlafsäcken und Proviant ausgerüstet hatten. 50 000 Tickets wurden verkauft.

Ärger gab es dann in Boston. Der Grund : Einige tausend außer Rand und Band geratene Jugendliche, die um Eintrittskarten anstanden. Die Hallendirektion hatte, um den Fans eine kalte Nacht unter dem frostigen Himmel von New England zu ersparen, die Halle für die Übernachtung zur Verfügung gestellt. Das Ergebnis : Beschädigtes Inventar im Werte von 30 000 Dollar. Die Stadtväter untersagten daraufhin das Konzert und verhängten für die Zukunft generelle Rock-Sperre über den "Boston Garden".

Ein Konzert in Palm Beach (Florida) wird unter freiem Himmel veranstaltet : Auf einer Rennbahn in der 150 000 Menschen Platz finden können.
Led Zeppelin ist zur Zeit dabei, die eigenen Besucherrekorde zu brechen, oder die, die die Beatles einmal aufgestellt haben.

WEA Musik GmbH · A Warner Communications Company · 2000 Hamburg 76 · Gustav-Freytag-Str. 13 · Telefon Hamburg 2 20 14 81-7 · Telex 2 14 861 wea

Interpret:	LED ZEPPELIN	Best. Nr.: SSK 89 400 G
Titel:	PHYSICAL GRAFFITI	
Seite A:	Custard Pie (4:20)/The Rover (5:54)/In My Time Of Dying (11:08)	
Seite B:	Houses Of The Holy (4:01)/Trampled Under Foot (5:38)/Kashmir (9:41)	
Seite C:	In The Light (8:46)/Bron-Yr-Aur (2:07)/Down By The Seaside (5:15)/ Ten Years Gone (6:55)	
Seite D:	Night Flight (3:37)/The Wanton Song (4:10)/Boogie With Stu (3:45)/ Black Country Woman (4:30)/Sick Again (4:40)	
Produzent:	Jimmy Page / Executive Producer: Peter Grant	

"Wenn schon eine neue Platte, dann soll sie auch perfekt sein," sagt Led Zeppelin-Sänger Robert Plant. Während andere Gruppen mit neuen Plattenveröffentlichungen nur so um sich werfen, glänzt Led Zeppelin durch eine für seine Fans quälende Zurückhaltung: Jedes Jahr nur eine Platte. Doch auch dieses Konzept haben sie nun durchbrochen: Auf "Physical Graffiti" mußte man zwei Jahre warten. Doch dafür ist es auch eine Doppel-LP. Noch einmal Robert Plant: "Wir peitschen uns nicht in den Tod. Wenn wir keine Lust haben, oder keine Einfälle, dann machen wir eben Pause - zum Auftanken."

"Physical Graffiti" ist Zeps sechstes Album - und das erste Doppel-Album.
Vor etwa einem Jahr begannen die Arbeiten in verschiedenen Studios. Robert Plant berichtet: "Es begann eigentlich wie immer ziemlich planlos. Wir blödelten herum, spielten alte Sachen, probierten neue aus. Und nach einigen Tagen merkten wir, daß wir ein Doppelalbum machen würden."
Die Aufnahmen dauerten dann - mit Pausen - vier Monate. Robert Plant: "Wir lassen uns von keinem hetzen. Wir lassen uns auch keine Deadline aufzwingen. Wir geben die Platten auch erst frei, wenn wir sie perfekt finden. Wenn wir noch Fehler entdecken, geben wir die Veröffentlichung eben nicht frei. Die Philosophie der Band ist, daß wir etwas tun, wenn wir es wollen und wann wir es wollen."

Page, Bonham, Plant und Jones sind inzwischen auch Mitbesitzer einer eigenen Produktionsfirma : "Swan Song". Dies ist die erste eigene Schallplatte, die auf dem neuen Label erscheint. Sie ist 82 Minuten und 39 Sekunden lang.

CUSTARD PIE

Ein klassischer Zeppelin wie "Black Dog" oder "Immigrant Song". Page spielt die Gitarre wie ein Maschinengewehr. Eine Komposition von Page und Plant, aufgenommen in Ronnie Lanes "Mobile Studio".

THE ROVER

Aufgenommen im fahrbaren Studio der Rolling Stones. Hier wird besonders deutlich, daß sich die Zeppelin nicht als Stars empfinden, sondern als ein Kollektiv. Textzitat : "It's the new world rising from the ashes of the old, if we can just join hands, that's all it takes."

IN MY TIME OF DYING

Mit 11:08 Minuten die längste und eine der wildesten und tanzbarsten Nummern der Gruppe. Als Komponisten zeichnen alle vier.

HOUSES OF THE HOLY

Das war auch der Titel der letzten Zeppelin-Veröffentlichung vor zwei Jahren. Ein ausgesprochen "freundliches" Rock-Stück. Der Text ist sogar lyrisch : "There's an angel on my shoulder, let me wander in your garden."

TRAMPLED UNDERFOOT

Das sind die vitalen Hardrocker, wie das Publikum sie mag. John Paul Jones diesmal am Clavinet.

KASHMIR

Ein völlig untypisches, aber sehr schönes Stück von Bonham, Page und Plant. Was nach einem ganzen Streichorchester klingt, ist Page an der Gitarre, die er mit dem Bogen streicht. John Paul Jones spielt Mellotron. Eine Impression aus dem Vorderen Orient.

IN THE LIGHT

Der Anfang erinnert stark an George Harrisons indisch beeinflußte LP "Wonderwall". Doch dann geben sich die Zeppeline wieder zu erkennen. Ein sehr spannendes Stück mit starken rhythmischen Spannungen.

BRON-YR-AUR

Fast ein Zwischenspiel zur Entspannung. Ein Solo von Jimmy Page auf der akustischen Gitarre.

DOWN BY THE SEASIDE

Eine einfache Ballade im Stil Neil Youngs. "But in the country hear the people sing, see what they are growing, know where they are going. The people turn away." John Paul Jones am Electric Piano.

TEN YEARS GONE

Ein schwermütiges, ruhiges Stück, wie man es eigentlich von Zep nicht erwartet. Page ist wieder überall - er spielt sechs Gitarren, u.a. eine zwölfseitige. "As it was then again it will be, rivers always reach the sea."

NIGHTFLIGHT

Ein Ohrwurm nach Art der Stones. Sehr leicht, lustig und "kommerziell". Fast ein "Schlager". Ein verschleppter Boogie Woogie.

THE WANTON SONG

Das ist der Sound mit dem die Zeppelin zur Zeit die amerikanischen Konzerthallen füllen. Laut, kraftvoll, Robert Plant nannte es mal "männlich".

BOOGIE WITH STU

Stu ist Ian Stewart, der Hauspianist der Stones, der mit Page in den frühen Yardbirds-Tagen gearbeitet hat. Man bekommt Angst um die Stimme von Robert Plant.

BLACK COUNTRY WOMAN

Zunächst Solo für Gitarre und Stimme, dann steigt Bonham mit der Fußtrommel ein. Archaischer Baumwollpflücker-Blues. "If you don't love me your sister will". Bestechend durch seine Einfachheit.

SICK AGAIN

Mit einem typischen Zeppelin-Stück verabschieden sie sich, rhythmisch kompliziert, satter Sound. Bitte laut hören !

Hamburg, Februar 1975

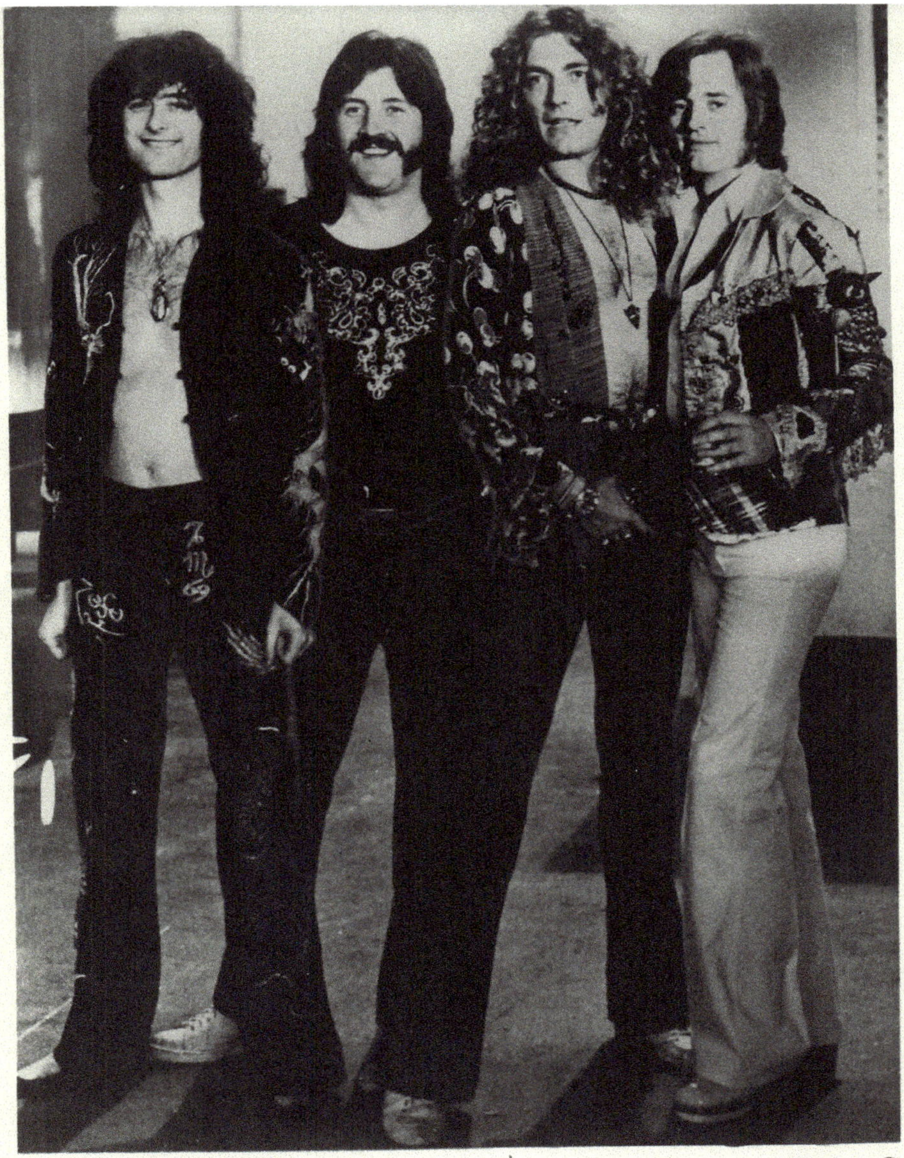

LED ZEPPELIN
From left to right: Jimmy Page, John Bonham, Robert Plant and John Paul Jones.

LIMITED EDITION PROMO PACK MAY 1997

The Led Zep Scrapbook Volume One

> "When Led Zeppelin played a concert it wasn't just a concert. It was an event." — Peter Grant 1993

POP SCENE — MONDAY, FEBRUARY 3, 1969

Led Zeppelin: fast becoming Cream of crop

Of all the memorable things which happened during Toronto's two heavy rock shows last night (Led Zeppelin at the Rock Pile; the Turtles and Iron Butterfly at Massey Hall) one visual image easily stood out.

It was the sight of Led Zeppelin's hero-worshipped lead guitarist, Jimmy Page—resplendent in avocado velvet suit, bent over as if in agony to the audience, his fingers working like a touch typist's, his foot thumping like a kangaroo's tail, the sounds as clear and as piercing as a bedside phone in the stillness of 3 a.m.

Above all else, and there were highlights aplenty, it was Page's night. He arrived in Toronto, without a record on the market but with a reputation that long ago preceded him.

Several critics, myself included, had suggested Led Zeppelin just might be the next so-called super group, the likes of Cream and Hendrix. Advance airplay and reviews of the debut Led Zeppelin album (to be issued on Atlantic shortly) brought over 1,200 people to the Rock Pile. They expected a lot, and few were disappointed.

Led Zeppelin is a quartet, consisting of John Paul Jones on drums, John Bonham on bass and singer Robert Plant, as well as Page. Considering the group was only formed a few months back, it's remarkably tight and together.

Comparisons with Cream are as inevitable as they are unfair. Page is not yet in Eric Clapton's class, but he has the potential. Bonham is not Jack Bruce but, likewise, he's on the right road. Jones is a fine drummer with precision timing, but Ginger Baker had that scene all wrapped up.

Led Zeppelin is not Cream, nor will it fill the spot left behind by Cream. Nobody will. But the Zeppelin outfit has a thing going of its own, and there's little doubt that that thing is going to be very successful.

Page came off as the finest group guitarist to emerge since Clapton. Already, he is way above Jeff Beck, Mike Bloomfield and Elvin Bishop. His spotlighted work, including the riffs with the violin bow, was executed expertly, without pomp or pretension.

Singer Plant is from the English blues school—hard, angry, defiant, gutsy. He could well develop into one of the big name group singers of the year.

Seattle, Wed., July 18, 1973

Dedicated Fans Enthralled By Led Zeppelin

A rainbow of color shot up from behind Led Zeppelin at the mid point of their concert last night at the Seattle Center Arena.

Above their heads, cut glass globes spiraled in the darkness, scattering bits of white light off the Coliseum dome to create the glow of a thousand shooting stars.

'n front of and below this visual onslaught stood the four Englishmen whose phenomenal appeal with Seattle youth remains an enigma that only a dedicated fan could unravel.

This group made their initial Seattle success in 1969 at the short-lived Seattle Pop Festival.

One would think that because of the band's complex approach that their popularity would center on high school and early college students who find themselves on the outer fringes of general society.

But if last night's teeming throng of some 14,000 spectators is representative of Led Zeppelin's audience as a whole, then it is clean-cut, well-dressed, and uniformly attractive youngsters who dig their music.

It is difficult to analyze the reasons behind a sellout crowd and album sales in the millions. Jimmy Page's guitar never quits. The burden of melody falls on his shoulders, except when bassist John Paul Jones doubles on organ.

Page is at home in the blues — but Led Zeppelin is a much more inventive group, and instead of staying with a familiar blend of bass and guitar patterns used by many "heavy" British musicians, they go on to explore the extremes of electronic sound which on occasion breaks away from music and into a dark and primitive area of human experience.

Maybe this is one reason why Led Zeppelin reaches middle-class Seattle youth. Their music, their lighting, such stage effects as smoke pouring out across the expanse of stage, and their almost satanic individual appearances, may offer the extreme contrast to comfortable contemporary living that is offered.

The music is obviously intended to heighten or prolong a drug experience, or may be a drug experience in itself.

The far-reaching effects of ethereal key changes, sharp dynamic contrast from very soft to very loud, and the use of the organ at key intervals, can produce a sense of spiritualism that works on the same principle as a church choral service.

But these are only guesses. Led Zeppelin's music has secrets which a generation that has been schooled in rock music intuitively feels. Part of the financial success of such concerts as last night's is due to the social bond felt by 14,000 kids raising their voices in unison.

This group speaks a dialect that only a select audience can adequately interpret. Just as the elderly bear wisdom that the young cannot understand, so also do the young share rituals that are meant for no one's ears but their own.

OMNIBUS PRESS

Led Zeppelin
The Concert File
Dave Lewis & Simon Pallett

This major new Led Zeppelin publication explores in greater detail than ever before the in concert history of one of the most successful bands of all time. Every known Led Zeppelin concert is logged in a day to day style accompanied by countless set lists, first hand views and group anecdotes.

Much more than a mere reference list, **Led Zeppelin - The Concert File** offers a new angle on the story of how Led Zeppelin developed into the greatest live rock attraction of their era - from one night stands at the Fishmonger Arms in London, across the ballrooms of the famous American Fillmore venues to the record breaking massive stadium achievements of the late 70's, the final UK appearances at Knebworth and last tour over Europe in 1980.

The book is illustrated throughout with nearly 300 photographs - many of them rarely seen, with over 50 spread over a 16 page colour chronology section.

Photo highlights include rare off-stage shots taken on their first tour of Copenhagen in 1968 - the first known live shot of the group taken as the New Yardbirds on October 18, 1968, unpublished live photos from the Brondby Pop Club 1969, soundcheck scenes from Perth Australia 1972, the unscheduled show in Jersey in 1975, plus candid offbeat pics from their final US tour in 1977. The cover illustration is a striking sepia tinted shot from an open air appearance that accurately reflects their on-stage pulling power.

There are also over 200 reproductions of rare Zeppelin concert memorabilia items including original adverts, posters, ticket stubs, backstage passes, press reviews etc - presenting a stunning visual history that compliments the text.

A DIVISION OF BOOK SALES LIMITED/
MUSIC SALES LIMITED
8/9 FRITH STREET, LONDON W1V 5TZ
TELEPHONE 0171.434.0066
FACSIMILE 0171.734.2246
WEB http://www.musicsales.co.uk
E-MAIL music@musicsales.co.uk

PRESS RELEASE

The Led Zep Scrapbook Volume One

The main Concert File text not only profiles every Zeppelin tour, there are summary asides on key songs and events plus full details of group members' guest appearances and all the post Zeppelin reunions such as Live Aid and the Atlantic 40th Birthday show - leading to full coverage of the Page Plant MTV filming thus bringing the story full circle.

In addition to the main Concert File text, the book includes full appendices of the respective solo careers of the ex members with tour by tour gig itineraries - logging over 400 Robert Plant shows and 150 Page appearances. There's also complete coverage of the 115 shows that formulated the Page Plant World Tour of 1995/6 with relevant set list details.

Finally the Bootleg File section offers a perspective on the abundance of releases that make up the vast catalogue of Led Zeppelin live unofficial CD's with a guide to 85 essential titles.

It all adds up to one of the most comprehensively researched rock publications ever attempted - a lavish publication that sets the record straight on what happened and when from the place where Led Zeppelin functioned best - live on stage.

This is the definitive on stage chronicle that will delight and enlighten the band's countless fans throughout the world.

For further information contact: Dave Lewis (01234 267515)

LED ZEPPELIN THE CONCERT FILE
BY DAVE LEWIS AND SIMON PALLETT
THE PROMO PACK

This Promo Pack has been designed to offer a background perspective to the Omnibus Press publication Led Zeppelin The Concert File

THE AUTHORS:

DAVE LEWIS
Dave Lewis is a well-known and respected authority on Led Zeppelin. He first saw the group play live when he was 15 years old and the effect has been a lasting one. He is the author of several previous books on Led Zeppelin including the highly acclaimed 1991 publication *"Led Zeppelin A Celebration"*. He also edits and publishes the long-running Led Zeppelin magazine *Tight But Loose*. He views the publication of *"Led Zeppelin The Concert File"* as the natural successor to *"A Celebration"*, unfolding the story of the group from the place they functioned best – live on stage.

Dave is a record shop retail manager by profession and lives in Bedford with his wife Janet and two children, Samantha and Adam.

SIMON PALLETT
Simon Pallett is widely acknowledged as one of the world's foremost authorities on Led Zeppelin's live legacy. Over the past 20 years he has researched and analysed a vast collection of Zeppelin's live recorded output. Simon has been involved in several previous Led Zeppelin books, including the final edition of *Live: The Exploration Of Underground Tapes*. The *Concert File* is his first major work. Simon lives in Buckinghamshire with his wife Janet, son James and Ajax the great dane.

THE CONCERT FILE INTERVIEW

The following interview with Dave Lewis and Simon Pallett offers an insight into their thoughts on the collation of the book and Led Zeppelin's live legacy in general. It was conducted in March 1997.

Q: How long has it taken to write and research the book?

DL: The actual writing and collating of information went on non-stop for some 18 months. The idea to do the book had been in the air for a couple of years so I'd been amassing material since 1994. There had long since been a plan to follow up *A Celebration* in some way and Chris Charlesworth at Omnibus came up with the concert log idea. The enormity of the task to get the concert listing as accurate as possible really hit home when we began contacting the many sources for information. Meeting up with Anne Bjorndal who unfolded tales of their early days and the assistance of collectors such as Hugh Jones in Seattle opened up many new avenues for us to pursue.

SP: Dave first suggested the idea to me in late '94 after one of the *Unledded* recordings, so I began collating material for use from that point, although work didn't start in earnest until after the Page/Plant UK tour in the summer of '95. Much of the source material came from Dave's collection and my own collection, so you could say the research began 20 years ago when I first started collecting.

Q: How easy was it working in collaboration?

DL: It became obvious when I was initially approached to do the book that it was a project that demanded much time and attention. To that end I quickly decided to ask Simon to co-author it with me, knowing of his immense knowledge of their live history. The main difficulty was the fact that we lived some 100 miles apart and co-ordinating meetings with our respective schedules was a strain. On top of that there were the endless phone calls and exchanging of info via the post. The latter was not helped by several one day post strikes last summer. It often seemed like we'd never get through it - but hopefully the end result will have been well worth the worry.

SP: With rgard to the content of the book, it was very easy. Dave and I agreed very early on exactly what format the book should take, so there was little conflict in that respect. We both knew what we wanted and it was then just a case of organising the monumental workload to achieve those goals. Most problems we encountered were of a technical nature - computer malfunctions, postal strikes etc.

Q: What was the most difficult period of their live history to gain accurate information from?

DL: Unsurprisingly 1968 and 1969. As so little official data remains from back then, those early itineraries have been a maze. We were still undecided about the opening Scandinavian dates right up to the point of the book being printed. Again the likes of Hugh and Robert Godwin proved to be most helpful when it came to trying to piece together the 1969 dates. In fact in the writing process we actually went backwards commencing with the 1977 to 1980 period, partly to establish a format and pattern but also to avoid confronting 1968 and 1969 until we were good and ready!

SP: Yes, obviously the early years. Local newspaper reports proved invaluable here in trying to piece together exactly what happened and where. Mainland Europe also proved to be a problem area. There seem to be very few rock publications from some countries in the early seventies, and little or no records held at venues, so verification was difficult. Even the 1971 European tour is shrouded in mystery. It's possible they played a full tour, but it's more likely they played selected dates and spent time in the studio re-mixing the fourth album.

Q: There are already many Led Zeppelin books - why is there room for this one and what fresh revelations does it include?

DL: We are aware that there can be only so many ways of telling the story but in doing it this way - in a day to day format

THE CONCERT FILE: THE INTERVIEW

through their on-stage progress - I think it really brings home the various peaks and troughs the band went through. The good nights, the not so good nights and all the craziness that accompanied them in America. This is evident from their formative days - the spring tour of the US in 1970 was fraught with rioting crowds often incited by a heavy police presence. I also think their plight after the misfortune and tragedies post-1975 is chronicled in a way that highlights how they vainly tried to recreate the glory days of their early career.

SP: This is the first book to tell the whole story right from the start through to the current Page/Plant reunion. Most books tell the story vaguely to 1980; this book covers the complete history. This book is also based on fact - something that is often missing from Zeppelin books. I think also presenting their live achievements in log form really recreates the atmosphere and captures the true excitement and mayhem that was life on the road with Led Zeppelin.

Q: They were often riled in the press - are there any scathing reviews that come to mind?

DL: There was certainly no shortage of these to choose from. It's well known that they had a decidedly uneasy ride with the press. There are plenty of examples of that via the less than complimentary press comments included in the book. Some of them may have been justified - but some were well over the top. For pure out and out vitriol the reviews we pulled out of their August 9 '69 Anaheim show and the Copenhagen July 23 '79 show take some beating.

SP: This book is not an exercise in hero-worshipping through rose-tinted spectacles. Zeppelin were not always good. They had bad days and these are covered objectively in the book. Extracts from bad reviews are published as well as the good reviews. Some journalists apparently just did not like Zeppelin and their reviews are more of a personal attack than a comment on music. Some of these are reproduced also, mainly for the humour content and to show just how wrong the press can be!

Q: Much has been previously chronicled about their infamous off-stage antics - do you think this influenced their live performances?

DL: Inevitably it did - and that side has alrady been well covered in the likes of the *Hammer Of The Gods* etc. Whilst we did not need to repeat those antics, there's a constant air of chaos as each tour progresses. You only have to look how often they arrived at a gig on time. The on-the-road fatigue did take its toll although at times they seeed to just get carried along with it all. I think Plant summed it up best after arriving some two hours late for the June 2 1973 Kezar show when he stated, "Now that we've been awake for three hours, we should start feeling like a rock 'n' roll band!"

SP: Most definitely. I think when the band were enoying themselves offstage this certainly added something positive to their on-stage performances. Much of the reported Zeppelin 'road fever' occurred at the Continental Hyatt in Los Angeles (known affectionately as The Riot House), and the Edgewater Inn in Seattle. Concerts in these cities were always among the best of each tour!

Q: Which gigs do you think best chronicle the development of the group through the years?

DL: Well, there are obvious ones such as the Boston Jan 26 '69 show and the early Fillmore dates where they made an immediate impact. Equally important I feel were the lesser high profile tours such as the Japan visit in 1971 and to a greater degree their 1972 US tour. They were vastly overshadowed in the press by the Stones visit that year - but on stage they were just on fire - spurred on by the recent recording of the *Houses Of The Holy* album. You get the situation where they arrive in Seattle on June 19 1972 and proceed to play a three hour set that features four unreleased numbers - one of them twice! They knew they were on the crest of something really special. And Grant knew it too - making sure they had a press agency working with them when they went back the next year. That 1973 US tour was the moment they stopped being a mere rock 'n' roll band and became just about the biggest thing in America since The Beatles.

SP: I think the Winterland show on April 26 1969 was a major show in Zeppelin's development. It was the first show where they performed *Whole Lotta Love* and also the first where Jimmy used the Theremin. The Bath Festival in 1970 was important because it was here that they were first widely accepted by the British public and given the recognition they deserved. There were so many important shows in such a wide and varied career that it's difficult to select just a few. You'll have to read the book to get the full picture!

Q: Which show stands out for you personally?

DL: Obviously the ones I attended are very memorable - the Electric Magic show at the Empire Pool - the five Earls Court shows - that really opened my eyes to how impressive the level of on-stage improvisation had become - and how their shows really had become events. Then there was the sheer emotion of Knebworth and some of the Over Europe dates particularly Cologne where it did seem a rejuvenation was in the air. Luckily we also have first hand evidence of many of their gigs via the tapes and unofficial CDs. As a night of nights, the famous LA Forum June 21 show known as *Listen To This Eddie* takes some beating. That really does display the power they wielded and the ecstatic audience reaction is captured in a way that takes you right back there.

SP: Again, so many it's difficult to choose just a few, but if I was pushed it'd have to be Boston '69, Winterland '69. the Royal Albert Hall '70, Bath Festival '70, any show in Los Angeles or Seattle, Earls Court '75. My favourite tour is probably the brief Japanese visit in 1971. The band were on top form and every show was different - Zeppelin at their improvisational best.

Q: Which individual tracks do you think best personifies Led Zeppelin's live prowess?

DL: For me it's *No Quarter*. This developed into an instrumental tour de force around the 1975 era. The middle section was employed as a very loose improvisation section where John Bonham and Page would drift around the time signatures. One night it might emerge in a jazz vein, another a funk work-out. It was this air of unpredictability that made it so engaging - there were times when they just drifted off into their own little world. And John Bonham's drumming on this track was always superlative - never flashy but always precise and ready to allow Page the freedom to meander around the rhythm. There were similar moments to be enjoyed within the middle section of *Dazed And Confused* during the

THE CONCERT FILE: THE INTERVIEW

same period when they experimented with versions of *Woodstock*.

SP: One of the main attractions of Zeppelin's live show was that they were not just content to reproduce their album tracks onstage. They would use the original recorded arrangement as a basis and then often continue to develop the composition. The original recording of *Dazed And Confused* on the first album runs for just over 6 minutes. By 1975 they were regularly improvising and experimenting so much that the piece was often extended to over 45 minutes in length. *Whole Lotta Love* is also representative of Zeppelin's ability to improvise at will. Onstage this number would often be extended to include numerous rock and roll numbers from the depths of their memories. Rock, blues, soul, funk - were all represented when Zeppelin experimented.

Q: With the onset of punk, Led Zeppelin were at the forefront of the Dinosaur backlash - in studying their live performances during that period, was that criticism justified?

DL: To a point it probably was. There was a need for a fresh re-think when it came to returning to the spotlight at Knebworth. The fact that much of the set was based on the previous 1977 tour hinted at their lack of conviction to rehearse new material. Matters did improve when they did the *Over Europe* tour which was a genuine effort to get away from the big show mentality of the past. They took that particular route as far as it could go in 1977. The *Over Europe '80* tour was a partial success in getting back to basics - although the physical well-being of the group was still in doubt. Maybe they would have put that right had they gone to America as planned in the fall.

SP: Certainly Zeppelin were still very excessive in 1977 While two to three minute songs were the norm with the up-and-coming punk bands in London, Zeppelin were touring America providing 30 minute versions of *No Quarter* and 25 minute drum solos! However the 1977 tour was their biggest ever, so it would appear the public were more than happy with their particular brand of musicianship. The sets were dramatically streamlined for the 1980 tour but I think this is probably the way the band would have wanted to develop anyway. I don't think Zeppelin took the criticism seriously - the press had been proved wrong far too often. Zeppelin made music for themselves, not to appease anybody else.

Q: Had they have kept going, how do you think Led Zeppelin would have fared in the '80s?

DL: A very difficult question to answer. You do get the feeling that Robert had begun to tire of it all. On the other hand if the 1980 US tour had gone ahead and they'd have rekindled that love affair with the American audiences, it may well have motivated them all and opened up a whole new era. I could have envisaged them encompassing things like video and adapting their creativity to that medium and moving with the times. I'm sure the need to do solo projects would have occurred - maybe they would have got together periodically between breaks in the way the likes of Genesis do.

SP: I think that the success or failure of the proposed 1980 US tour would have been important in determining the group's future. Robert had only agreed to do the tour after much persuasion and if he hadn't enjoyed himself I think it may have proved difficult to continue. Also there were health problems, both within the band and the management structure, so Zeppelin may have been on borrowed time anyway. If they had continued I think they would have developed in their usual manner - pushing ever forward, utilising new technology and experimenting with different forms of instrumentation. The results eventually may not have been dissuimilar to what we have today with the Page/Plant reunon.

Q: Why do you think there is so much interest in the group some 16 years after they retired?

DL: Well, Led Zeppelin have proved to be one of the most durable acts of the last 40 years. I think it's a combination of the strength of their studio catalogue, their live reputation which the book highlights, and the mystique that still surrounds them. They enjoyed a relatively short career and the need to examine what happened and when in great detail seems to grow with the passing of time.

SP: The quality of their recorded legacy must be a major factor. Page went to great lengths to ensure that each album was not released until it was as good as he felt it could possibly be. Release dates were often delayed to enable one final remix or even for the colour tone to be adjusted on the album sleeve. Zeppelin's awesome live reputation has continued to impress even among those who never witnessed the group live on stage. I think interest seems to have been perpetuated, in part anyway, due to the countless bootleg releases.

Q: How important are the bootlegs to the story of their live history?

DL: Absolutely essential - whatever the moral standing might be, they offer first hand evidence of just what Zeppelin sounded like on any given night. The market may be over saturated now, and the quality variable, but the fact that so many of those famous shows are available on CD is also another key factor in maintaining the interest of their following. And in producing a book of this kind, the extent of their unofficial catalogue has proved to be a major asset.

SP: Bootlegs are vital evidence of Zeppelin's on-stage power. Without them *The Song Remains The Same* soundtrack would be the sole example of the group's live history and, although it's not a bad album, it's hardly representative of their achievements throughout the band's twelve years of performing live.

Q: Can you see Jimmy Page ever getting around to that long mooted official live chronological live album?

DL: I think that such a project is definitely still in the air - the fact that Page didn't bother remastering *The Song Remain The Same* live soundtrack points to his desire to one day produce a better alternative. Of course, Jimmy is well aware of the amount of live stuff that has made it on to unofficial releases and this has possibly been the main reason for it not happening. I think The Beatles' *Anthology* might be a catalyst in spurring other established acts to chronicle their history. An anthology-type Zeppelin project is a mouth-watering prospect as it could combine the live soundtrack/studio outtakes with the visual material lining their archive such as the Earls Court video footage. It may be a while off in the light of the current Page and Plant activity, but I think Jimmy will want to turn his hand at this in the future.

SP: A live chronology box set would prove an ideal companion to the studio box; and from the sales figures for *Remasters* and the studio box it would certainly seem a financially viable proposition. Robert has always been reluctant in the past to consider a project such as this, preferring to look forward rather than retrospectively back to their former glories. However Robert's views have changed dramatically in recent years and he may now be susceptible to such an idea. Time, therefore, may now be the main consideration. A project of this size would require listening to vast quantities of tapes and selection would not be easy. The next Page/Plant album is obviously now taking up most of their time, and I doubt whether Jimmy will have enough free time for the foreseeable future.

Q: It's good to see their solo careers are covered in the Appendix sections - how do you look back on that era?

DL: Some fond memories. And some strange times. The low point for me was The Firm's inability to gell into what on paper looked a winning combination. In the end it was a mismatch of

The Led Zep Scrapbook Volume One

THE CONCERT FILE: THE INTERVIEW

talent that seemed to hold Jimmy back. Those early Plant tours also seem very quaint now as he attempted to turn away from the past - only to succumb to the inevitable by 1988. When compiling those itineraries it becomes more than evident how prolific Robert was as a solo performer. For me he really excelled on the *Fate Of Nations* tour, turning in some terrific performances - notably Birmingham in July '93.

SP: Both Robert and Jimmy produced some very good work during the '80s, although none of it comes close to the quality of Zeppelin material. Robert worked very hard at trying to establish an identity as a solo performer (in fact several identities) and proving that he could cut it on his terms and without relying on the Zeppelin tag; while I think Jimmy spent a lot of time searching for his previous persona. I don't think Jimmy ever really wanted a solo career; in fact, I don't think Jimmy ever really wanted to do anything else other than Zeppelin. I do however think that *Fate Of Nations* and *Coverdale/Page* were their best solo projects and I think the timing of the reunion was just right.

Q: Before the Page Plant *Unledded* MTV show and world tour, there were several attempts at getting back together such as Live Aid and the Atlantic '88 show - did your research reveal why it took so long for Page and Plant to finally reunite?

DL: It's no real secret that Robert was the continuing stumbling block. He continually made it clear that recreating Led Zeppelin would do irreparable damage to their legacy. The Live Aid and Atlantic reunions were prime examples of the spirit being willing - but other elements clearly spoiling the overall effect. However I think he was beginning to give in around 1990. The Knebworth Silver Clef show with Jimmy really did look as though it would spark something of a permanent reunion of the pair. On the evidence of *Wearing And Tearing* they really should have got together the next week! In the end I think it was the influence of Robert's manager Bill Curbishley that really swayed the balance.

SP: Robert adopted the admirable stance of wanting to move ever forward and not just retreading old glories. In the end, I think it was Bill Curbishley who convinced Robert that he could still achieve this by working with his former partner. There had been previous attempts at re-uniting. In 1985, after Live Aid, they rehearsed in Bath with drummer Tony Thompson, but these rehearsals were fraught with difficulties and eventually abandoned. In 1990, after *Remasters*, there were plans to rehearse, but Robert again is supposed to have vetoed these.

Q: What are your views on the non-involvement of John Paul Jones in the MTV *Unledded* filming and subsequent world tour?

DL: They have gone some way to defending it by stating the need to keep it simple which I can appreciate. There was also the stigma to call it Led Zeppelin had Jonesy been involved. On a pure musician's level though it has to be viewed as a missed opportunity. What I still find bemusing is the decision to name the album *No Quarter* - which surely was a composition that will always be associated with Jonesy.

SP: Obviously who Jimmy and Robert choose to work with is up to them and it's not for me to question their decisions. It could be that they felt the involvement of Jones would push the project a bit too close towards Led Zeppelin or it could just be that they feared it would have caused further problems. It took long enough for Robert and Jimmy to agree on the terms for a joint venture; if things had to be agreed three ways it could only have led to delays and complications. I do, however, think that a little more diplomacy could have been involved in letting Jones know what was going on.

Q: In presenting the *Unledded* MTV special and subsequent world tour, do you think Page and Plant have done justice to their previous live legacy?

DL: Yes, undoubtedly. In re-arranging those old songs they really did add something new to them - particularly the likes of *Kashmir* and *In The Evening*. What was also very pleasing was the way *Calling To You* and *Whole Lotta Love* were used as vehicles for all manner of medley fun - a tactic employed so successfully in the Zeppelin era. Hearing the likes of *As Long As I Have You* and *Boogie Chillun* and *We're Gonna Groove* in this way was a real treat.

SP: Certainly. I'm also particularly pleased that they chose to perform and reinvent numbers that were never played live by Led Zeppelin, such as *Tea For One* and *Custard Pie*.

Q: Has the book turned out the way you originally envisaged?

DL: Yes - it's certainly fulfilled the vision that I originally had for it. Mike Warry, the designer of the book, should take much credit for successfully interpreting that vision in his superb layout. Luckily he was a fan himself which obviously helps when it comes to matching photos with the correct era. It was only when the typeset came back for checking that I saw the full extent of information we had collated. It really does present a complete picture of their entire live history from 1968 to the present day. I'm also pleased with the depth of rare visuals and photos we managed to locate. Coming across that New Yardbirds 1968 shot was like finding the proverbial penny black!

SP: It's better than I originally envisaged it. The finished book is actually double the size of the book originally commissioned by Omnibus. As the writing progressed we soon came to realise that the book would need to be extended to include the level of detail that we wanted to include. Chris Charlesworth was very patient and extended deadlines and budgets on several occasions. In the end, I think it was worth the wait to produce a book of such quality.

Q: Finally what do you hope readers of the book will draw from it?

DL: I hope it's viewed as a major reference work that offers a new angle from which to tell their story - from the place where Led Zeppelin functioned best - live on stage. It's also a book that needs to be listened to as well as read. Even the most casual of fans will have come into contact with their unofficial catalogue on some level and cross referencing the music to the text will certainly add to the enjoyment of the book. It certainly inspired us as we were writing it all! I'd like to think it reads as more than a mere list of dates. I detest the trainspotting criticism that is often levelled at the fascinating minutiae that books of this type present. If this is anorak wearing stuff then I'd better go out and buy one! We actually prefer to think of it as a thirst for knowledge that paints as complete a picture as it could on the subject. I'm very proud of the depth of detail we have amassed - but also hope that within that detail the true drama and musical prowess that surrounded Led Zeppelin as the premier live attraction of their era equally shines through.

SP: I hope readers will gain an understanding and appreciation of the Led Zeppelin live legacy and will be encouraged to learn more. I think it's a book that can be read from the start in normal fashion or could just be repeatedly delved into at random and still found interesting. I hope it's a book that will be enjoyed as often as Led Zeppelin's music should be played!

DL: That's a good tip actually - if you initially approach the book as a novel and read it from page to page the sense of drama that surrounded them is most apparent. In rock terms this really is the greatest story ever told, and telling it this way certainly re-emphasises that claim.

31

The Led Zep Scrapbook Volume One

RECORD COLLECTOR MAY 1997 FEATURE

LED ZEPPELIN THE CONCERT FILE

AUTHORS DAVE LEWIS AND SIMON PALLETT PREVIEW THEIR NEW BOOK ABOUT THE LIVE LEGACY OF THE GROUP AND EXAMINE THE THRIVING COLLECTOR'S MARKET

"When Led Zeppelin played a concert, it wasn't just a concert: it was an event." So said Zeppelin's manager, Peter Grant, in one of his last interviews before his death. It's a statement that introduces 'Led Zeppelin: The Concert File', which is published by Omnibus Press this month.

The book has been written and researched by regular RC Zepp correspondent Dave Lewis with another renowned expert on the band, Simon Pallett. Together they have pooled years of research to come up with a near-definitive, day-by-day log of every Zepp show — over 500 in all, with relevant set-list details, on the road reminiscences and press comments from the time, all illustrated with masses of memorabilia and rare visuals. The book recaptures the era when Led Zeppelin reigned supreme as the world's top live attraction.

Dave Lewis is keen to explain that this book offers much more than an anorak-coated bunch of song-lists and dates: "There are only so many ways the story can be told, and the Zeppelin bookshelf is already creaking under the weight. So rather than just listing the data we had unearthed, we realised that when we chronicled the band's movements on a day-to-day basis, their story unfolded from a new angle. I remember Peter Grant once telling me that Zeppelin was primarily an in-concert band — that's where it really mattered. And when you begin to examine their live history, that fact is entirely evident. Their studio work was just a starting point. Once they were out on the road, they would take the basic structures of the songs and experiment with them as they saw fit. That's what made their performances so unique.

'The Concert File' also presents a wealth of rarely-seen photos and visuals, and the collation of this material presented another real challenge. "It was a priority from the start," Lewis explains. "A call for assistance went out 18 months ago via my Zeppelin mag, 'Tight But Loose', and luckily we had some fantastic responses. Rarest of all was a solitary slide that came in from photographer Graham A. Wiltshire. This was taken at the Marquee on 18th October 1968, when Zepp were still being billed as the New Yardbirds, and it's certainly the earliest colour live shot I've seen."

In detailing Zeppelin's live career, accurate information was essential, as Simon Pallett notes: "We've overhauled all the previous information that has come to light over the years, and studied original cuttings and first-hand accounts to come up with the most accurate gig listing possible. There are no official records in existence for many of Zepp's early tours, so it was a case of painstakingly piecing all the evidence together."

"Something that really became apparent as the text evolved," adds Dave Lewis, "was the sense of drama and chaos that surrounded them as they moved from city to city. It's no wonder that some of their performances were somewhat erratic! The speed of their rise to prominence really hits home as well. From their humble beginnings playing one-nighters at venues like the Toby Jug in Tolworth, they were soon making immediate impact in the States via the Fillmore halls, and then reached superstar stadium status. We've tried to present a front-row seat from which to relive the whole Led Zeppelin concert experience. This is their story as told from the place where they functioned best — the stage.

'Led Zeppelin: The Concert File' by Dave Lewis & Simon Pallett is published by Omnibus Press in May.

WITH THANKS TO PETER DOGGETT /COPYRIGHT RECORD COLLECTOR

LED ZEPPELIN:
The Concert File
Dave Lewis & Simon Pallett
Explores in greater detail than before the in-concert history of one of the most successful bands, telling how the group developed into the world's greatest live rock attraction. Logs every Led Zeppelin concert played and presents appendices of the solo careers of the ex-members, including full coverage of the Jimmy Page/Robert Plant world tour. Masses of rarely seen memorabilia and photographs.
Omnibus Press

Zeppelin's Concert Legacy

LED ZEPPELIN: THE CONCERT FILE
By Dave Lewis & Simon Pallett
Omnibus Press, May 1997

In the last six years it seems that accurately compiling the complete performance chronology of Led Zeppelin's career has grown into something akin to a competitive sport—and the Michael Jordan, Gary Payton and Hakeem Olajuwan of this league have undoubtedly been *Tight But Loose* fanzine editor Dave Lewis, *Collector's Guide* creator Robert Godwin and *Led Zeppelin Live* author Luis Rey.

Now with the release of *The Concert File*, Dave Lewis (in collaboration with UK Zep expert Simon Pallett) has made an ambitious and convincing bid for the championship in 1997.

With the clout and budget of a major publishing company behind them, Lewis and Pallett have undertaken to confirm and compile every live concert, radio performance and incidental appearance Led Zeppelin were party to in their twelve year career (as well as the members' post-Zeppelin activities), lay it out in a chronolgical form liberally peppered with graphics and photographs, and tell the story of what was arguably the greatest live band in rock history. And for the most part, they have succeeded.

The trick with a book like this, at least from a publishing standpoint, is to create something that will reach people beyond the hardcore fans who will buy it sight unseen and produce a book that will appeal to—and educate—those with a more casual interest in the subject.

This goal is achieved largely thanks to the concise and well-written text. Offering a minimum of editorializing and a wealth of hard facts, the story is brought to life by extensive quotes from Peter Grant as well as comments from reviewers, promoters, people who attended Zeppelin concerts and occasionally even members of the band themselves.

With the multitude of previously unseen photos, concert ads, press clippings and ticket stubs, there is no question that the average *Proximity* reader will find much to thrill them in this book; what's most impressive is that anyone else who takes the trouble to get into it will find the fascinating story of a unique and influential band, and in turn a snapshot of a time period in rock music and pop culture that is justifiably considered to be a golden age.

Beautifully designed, laid out and printed, *The Concert File* is a feast for the eyes of any Zeppelin fan. And for the time being, it stands as the *definitive* source for information on the band's performing career—nice job, chaps!

- HJ

REVIEW FROM PROXIMITY / LED ZEPPELIN COLLECTORS AMERICAN MAGAZINE
APRIL 1997

INTERVIEW FROM PROXIMITY / LED ZEPPELIN COLLECTORS MAGAZINE APRIL 1997   (Subscription details from Proximity : PO Box 45541, Seattle, WA 98145 0541, USA)

Dave Lewis talk about Simon Pallett
THE CONCERT FILE

On the eve of the release of The Concert File, here is an inside glimpse into how the book was put together by the authors themselves, via trans-Atlantic interview.

How much freedom did Omnibus Press give you in putting the book together in terms of content, layout and design?

DAVE LEWIS: Omnibus' Editor in Chief Chris Charlesworth oversaw the text but overall we had total control in terms of the content. I had a clear vision of the format I wanted from the start, i.e. a summary before each touring segment, relevant asides, full solo years appendix etc.

In terms of layout—having experienced the compromises that losing control can cause when I did *Led Zeppelin: A Celebration*—I was very keen to have a strong advisory input into how the book looked. The designer Mike Warry worked very closely with us on the selection of photos and general layout. Luckily he is a Zeppelin fan himself and was very aware of the need to match the correct visual with the relevant date and era concerned. To that end I'm glad to report that there are no beards mysteriously infiltrating the visual side of things post-1971!

The book is full of incredibly rare photos—such as Page with the Mickey Finn in the mid '60s and the 'New Yardbirds' in Scandinavia '68—how did you go about finding and getting clearance for all those choice shots?

DAVE LEWIS: One of the priorities with the book was to compliment the information being presented with some fresh visuals. There have been so many Led Zep books now that getting away from the standard Neal Preston-type of shot can be very difficult. Luckily by leaving no stone unturned we came up with a variety of discoveries. In some cases this took months of careful negotiation, others I just stumbled upon.

The Mickey Finn shots turned up in a photo file from an agency Omnibus often uses. In the case of the Scandinavian photos, journalist Anne Bjornfeld, who saw them many times during those early tours, is a reader of *Tight But Loose* and has often told me of the material she had in her possession. Anne came over to London early last year and we met up. It was really like uncovering buried treasure when she brandished a set of photos that had been unseen outside of her collection for 27 years!

Above: The very first tour, Scandinavia 1968. Photo from The Concert File (Omnibus Press)

Below right: Example of a two-page spread from The Concert File, profusely illustrated with rare photos and discussing the U.K. dates of January, 1970.

What was the most exciting find you uncovered while doing your research?

DAVE LEWIS: Visually it has to be the photo of The New Yardbirds taken on October 18, 1968. This arrived at Omnibus from a freelance photographer, Graham A. Wilshire, who was on the rock and pop circuit during the late 60's and early 70's. It was a single transparency that Nikki Russell, the picture researcher at Omnibus, said looked "quite interesting" I could hardly believe my eyes when I had it sent over. Graham told me it was the only photo he took that night. As an image of their embryonic days it really was some find.

With the text itself, one of the most vital additions to our research was the batch of U.S. cuttings provided by a certain H. Jones! We had no shortage of U.K. press material but reviews of dates such as the night they played in Kansas City using borrowed equipment were such an asset.

SIMON PALLETT: For me the whole experience has been one of discovery and rediscovery. In listening to so many tapes I found that previously underrated periods took on new meaning. The 1972 U.S. visit is a prime example. Writing and logging their progress through the years has certainly enhanced my own appreciation of the enormity of Led Zeppelin's achievements as a live band. That's something we hope all readers of the book will share.

How many new dates do you reckon you've uncovered, or wrong dates corrected, based on Godwin's 1995 itinerary as the most comprehensive (and recent) one?

SIMON PALLETT: It's difficult to put a figure on it at all. It's really been a case of overhauling all the informational data we have at our disposal and assessing it. We've certainly benefited from Robert Godwin's unselfish sharing of information. He took the time to verify some of our findings and add his own new discoveries.

What criteria was used for being absolutely certain of a 'suspicious' date?

DAVE LEWIS: A combination of factors. Press ads from the time, firsthand reviews, reminiscences from those that were there. We took all the available evidence and then made a decision. In the case of some dates, particularly the Scandinavian '68 period and various '69 dates, the jury may still be out on our outcome! We await the deluge of feedback from those that may question some of the listings, and I'll certainly be using the next issue of *Tight But Loose* as a platform for future Concert File discussion and revision.

SIMON PALLETT: We don't make any claim to this being a definitive listing, so nothing's cast in stone. It's our own valiant attempt to get it as right as possible but obviously it's open to question.

Only two dates are listed on the mysterious Spring tour of Europe in 1971. What kind of efforts did you put into researching this period, and could you confirm the June 1971 tour dates that Luis Rey listed in the last edition of his book?

SIMON PALLETT: One of the policies we stuck by was that if we were not one hundred percent sure on a date, we would not print it or speculate that it happened. With the earlier, in particular, spring '71 dates, as we state there may have been others performed but no clear evidence has come to light to verify them. One probable reason why that period saw them performing brief stints of dates rather than a full fledged tour is that they were very much tied up in remixing the fourth album at Island Studios, after the earlier stint at Sunset Sound in L.A. had not lived up to expectations. This would certainly have curtailed a full tour at the time. There seems to

Jimmy performing "White Summer" solo on the Julie Felix TV show in London. April 26, 1970, photo from The Concert File (Omnibus Press)

have been so little coverage in the European press for that period so it's all a little speculative. I believe Luis' new book makes the same point about this tour.

One of the outstanding things about the book are the many direct quotes from Peter Grant and others closely connected to the band. Did you have one major source for this material or did you simply compile it from various interviews over the years?

DAVE LEWIS: From the onset we made a conscious effort to make sure the book did not just read like a list of dates and setlists.

Source material to illuminate the spirit of the times was where the bulk of our initial research was directed. This material was garnered from Simon's collection, the TBL Archive, the input from contributors and also talking to associates who had come into contact with who were there over the years.

In the case of Peter Grant, much of the material comes from the two days I spent talking with him in June and October of 1993, the last major interview he gave before his passing. It was then that he made the statement, "When Led Zeppelin gave a concert it wasn't just a concert, it was an event." That really sums up the whole ethic of his steering of the group to become what they did, and as big as they did. I would view the strategy of their 1975 and 1977 touring operations as the blueprint for the big scale tour concepts that exist today with the likes of U2.

Obviously, musically they had to have the chemistry to make it happen, but Peter Grant's re-writing of the rulebook on how this band should be presented live was equally important in carving their lasting live legacy—which is why the book is dedicated to him.

In addition to your input from Peter Grant, how much cooperation did you seek and/or get in working on the book from the current Zeppelin organization?

DAVE LEWIS: Chris Charlesworth is very active in the Trinifold camp with the Who reissue programme, so they had knowledge of the project. However with their schedule it's always very difficult to get direct involvement.

This is an independent Omnibus Press publication but we obviously hope they view the end result favourably—it's certainly a book that should jog their memories on the many remarkable moments they shared on stage all those years ago.

Posing with Julie Felix, April 26, 1970, photo in The Concert File (Omnibus Press)

WITH THANKS TO HUGH JONES/COPYRIGHT PROXIMITY

Kinky Led Zeppelin still king of the funky

By Jack Hafferkamp

Led Zeppelin brought its urban kids' electric circus and hydraulic lift traveling light show to town Monday for the first of three successive nights at the Chicago Stadium.

Think of that—60,000 (give or take a few) tickets gobbled up in a matter of hours. This is no small-time operation.

Led Zeppelin is, of course, the reigning champion of British heavy-kink rock. And they can prove it. The band is the largest selling group in Atlantic Records' sweet history.

All five Led Zeppelin albums have gone platinum (which is to say, over a million units sold).

And in 1973 the band attracted the largest paid attendance to ever line up for one rock act, when 56,800 people crammed into a Florida stadium to see them strut their heavy-duty stuff.

MONDAY'S audience was, not surprisingly, what might be termed basic Chicago downer-teen funky. The kids were there to, you know, get down.

But actually, I don't remember seeing quite so many never-been-shaved cheeks at previous Zep extravaganzas. And I know I've never before heard so many boys with prechanged voices.

Just before the show began, an announcer came on to brief the crowd on what it could and could not do. I wouldn't want to imply he was condescending or scornful, but his rap went something like:

"The request of the group is that you stay in your seats. That's the group's request, OK? And don't climb over the barricade, OK? And don't stand up in your seats, either. OK?..."

FOR ITS PART, the band played a new variation on its standard heavy-heavy, super-loud, bare-chested, Victorian decadent, fingernail polish and lipstick, kiss-me-because-I'm-really-funky, cartoon performance. Two hours worth.

Still, there were a few surprises. My companion, for example, noted she owns a blouse just like the one singer Robert Plant was wearing.

Drummer John Bonham played what must have been the longest drum solo in the history of mankind.

Caz, the fan who stops at nothing

SOME pop music fans will go to any lengths to worship their heroes — but not many will go as far as 19-year-old Caz Frattley who decided in fact was the right length as far as her favourite group — Led Zeppelin — was concerned.

Caz, of Westmorland-close, Leyland, decided to show her affection for one of the world's leading underground groups by writing a 31-ft. long fan letter to them.

She fitted 25 song titles — distinguished from the rest of the words by "deep purple" letters — into her fan letter. The letter took two days to work out and three nights to write on to the back of several rolls of wallpaper.

"By the time she had finished, the heavy letter had her rocking and reeling almost as much as the heavy music of Led Zeppelin.

"I was relieved when it was finished, my back was aching," admitted Caz, a telephonist.

She posted the letter to the Guildhall in the hope it would find its way to the group before tonight's sell-out concert. Caz now hopes that the fan letter might get her the introduction she has been after to her favourite member of the band — singer Robert Plant.

A Led Zeppelin fan for more than three years, Caz has not been able to meet the group at either of the two other concerts she has seen.

Her husband Eric got tickets for the concert scheduled for January 2nd in Preston but the group had to cancel the date because of illness.

live & recorded
...comes Led Zeppelin

by Ben Blummenberg

The Led Zeppelin landed in Boston, Thursday Jan. 22, and for four consecutive evenings virtually blew an overflow Boston Tea Party crowd clear into the Charles River. Playing long sets, well over an hour in length, the Zeppelin lived up to its advance billing as a group of exceptional power and drive. What also emerged, however, is that the L.Z. possesses extraordinary complexity as well.

Both the official publicity on the band, and the unofficial rumor mill, told of a blues rock unit built around the guitar genius of Jimmy Page. (Jimmy Page is the last of the three exceptional lead guitarists produced by England's amazing Yardbirds. The other two are Eric Clapton and Jeff Beck.) This description just scratches the surface. The Led Zeppelin is launched from a blues-rock base but is no means limited by it. Furthermore, the L.Z. is truly a talented and diversified unit, not just a backup group for Jimmy Page.

In concert, the L.Z. went through most of the material on their first album (Atlantic 8216) plus some newer, unrecorded songs. The titles and lyrics may be basic blues, but the approach and performance is of a much wider scope. Perhaps the most outstanding feature of the Zeppelin is that they employ three of four major instrumental concepts in almost every song. The impression, to say the least, is staggering! Indeed the L.Z.'s only fault is a tendency to compress too much into a short space of time.

Rhythm changes abruptly, time patterns change abruptly, volume levels change abruptly, yet melodic lines and chord skeletons manage to merge kaleidoscopically as each member of the band feeds one another and in turn plays off the ideas thrown out. The entire approach is very loose and very improvisational. The result is a surprising intricacy developed out of a form that is usually considered to be quite simple. Yet the basic power is never lost.

In one sense, the Led Zeppelin represents the best of two worlds.

A few things that particularly got me: 1) At various times during "You Shook Me" Robert Plant (vocals) and Jimmy Page (lead) play riffs off against each other with Plant's voice frequently acquiring the electrical qualities indistinguishable from Page's guitar. 2) A 5-minute drum solo by John Bonham that includes some fantastic and hysterical hand drumming but really defies description. 3) The frequent quiet passages in "Black Mountain Side" by Jimmy Page, which approach the best of pure mountain music.

For my taste, the Led Zeppelin really gets it all together on "How Many More Times," with which they like to close an evening. This ten-or-more-minute master-piece has one of the most infectious rythmns core I ever heard. If you don't want to jump, dance, and smile after hearing this, you must be dead. This core, which involves everybody, provides the departure point for extended individual solos by each member of the band. The technically impressive pile driving bass of John Paul Jones is a spiritual gift. Plant's amazing vocal power is at its best. Jimmy Page's virtuosity runs the gamut from explorations into abstract electronics to down-home funk. "How Many More Times" is one of those rare rock developments that could literally never end. The wild, screaming reception accorded the Led Zeppelin certainly bears this feeling out.

I expect the Led Zeppelin to be flying high for some time. They and the Jeff Beck Group are to rock what Formula One cards are to road racing. Their raw power is compelling and hypnotic while their complexity makes repeated exposure a pleasure. The L.Z. vary the arrangements of the same song on successive nights quite widely. As Jimmy Page who has little sympathy with complicated synthetic studio effects, said to me: "If we can't do it live, we won't do it." That L.Z. hits me just right, as does the entire Led Zeppelin from stem to stern.

ZEPPELIN PACK 'EM IN

ROBERT PLANT, lead singer of the high-flying Led Zeppelin, said recently in London the group wanted to tour America again because audiences here are so "ultra responsive."

His observation was correct, but even the Led Zeppelin was obviously not prepared for the reaction they caused Saturday at the Pacific Coliseum as nearly 19,000 rock fans jammed the building for the group's first concert in a 19-city tour. Although it started before/an hour late, the concert was already blasted by the fact that there were none of the often tedious and time-consuming supporting acts.

Led Zeppelin walked onstage at 8:30 p.m., took control and didn't stop through two and a half hours of glorious, ear-splitting rock.

They are essentially the same group they were here last year, with as many new builds as there were noticeable improvements.

Except for a few minor mechanical problems during the opening of Dazed and Confused, Led Zeppelin succeeded in their heavy brand of rock that everyone craves to hear.

The only new material offered was the song Since I've Been Lovin' You, to be released soon on Led Zeppelin III. Its raw, physical qualities make the album one worth looking forward to.

And no one really opined that they played songs from their first two albums. From the raw, gutsy sounds of How Many More Times, to the beauty of Heartbreaker, there was a complete improvisation that is Heartbreaker.

Robert Plant, the physical and vocal ground of the group, turned the crowd on at will with his shaggy blond mane and his searing three-octave voice.

The lead guitar of Jimmy Page was a constant delight to the senses, particularly in his much-improved White Summer solo.

Drummer John Bonham demonstrated his talent in a 15-minute stick-twirling and bare-handed exhibition that exhausted himself and the listener, while bass guitarist John Paul Jones more than kept the beat alive.

As the concert drew to a close during the heavy pitch of Whole Lotta Love, the massive crowd surged forward and about 70 ecstasies fans spilled it for the group and the audience by rushing up onto the 15-foot-high stage.

"Never before in the history of Led Zeppelin has this happened," Plant shouted mockingly into the microphone, not knowing whether to be offended or flattered.

The one stage was finally cleared, Led Zeppelin came back for two encores and a standing ovation that was a fitting tribute to one of the most talented rock groups in the business today.

String quartet in concert

Guest artists at the next concert in the Vancouver Women's Club Musical Club current concert series will be the Purcell String Quartet of the Queen Elizabeth Playhouse, in a program starting at 8:15 p.m.

The quartet, which is made up of leading members of the Vancouver Symphony Orchestra, is currently in the middle of the second major concert series in the Vancouver Art Gallery, and has received widespread critical acclaim.

"When Led Zeppelin played a concert it wasn't just a concert. It was an event." Peter Grant 1993

Pop i Reventlowparken
NUSK
I MORGEN SPILLER
YARD-BIRDS (England)
og
BEATNICKS (Norge)
Ang. busser: Se annoncern ovrsl.

ELECTRIFYING ZEPPELIN

WELL over a thousand people were packed into the dance hall of the Belfry, Sutton Coldfield, for what turned out to be the greatest rock concert ever seen there. No strangers to the Birmingham area, Led Zeppelin put over the heaviest rock sound for three hours powering through new and old numbers.

To see them perform is quite an experience. With Robert Plant shaking his head and madly hopping round the stage. Jimmy letting loose some fluent licks and John and Bonzo piling on the power. There is a good deal of co-ordination between Jimmy and John. Each seems to know what the other will do — no mean task and the well known riffs seem to possess an electrifying intensity as they reverberate from the massive stacks.

The material battering the fans from all sides included the old favourites "Since I've Been Loving You," "Communication Breakdown" and the immortal "Whole Lotta Love," with "Black Dog," "Going To California" and the aesthetic "Stairway to Heaven" from the fourth album.

Their stage show is so exciting that you have to become involved as they go from side to side. Their albums don't seem to make you realise this, but are a good second-best if you are one of those who couldn't manage the concert tour. — **TONY McNALLY.**

YARDBIRDS CHANGE

THE YARDBIRDS are to change their name after two farewell performances this weekend — at London's Marquee tomorrow (Friday) and Liverpool University on Saturday.

From Sunday the group will be known as Led Zeppelin. The line-up is Jimmy Page (lead and steel gtr), John Paul Jones (bass gtr, organ), John Bonham (percussion) and Robert Plant (lead singer, bass gtr., harmonica).

The Led Zeppelin will make its record debut with an album which they have just completed and which will be released in December. A single will also be released around the same time.

Led Zeppelin
(MADISON SQ. GARDEN, N.Y.)

Madison Square Garden was packed for three concerts by rock supergroup Led Zeppelin, who wound up their successful U.S. tour with the Britishers' first Gotham appearance in almost two years. The quartet led by vocalist Robert Plant and lead guitarist Jimmy Page, gave the young crowd their money's worth the first night, Friday (27).

The only act on the bill, the Atlantic disk artists performed for 275 minutes with the sole pause being between finale and encore. The three Concerts East sellouts grossed an aggregate $390,000 at a $7.50 top.

Led Zeppelin, the combo who displaced the Beatles as British's top group before that famed act broke up, delivered an almost-nonstop program of faves and newer tunes, from blues-rock to rock 'n' roll. Plant started weakly, but soon caught fire as he strutted and sang with drive.

Plant's classiest moment, perhaps, came when he saw security forces having difficulty clearing the centre orchestra aisle. He admonished the fans to "stop acting like children," a far cry from the taunting of security personnel which is considered "in" by too many acts.

Page, one of rock's premier guitarists, was in top form on regular electric and doubleneck. John Paul Jones, an addition to his steady work on bass guitar, had more action on keyboards than previously, playing organ, synthesized piano and mellotron. Page also had a turn on synthesizer. The drumming of John Bonham was steady throughout, but his solo had little to offer, but length, bettering 15 minutes.

Led Zeppelin's gimmicks included mirrors at the rear of the stage, smoke, smoke-flash torches, and a fired ring around a gong. But all that was really needed was the quartet and their overpowering music. — **Kirb.**

Led Zeppelin's excited fans given shower

Although they won't even arrive for another month, the hard-rock group Led Zeppelin created a commotion here Sunday which brought down the house in spots around town and unleashed a fire hose on some exuberant fans.

In South Houston, the police had to call fire trucks to "hose down" about 3,000 fans of what critics have called "the world's most popular band."

They were part of the stampede in this area for tickets to the group's Feb. 28 concert at The Summit. Tickets went on sale for one day only at 8:30 a.m. at four Warehouse Records and Tapes stores.

With only 18,000 seats available, the faithful camped out Saturday night waiting for a chance to buy them. And when the doors of the record stores opened Sunday morning the crowd began to roar.

Cleve Howard, owner of the stores, said it is the last Zeppelin concert he will serve and added that Zeppelin does not allow promoters to sell tickets by mail because the group "thrives on the publicity these things create."

Bill Paustenbach, 20, arrived to work at the company's Westheimer location just after the windows had been broken and a customer taken away in an ambulance, his face cut open.

"All we could see were police cars," said Paustenbach. "People really wanted to go to this thing. If they got tickets they would walk out in a daze saying how great it was."

Store officials instructed the successful buyers to hide their tickets and leave by the rear to avoid having them stolen by the crowds which remained.

South Houston police confirmed that a line of "3,000 or 3,500" outside the 1400 Spencer Highway store was scattered with high pressure fire hoses.

"Instead of moving back and straightening up, they just sat down. We kept them in line with the water," a police officer said. "It seemed to work." The temperature ranged in the upper 30s.

No one was arrested at the ticket sales locations.

Lon Bozarth, supervisor for the record stores, criticized the Houston police: "They didn't do anything. Maybe they figured we should hire private guards to handle it."

Bozarth called Sunday's stampede the worst incident in the store's concert ticket sales history.

GRÖNA LUND
STOR POPFINAL!
Engelska Yardbirds på Stora Scenen kl 20. I morgon Hep Stars.

YARDBIRDS

4 da'r kvar tills Gröhan stänger.
Så än finns det hopp. An lyser Tornet.
An striker man'j Bergbanan, Dansar.
Kör Go-Cart. Spisar. Har kul.

Gröna Lunds-varieten med fint program på Gamla Scenen kl 21.30.

Snurrmästakrobaterna Golden Maet historiens högt över Stora Scenen kl 23.

Lecuona Cuban Boys på Tyrol. Spansk-show. Bord 62 18 82 från kl 18.

Lennart Wärmells orkester på Dans Ut. Fri entré till discoputen på Dans In.

Mera pop! Pete Proud och Merry Go Round på Jump In!

Hela Grönan öppnar kl 19. Tel. 67 01 85.

Thunderstorm, stormy fans end concert

TAMPA, Fla. (UPI) — City officials, reeling from a mini-riot which erupted when a thunderstorm washed out a Led Zeppelin concert, canceled a rain-check re-run yesterday, leaving fans from as far as Michigan and New York holding "rain or shine" ticket stubs.

"If I were in Buffalo, I'd go home right now," said Donnie Strickland. The 19-year-old man and three companions had driven 24 hours to get to Florida for the concert.

Strickland said they were the first ones in the stadium when the doors opened at 11:30 a.m. Friday for the 8:30 p.m. concert. After spending the day in 90-degree weather on the sun-baked football field, they settled down for the concert.

The British band played for 20 minutes before the thunderstorm hit. About 45 minutes later the concert was called off.

The cry, "We want Zeppelin! We want Zeppelin!" came from the 70,000 fans as rocks and bottles began flying onto the stage.

"We had what had to be called a small riot," a Tampa police spokesman, Johnny Barker, said. "There were between 3,000 and 4,000 people who were unruly and disorderly."

About 250 police officers, all in riot gear and using billy clubs, broke up the rioting and herded the fans out of the stadium.

The melee left an estimated 100 fans with injuries. Eight were arrested.

LED ZEPPELIN THE CONCERT FILE PROMO PACK INSERT: WITH THANKS TO STEVE CONNOLLEY AND HUGH JONES. WHERE ARE YOU NOW CAZ?!

LED ZEPPELIN THE CONCERT FILE
50 BRAINTEASERS FROM THE FILE...

1. Which blues legend did Led Zeppelin share top billing with at The Roundhouse, London on November 9 1968?

2. In which American city did they make their US live debut?

3. Which Yardbirds hit did they perform during the second set at their Jan 10 1969 Fillmore West appearance?

4: Who previously recorded *Fresh Garbage* and *As Long As I Have You* - two often performed cover versions on their early tours?

5: Name the only occasion they shared the bill with The Who.

6: When was *Whole Lotta Love* first heard on the radio?

7: "A lot of people thought we weren't gonna come here today" - Plant to the audience at which July 1969 US gig?

8: Name three acts who appeared with Zeppelin on the 1969 Bath Festival of Blues.

9: Who amongst their touring entourage of the time inspired the name The Nobs which they adopted for the Feb 28 1970 KB Hallen show?

10: Which band did Robert and Bonzo jam with at Birmingham Mothers' Club on May 24 1970?

11: Who invented the Theremin?

12: Which US DJ introduced them on stage at the LA Forum on September 4 1970?

13: At separate shows on the 1971 UK spring tour Plant made reference to hits of the time by The Mixtures and Ray Stevens. Name the two songs mentioned.

14: When and where was *Stairway To Heaven* first performed live?

15: True or false - *Gallows Pole* was only ever performed live once?

16: "You should have come last night. Last night there were several bowler hatted beatnics". Plant to the audience at which 1971 US show?

17: Which film theme did Page incorporate into *Dazed And Confused* during a performance in Manchester on the 1971 November UK tour?

18: What's the connection between Kylie Minogue and their appearance at the Coventry Locarno in December 1971?

19: At which show did they perform *Dancing Days* twice?

20: "Jimmy sprained his finger two days ago and we had to cancel last night. He's been playing tonight and putting his hand in a bowl of cold water to keep the swelling down". Plant to the audience at which 1973 US gig?

21: Which film studio did they rehearse at prior to the 1973 US tour?

22: Who eventually headlined the Knebworth festival bill that Zeppelin turned down in July 1974?

23: Name five musicians who jammed on stage with Zeppelin during their career?

25: What's the connection between the film *Deep Throat* and their appearance at the LA Forum on March 27 1975?

26: Which five DJs introduced the band on-stage at the Earls Court shows in May 1975?

27: "I think football's a load of bollocks" - John Bonham to the audience at which 1975 UK gig?

28: What number did Page and Plant perform with Bad Company at the LA Forum on May 23 1976?

29: Name two musicians who jammed with Zeppelin during their rehearsals at Manticore Studios in early 1977.

30: True or false - *Black Dog* was not played live on their 1977 US tour?

31: "The man who played the Los Angeles Aztecs and beat them 10-1 by himself" - Plant to the audience at which 1977 US gig?

32: Name three UK journalists who were name checked on stage by Plant during their career?

33: When was *Over The Hills And Far Away* first performed live on the 1977 US tour?

THE CONCERT FILE: BRAINTEASERS

34: What was the last song Zeppelin performed live in America?

35: Which UK group did Page jam with in September 1977?

36: Under what pseudonym was Plant credited for on the sleeve of the Dansette Damage single he was involved in?

37: When and where was it first announced that Zeppelin would be appearing on the 1979 Knebworth bill?

38: Name four acts that were originally touted for the Knebworth '79 bill but did not appear in the final line-up.

39: At which show did Jimmy's Zoso symbol last appear attached to his amp set-up?

40: "We'll shortly be doing Eleven Years Gone" Plant to the audience at which 1979 gig?

41: How much did the Knebworth tickets cost?

42: Name three Zeppelin shows that were curtailed before their scheduled finish?

43: "Good evening. Right, well we're here, aren't we? We've go a little number now . . . it's called with a bit of rough translation 'Schwartz Hund' " - Page to the audience at which 1980 Europe show?

44: Which city was their 1980 American tour due to commence at?

45: Which Led Zeppelin songs did Robert Plant perform without Jimmy Page at the 1990 Silver Clef show at Knebworth?

47: Which former Zeppelin set opener did Page and Plant perform as an encore at the 1994 Alexis Korner benefit show at the Buxton Opera House?

48: Which number did Page and Plant open with at their August 25 1994 *Unledded* filming performance?

49: Which artist jammed with Page Plant and Jones on the performance of *When The Levee Breaks* at the Hall of Fame Induction on January 12 1995.

50: At which show was *Custard Pie* first played live by Page and Plant on their World Tour?

The answers are all revealed within the text of Led Zeppelin The Concert File.

COMPETITION ANSWERS OFFER:
If you think you can search the answers out, submit them to the TBL address, 14 Totnes Close, Bedford MK40 3AX.
The first three most correct answers to the 50 questions will each receive a special Concert File promo item. Closing date is 1/8/97. Full details and answers will appear in the next issue of Tight But Loose.
Dave Lewis and Simon Pallett welcome any feedback on the text and general comments on the book. Write to TBL Concert File Feedback, 14 Totnes Close, Bedford MK40 3AX,
or via the TBL website at
http://www.linwood.demon.co.uk/index.html
E-mail address is: david@linwood.demon.co.uk.

For details of the Tight But Loose magazine/Page Plant Information Service send an sae to TBL, 14 Totnes Close, Bedford MK40 3AX.

LED ZEPPELIN THE CONCERT FILE PROMO PACK compiled March 1997. Text: Dave Lewis/ Simon Pallett. Layout and design Dave Lewis/ John Jones.

THE CONCERT FILE UPDATE STARTS HERE

As with any bank of information of this nature, 100% accuracy is always hard to maintain. Despite many hours of checking we've already noticed some gremlins affecting one or two of the photo captions in the finished book.

"Premiering Hot Dog, Knebworth August 4 1979" on page 132 should have read "Premiering Hot Dog in the UK at Knebworth August 4 1979" (it was first aired at the Copenhagen show on July 23).

A last minute photo switch led to the live Page Plant photo on page 170 being wrongly captioned: It's not as listed, from the Poole Arts Centre, but taken earlier on the first leg of the US tour. We knew it - you probably knew it but somehow it didn't get corrected at the right moment.

Other factual amendments to note: The re-scheduled date at Liverpool University on May 10 1971 occurred on a Tuesday not a Monday as we list it. The show at the Coventry Locarno we had listed as Tuesday, December 7 1971 actually took place two days later on Thursday December 9.

Those are some of the amendments that have come to light at the time of writing - we welcome any further feedback and additional information/corrections etc. A full update of all revisions and comments received will appear in the next issue of **TIGHT BUT LOOSE**.

LED ZEPPELIN THE CONCERT FILE
50 FACTS FROM THE FILE

- Their first tour together was a trip to Scandinavia in September 1968 where they were still billed as The Yardbirds. Early dates included support from a topless go-go dance act known as The Ladybirds.

- Their first concert billed as Led Zeppelin occurred at Surrey University on Friday October 25 1968.

- Their first US tour saw them supporting the likes of Vanilla Fudge, Iron Butterfly and Alice Cooper. They were quickly elevated to top billing after making an immediate impression on the American college circuit.

- On January 26 1969 Led Zeppelin performed at the Boston Tea Party venue. After playing their standard set, the ecstatic crowd refused to let them leave the stage. They carried on playing old rock 'n' roll standards and Beatles covers, finally clocking in a four-hour set. "For me that was the key Led Zeppelin gig" recalled John Paul Jones. "It was then I realised what Led Zeppelin was going to become."

- Their early set lists were fleshed out with cover versions such as of *Train Kept A Rollin'* which The Yardbirds had featured, Garnet Mimms *As Long As I Have You* and Chester Burnett's *Killing Floor*.

- On March 5 1969 the group had trouble gaining entry to a show they were due to play at the Locarno Ballroom, Cardiff - because they did not have the regulation collar-and-tie on. A fact recalled years later on stage by Plant during their May 24 1975 Earls Court show.

- Led Zeppelin's one and only live TV appearance in the UK took place in Studio G at the BBC's Lime Grove studio on March 21 1969. At short notice they replaced The Flying Burrito Brothers to perform *Communication Breakdown* on the BBC1 arts show *How Late It Is*. The tapes of this show have long since been wiped.

- On June 27 1969 the group recorded a pilot show for BBC Radio One in front of an audience at London's Playhouse Theatre. The resulting broadcast on August 10 set the pattern for the station's long running *In Concert* series.

- Zeppelin played a host of summer outdoor shows in the US in 1969. This included a date on the Woodinville Park Pop Festival in Seattle on July 27 where they shared the bill with, amongst others, The Doors, Chuck Berry, Vanilla Fudge and Ike and Tina Turner. The next day the infamous mud shark groupie incident took place at The Edgewater Inn, Seattle.

- At a date at the Kansas City Memorial Hall on November 5 1969 when Zeppelin found themselves having to borrow equipment from support act Morning Star after their PA and instruments were inadvertently shipped to San Francisco.

- Their January 9 show at the Royal Albert Hall in 1970 was filmed by noted '60s film director Peter Whitehead for an intended group financed TV documentary; however they were unhappy with the end result and the film remains unreleased.

- At a date in Copenhagen on February 28 1970 they appeared under the name The Nobs when Count Eva von Zeppelin - a descendant of the original airship designer - threatened to sue the group if they used her family name whilst in Denmark.

- The UK and European tour dates in early 1970 were the last time Page was seen playing a rare Gibson Les Paul Black Beauty guitar he'd had since 1962. Usually kept back for the studio, he began using it on the early tours. However during a flight switch in Canada it went missing. Despite an advert being placed in the *Rolling Stone* for information leading to its return it was never seen again.

- Page returned to the BBC's Lime Grove Studio in the spring of 1970 to perform a solo version of *White Summer* on the Julie Felix TV show. The show, which also featured a guest appearance by The Hollies was aired by BBC1 on April 26. This does exist in the BBC archive, albeit with slight line interference.

- On June 28 1970 Led Zeppelin played to over 150,000 at the giant Bath Festival near Shepton Mallet. It was this festival that inspired the attending Michael Eavis to begin the Glastonbury Festival, staged nearby which is still going strong today. The group's headlining act that day was a turning point in their recognition in the UK.

- Following their appearance at the LA Forum on September 4 1970 (immortalised on the *Live On Blueberry Hill* bootleg), the band jammed with Fairport Convention at the Troubadour Club. Fairport were recording a live album on the night but the Zepp/Convention jam tapes were soon in the hands of Peter Grant and never released.

- Zeppelin were approached to perform a show in Germany on New Year's Eve 1970 which would have been relayed via satellite coast to coast to America. Their manager Peter Grant turned down a fee reported to be in the region of $1,000,000 when he discovered the quality of such a link could be affected by bad weather.

- *Stairway To Heaven* was first heard on the radio during the April 4 1971 Radio One *In Concert* broadcast of Led Zeppelin. Over the next two decades, the celebrated anthem went on to rack up 3 million plays worldwide on its way to becoming the most requested song of all time.

- The group's May 3 1971 show at the KB Hallen, Copenhagen featured the only know appearance of *Four Sticks* and one of the few occasions they played *Gallows Pole* live. Both numbers would enjoy over 100 performances apiece when Page and Plant undertook their World Tour some 25 years later.

- Their appearance at the Vigorelli Stadium in Milan on July 5 1971 was cut short when a riot broke out between tear gas throwing police and the fans. They vowed never to return to Italy again.

- Zeppelin set lists were littered with rock 'n' roll cover versions. Their visit to Japan in September 1971 found them in particularly playful mood offering up versions of The Beatles *Please Please Me*, Cliff's *Bachelor Boy* and Ricky Nelson's *Hello Mary Lou*.

- By 1972 their set lists were regularly clocking in at over 3 hours. A prime example was the Seattle Coliseum show on June 19 of that year. This saw them premiere

The Led Zep Scrapbook Volume One

50 FACTS FROM THE FILE

- *The Ocean*, *Dancing Days*, and *Over The Hills And Far Away*, tracks from the yet to be released *Houses Of The Holy* album and perform a rare complete version of *Black Country Woman* - which was eventually released on the *Physical Graffiti* album in 1975.

- All 110,000 tickets for their 24 date UK tour that spanned December 1972 and January 1973 sold out in just four hours.

- The two opening dates on the group's ninth US visit in May 1973 attracted over 100,000 alone. The 56,800 who crammed into the Tampa Stadium on May 5 helped establish a record previously held by The Beatles for the largest audience for a single act performance in entertainment history.

- For their 1973 and '75 American tours, the group rented their own personal jet - a full sized Boeing 720B known as The Starship.

- Just prior to their final date at Madison Square Garden on July 29 1973, Zeppelin's road manager Richard Cole discovered that $180,000 of the group's money had been stolen from a safe deposit box at The Drake Hotel New York. The theft and money went undetected.

- The group made no live appearances together during 1974, concentrating instead on recording their sixth album *Physical Graffiti* and setting up their Swan Song label.

- There was no shortage of offers for them to perform during that year - promoter Freddie Bannister thought he had secured them to top the bill at the Knebworth Festival but Peter Grant had second thoughts before signing. Bannister was to be more successful five years later.

- *Kashmir* made its live debut on a warm up date at the Rotterdam Ahoy on January 11 1975. It was performed at every show from then on.

- *Dazed And Confused* was played live for the last time in full at their final Earls Court show on May 25 1975.

- When Robert Plant suffered multiple injuries on the Greek island of Rhodes in August 1975, the group were forced to cancel a projected stadium tour of America for which over 100,000 tickets had already been sold.

- The group made an unscheduled return to the stage on December 10 1975 with an impromptu appearance at Beehan's West Park night club in Jersey in front of an audience of just 350.

- The film of their 1973 Madison Square Garden shows *The Song Remains The Same* was premiered in October 1976. It was voted Best Documentary and Best Soundtrack by the prestigious Films And Filming magazine. The resulting film soundtrack album is Led Zeppelin's only official live release.

- There are of course countless unofficial live Led Zeppelin bootleg albums and despite legal clampdowns the market continues to flourish, making it possible to hear many of the gigs featured in the *Concert File* book. There are now over 700 Led Zeppelin CD bootleg titles covering live and studio material.

- Their final tour of America in 1977 was the biggest of them all - over a million fans attended the 43 shows. Logistically and technically it was a tour that would pave the way for the large stadium mega shows that are commonplace amongst today's major artists.

- The group's live sound was projected by a massive PA system supplied by Showco Inc, containing an output of 100,000 watts - a further 80,000 watts of power was used by a complex lighting system, including the use of krypton lasers.

- In attracting 76,229 fans to the Silverdome Pontiac on April 30 1977, the group broke their previous record set up in Tampa four years earlier for the largest single act attendance in history.

- A return date to the scene of that 1973 feat in Tampa on June 3 1977 ended in chaos when the group was forced to leave the stage after just 20 minutes when a thunderstorm broke out.

- Their final US concert at the Oakland Stadium in California was played out under something of a cloud after Bonham and Grant were involved in a violent backstage row with promoter Bill Graham's staff the previous day.

- Zeppelin's final UK dates took place on August 4 and 11 1979 when they attracted over 320,000 to the Knebworth Festival over the two weekends. This was considerably more than even Oasis attracted some 16 years later for their two appearances at the same site.

- Their final tour was a low key 14 date trek through Europe that was intended as a warm up for a full scale return to the US in the autumn. Their final show was at the Berlin Essporthalle on July 7 1980. The last song performed was a longer than usual version of *Whole Lotta Love*.

- Led Zeppelin were forced to retire after John Bonham was found dead at Page's Windsor home on September 25 1980, following a drinking bout. The group were preparing for a US and world tour that would have taken in America, South America and Europe.

- The first formal reunion of the ex-members of Led Zeppelin was at the Live Aid concert in Philadelphia on July 13 1985. Their 20 minute set was relayed live to the UK at 1 a.m. in the morning. In the hour following their appearance the monies pledged total increased by £200,000.

- They were back together for a less than successful reunion to celebrate the 40th anniversary of the Atlantic label at Madison Square Garden on May 14 1988. Jason Bonham filled his father's shoes on the drum stool. Jones, Page and Plant repaid the compliment by performing at Jason's wedding reception at the Heath Hotel, Bewdley on April 28 1990.

- During the solo years era, between 1983 and 1993, Robert Plant performed over 400 solo concerts. Jimmy Page was less prolific racking up some 150 performances either in a solo capacity or as a guest artist.

- After years of resisting the offers, Robert Plant finally reunited with Jimmy Page to recreate the spirit of Led Zeppelin - initially performing two invitation only shows at the London TV Studios on August 25/26 1994 for the MTV *Unplugged* series.

- The resulting film *No Quarter Jimmy Page Robert Plant Unledded* achieved the highest viewing rating in the *Unplugged* spot when it was aired on October 11 1994.

- Page and Plant subsequently took to the road performing 115 concerts on a year long world tour that crossed America, Europe, South America, Japan and Australia. In America the tour was one of the top grossing box office successes of the year, amassing over $30 million.

- In re-interpreting Zeppelin classics such as *Kashmir*, *Friends* and *In The Evening* with the deployment of the Egyptian ensemble and orchestra, Page and Plant successfully reconciled their past with the present bringing the live history of Led Zeppelin full circle.

- This tour also saw the return of the spontaneous medley tactic of the old era - as they randomly threw in the likes of *How Many More Times*, *We're Gonna Groove* and *As Long As I Have You* . . . ensuring that the Evolution of Led Zeppelin continues . . .

LED ZEPPELIN THE CONCERT FILE
50 QUOTES FROM THE FILE...

"The first time I saw them play was in Scandinavia. I remember standing on the side of the stage and being amazed. And Bonzo was only on £50 a week and I recall him coming back afterwards and offering to drive the van for another 50." *Peter Grant*

"The concert was cranked off by another heavy, the Led Zeppelin. Blues orientated (although not a blues band), hyped electric, the full routine in mainstream rock - done powerfully, gutsily, unifiedly, inventively and swingingly (by the end of their set). Singer Robert Plant - a cut above average in style, but no special appeal in sound. Guitarist Jimmy Page of Yardbirds fame - exceptionally fine. Used a violin bow on the guitar strings in a couple of tunes with resultant interesting, well integrated effects. Bassist John Paul Jones - solid, involved, contributing. John Bonham - a very effective group drummer, but uninventive, unsubtle and unclimactic in an uneventful solo." *Thomas MacCluskey, Rocky Mountain News.*

"Led Zepplin (sic), the re-grouped Yardbirds, made their Marquee début last week. They are now very much a heavy group, with singer Robert Plant pleading and ably holding his own against a powerful backing trio. One of the best numbers of the set was 'Days Of Confusion' (sic) featuring interesting interplay of Plant's voice and Page's guitar on which he used a violin bow, creating an unusual effect. Drummer Bonham is forceful, perhaps too much so, and generally there appears to be a need for Led Zeppelin to cut down on volume a bit." *Tony Wilson, Melody Maker.*

"As far as I'm concerned, the key Led Zeppelin gig - the one that put everything into focus - was one that we played on our first American tour at the Boston Tea Party. There were kids actually bashing their heads against the stage - I've never seen that at a gig before or since, and when we finally left the stage we'd played for four and a half hours. Peter was absolutely ecstatic. He was crying and hugging us all. You know.... with this huge grizzly bear hug. I suppose it was then that we realised just what Led Zeppelin was going to become." *John Paul Jones*

"It's nineteen minutes past the hour of ten o'clock... studio guests now... Led Zeppelin... Alright boys let's go underground. The girl I love she got long black wavy hair... right!" *Chris Grant*

"I remember seeing all three of James Brown's drummers stand around John Bonham at the Newport Jazz Festival in disbelief, wondering how one guy does what all three of them did." *John Paul Jones*

"Jethro Tull were great, playing to a sold out audience who really appreciated their efforts. Led Zeppelin, ostensibly stars of the show, came on for the second half. They were awful. Loud, pretentious, no subtlety, no nuance, just multi decibel riffs, echoed by Plant's frenzied 'singing'. He has obviously been watching Roger Daltrey. It would be nice if he listened to Roger Daltrey. And the crowd loved it! Perhaps I shouldn't blame Page and co. for performing undemanding material when all they have to do is stand there and whack out mediocrity to receive the reward of thunderous appreciation that greeted their every move." *Judy Sims, Disc*

"Imagine the sound of a tin bucket spiralling down a well and caught by a string at the very last instant, leaving a maelstrom of whirling concordal sounds. Jimmy Page catches the bucket with the strings of his guitar and the sound discharged belongs to Led Zeppelin." *James Brennan, Buffalo Evening News*

"They may be world famous but a group of shrieking monkeys are not going to use a privileged family name without permission." *Count Von Zeppelin*

"The concert started badly. Jimmy Page and Robert Plant were on the stage wiggling their hips and acting like two complete jackasses. The only thing that was coming out of the amplifiers was a lot of graunch and fuzz and feedback and the music was really poor. It went on like this for about twenty minutes and I was sitting there thinking how many Jeff Beck records I could buy with five dollars." *Tom Davis*

"A girl in Baltimore asked me if she could come backstage and watch the show from there. I thought this was the usual line from a girl just wanting to hang around with us. So I said: 'Why don't you go and sit in your seat and watch us?' She said: 'Because last time at this place, the cops tear-gassed the place and I'm frightened of being out there.' That's the sort of tension we keep finding. There's such a lack of understanding and trust between the audiences and the police." *Jimmy Page*

"To say that Led Zeppelin is an awful group is merely an understatement. 'Heavy' is the Zeppelin schtick. The volume is turned up high and each note sounds like an avalanche. False meaning is, thus, attached to each sound: listeners are conned into the belief that because Zeppelin is ridiculously loud then they must necessarily play important music. Nothing could be further from the truth." *Juan Rodriguez, Montreal Star*

"There were hordes of police with water-cannons ready to quell the anticipated riots, but Zeppelin left the audience too limp from the sheer excitement of the two and a half hour show. Even the police were toe-tapping and hand-clapping when Robert requested it! Led Zeppelin are really something else - they even made the tough Berlin police bop in the aisles!" *New Musical Express*

"The audience loved the acid rock band for its musical talent. It was not teeny-bopper idolisation. These fans respected

40

The Led Zep Scrapbook Volume One

50 QUOTES FROM THE FILE

"Zeppelin and Zeppelin respected them. Led Zeppelin is so much a part of today that it can easily transform into tomorrow. Its music cannot get much louder or its talent much better." *Milwaukee Journal*

"Who threw that firecracker? You ought to be locked up!" *Robert Plant*

"The difference between Nottingham Boat Club and Birmingham Odeon is not that much. You create an atmosphere wherever you go if you are 'at one' with the crowd. Going back to the clubs was probably a move for conscience sake, to get to where we started." *Robert Plant*

"A new kind of riot hit Ireland last weekend. A riot of fun, laughter and excitement, when Led Zeppelin paid their first visit to the troubled isle. The Britons who brought guitars instead of guns were given an ecstatic welcome. Violence and explosions raged only half a mile away from their concert in Belfast on Friday night. But the young people of the town, unconcerned with ancient conflicts, used their energy to celebrate the worthwhile cause of peace, love and music." *Chris Welch, Melody Maker*

"Please tell your readers we wanted to play here for some long, but the Italian police forced us to stop. We have played all over the world but I've never seen anything as bad as this!" *Robert Plant*

"What else can you say about a Led Zeppelin show? That the band makes good music to get stoned by? Certainly, there was a nice haze of marijuana hanging over the Gardens and the people from the St. John's Ambulance had lots to do. Or you could say, on a purely simplistic level, that Led Zeppelin is at times the most overwhelmingly stupefyingly loud band around." *Jack Batten*

"There were rows. One bloody amazing one in Japan when Robert came off stage with a split lip. It was over some dispute over some money from some tour. He still owed Bonzo some petrol money for 70 quid or something, but that's how it was!" *Peter Grant*

"They played non-stop for the best part of three hours. Enormous. They played about everything they've ever written. Nothing, just nothing, was spared. This was no job, this was no 'gig'. It was an event for all. So they get paid a lot of bread. Well, people paid that bread, and I'll reckon they got every penny's worth. It was a great night." *Roy Hollingworth, Melody Maker*

"Something has really happened this time. Something has really clicked. It's fantastic, the spirit within the band is just fantastic." *Robert Plant*

"All in all, there were five encores because the audience screamed and stomped like spoiled babies until they got what they wanted. I'm told that the group have performed ten gigs of this calibre over the last two weeks. It's easy to understand America's love for the group and vice versa. *Danny Holloway, NME*

"A nod, a wink, a drum roll or a wave of a fretboard and Zeppelin can turn a number back on its heels into songs totally unexpected. Who would imagine, for example, that 'Whole Lotta Love' could end up as 'Heartbreak Hotel'? It can, and it does when Zeppelin fly." *Chris Charlesworth*

"The latest Led Zeppelin tour is proving yet again that this is the top rock 'n' roll band in the world. There's never been anything like it. I am now convinced tha Zepp could outdraw the Stones, Alice Cooper, Carole King or Elvis Presley in any US city you care to mention." *Ritchie Yorke*

"How can I tell you about that show? Led Zeppelin and 50,000 San Francisco people got together to provide one of the finest musical events I've ever had the privilege to attend. There may be bands who play better, and there may be bands who perform better, and there may be bands who write better songs, but when it comes to welding themselves and an audience together into one unit of total joy, Zeppelin yield to nobody." *Charles Shaar Murray, NME*

"It's really been an incredible tour, but we're all terribly worn out. I went past the point of no return physically quite a while back but now I've gone past the mental point. I've only kept going by functioning automatically. We've kept up a ridiculous pace." *Jimmy Page*

"Kinky Led Zeppelin still king of the funky. For its part, the band played a new variation on its standard heavy-heavy, super-loud, bare-chested, Victorian decadent, fingernail polish and lipstick, kiss-me-because-I'm-really-funky, cartoon performance. Two hours worth." *Jack Hafferkamp*

"Karen Carpenter couldn't last ten fucking minutes with a Zeppelin number!" *John Bonham*

"It got to the point in 1975 where Grant said 'Look, there's nothing else I can do for you guys. We've had performing pigs and high wire acts. There's no more I can do, because now you really can go to Saturn'." *Robert Plant*

"In six and a half years Led Zeppelin are THE biggest and, judging by the excellence of their performance at Earls Court last Sunday, one of, if not the most exciting live acts in the world. I guess I came on the right night. It was one of those gigs that will remain scarred on my brain for life. It is difficult to describe the magic or the atmosphere of that Sunday." *Pete Makowski, Sounds*

"Last weekend we did a couple of warm-up gigs for these three. We believe these were the first three gigs to be sold out, so these must be the ones with the most energy stored up. You've been waiting!" *Robert Plant*

"Three hours, $14, Les Pauls, 'Achilles Last Stand'. For the money and the memory, there was not a single guitarist in the 1970s who put on a better show than Page. He may not have invented lead guitar, but in concert Jimmy Page defined it as a visual art form." *H. P. Newquist, Guitar*

"More than 20,000 hysterical fans in the Coliseum last night were transported into rock music ecstasy by Led Zeppelin. A handful of the 20,000, however, were transported to jail. " *Bruno Bornino, The Cleveland Press*

41

LED ZEPPELIN THE CONCERT FILE
50 GREAT PERFORMANCES FROM THE FILE...

50 outstanding live Led Zeppelin performances spanning their entire career from 1968 to 1980. This is the music that made the legacy.

A selection of worthy of consideration for that long overdue official live chronological box set . . . over to you, Jimmy!

TRAIN KEPT A ROLLIN'
Gonzaga University Spokane
December 30 1968

PAT'S DELIGHT
Fillmore West San Francisco
January 10 1969

YOU SHOOK ME
Fillmore West San Francisco
January 11 1969

BABE I'M GONNA LEAVE YOU
TV Byen Gladsaxe Denmark
March 17 1969

DAZED AND CONFUSED
TV Byen Gladsaxe Denmark
March 17 1969

AS LONG AS I HAVE YOU MEDLEY (including Fresh Garbage/Shake/Mockingbird)
Fillmore West San Francisco
April 26 1969

HOW MANY MORE TIMES MEDLEY (including The Hunter/Lemon Song)
Playhouse Theatre London
June 27 1969

COMMUNICATION BREAKDOWN
Texas International Pop Festival
August 31 1969

SOMETHING ELSE
Royal Albert Hall London
January 9 1970

LONG TALL SALLY MEDLEY (including Bye Bye Baby/Move On Down The Line/Whole Lotta Shakin' Goin' On)
Royal Albert Hall London
January 9 1970

WE'RE GONNA GROOVE
Dorten Auditorium Raleigh
April 7 1970

HEARTBREAKER
Civic Center, Ottawa April 14 1970

WHITE SUMMER/
BLACK MOUNTAINSIDE
Civic Center Ottawa April 14 1970

IMMIGRANT SONG
Bath Festival Shepton Mallet,
June 28 1970

BLUEBERRY HILL
LA Forum September 4 1970

OUT ON THE TILES
LA Forum September 4 1970

GOING TO CALIFORNIA
Paris Cinema London April 1 1971

FOUR STICKS
KB Hallen Copenhagen
May 3 1971

GALLOWS POLE
KB Hallen Copenhagen May 3 1971

BLACK DOG
Berkeley Community Theatre
California September 14 1971

WHOLE LOTTA LOVE MEDLEY (including Boogie Chillun'/Hello Mary Lou/Mess Of Blues/Tobacco Road/Good Times Bad Times/How Many More Times/The Hunter/You Shook Me)
Budokan Hall Tokyo
September 23 1971

WHAT IS AND WHAT SHOULD NEVER BE
Empire Pool Wembley
November 20 1971

LET'S HAVE A PARTY
Sydney Showground
February 27 1972

DAZED AND CONFUSED (including The Crunge)
Nassau Coliseum New York
June 15 1972

BLACK COUNTRY WOMAN
Seattle Coliseum June 18 1972

DANCING DAYS
Seattle Coliseum June 18 1972

STAND BY ME
Osaka Festival Hall October 9 1972

THE RAIN SONG
Alexandra Palace London
December 23 1972

ROCK AND ROLL
Tampa Stadium May 5 1973

SINCE I'VE BEEN LOVING YOU
Kezar Stadium June 2 1973

THE OCEAN
LA Forum June 3 1973

THANK YOU
LA Forum June 3 1973

KASHMIR
Madison Square Garden
February 12 1975

TRAMPLED UNDERFOOT
Long Beach Arena California
March 11 1975

NO QUARTER
Earls Court London May 24 1975

TANGERINE
Earls Court London May 24 1975

THAT'S THE WAY
Earls Court London May 24 1975

WOODSTOCK
Earls Court London May 24 1975

THE SONG REMAINS THE SAME
LA Forum June 21 1977

TEN YEARS GONE
LA Forum June 21 1977

STAIRWAY TO HEAVEN
LA Forum June 21 1977

IN MY TIME OF DYING/RIP IT UP
LA Forum June 25 1977

OVER THE HILLS AND FAR AWAY
LA Forum June 27 1977

ACHILLES LAST STAND
LA Forum June 27 1977

IN THE EVENING
Knebworth August 4 1979

WHOLE LOTTA LOVE
Knebworth August 4 1979

COMMUNICATION BREAKDOWN
Knebworth August 11 1979

TRAIN KEPT A ROLLIN'
Cologne Sporthalle June 18 1980

ALL MY LOVE
Cologne Sporthalle June 18 1980

HEARTBREAKER
Zurich Hallenstadion June 29 1980

The Led Zep Scrapbook Volume One

[50 QUOTES FROM THE FILE]

"The big one, Led Zeppelin, took over the Twin Cities this week, playing to a total audience of about 32,500. Only 'Up With People', the moral- uplifting-through-song extravaganza, has tried the same kind of booking, playing the two biggest auditoriums in the Twin Cities on consecutive nights in 1975. But the attendance and proceeds in the latter instance were paltry compared with those of the Zeppelin events, which grossed about $280,000. Perhaps only the four Beatles re-united could command the drawing power of Led Zeppelin, though even in their peak earning years, The Beatles never achieved the record sale and attendance figures set by Zeppelin." *Michael Anthony, Minneapolis Tribune*

"4,000 people swarmed all over the stadium floor and stormed the barricade in front of the stage, chanting, 'We want Led Zeppelin'. Witnesses said tension had already been building up because of some drug arrests and a large contingent of police in riot gear also riled nerves by standing guard at highly visible points in the Amphitheatre." *New York Post*

"Ever step in a pile of turd and couldn't get it off your shoe, no matter how hard you scraped it against the cement, no matter how much you wished it would just go away? About the only thing you could do was search for a nearby puddle of water. Unfortunately, at the first of Zep's six shows at the Garden, there were no such puddles to remove the group's excrement, which goes under the name of heavy-metal. Robert Plant screeches as though he's got a fist lodged up his rear end. And Jimmy Page: well, the guy's a great guiatrist, everybody knows, yet tonight he was sloppy, and his hesitation rhythms were convoluted. Still with a rock audience that never fails to confuse loudness for power and quantity for quality, the lumbering blimp can always reign supreme." *Mitchell Schneider, New York Post*

"Right now the man who fought the elements. The man who drinks Heineken, the man who fought food poisoning, the man who said he could go back to a building site anytime and we all agreed... the rhinestone cowgirl... the man who played the Los Angeles Aztecs and beat them 10-1 by himself... John Bonham... Over The Top!!!!" *Robert Plant*

"Going to a Zep show is still an endurance test - picking your way over passed-out people in the halls, trying to avoid flying firecrackers and smoke bombs set off by audience members, and, of course, struggling vainly to retain your hearing in the cruel onslaught of decibels." *Bob Claypool*

"It seemed logical to me that if we were to regain our position as the world's top group, we'd better play the biggest place possible!" *Peter Grant*

"It was an incredible thing really. I patrolled the grounds in a jeep on the night before the first gig and people had pushed down the stone pillars to get in early. It was a phenomenally powerful thing." *Robert Plant*

"The subdued lights were still much better than most bands will ever have! The powerful ascending riff of 'Kashmir' and the group's sense of simple melody and repetition combine to at least give an inkling of why they've attained such legendary status. Dazzling. Another Page solo, all without any backing. I went for a piss, bought a bar of chocolate, ate it, had a sit down, made some notes, went back in, and he was still playing it!" *Erik Von Lustbaden, Sounds*

"Dazed'n'Abused - They appeared sloppy and unrehearsed, sometimes seeming awkwardly lost, bewildered, stiff and reluctant to play. They were no more than a quartet of uninspired old men, a relic from the past. There was so little feeling inherent in the set that for the most part it was like watching a fully automated factory producing an endless string of chords that neither musicians nor audience cared about." *Eric Kornfeldt, NME*

"All the people that have come so far. It's been kinda like a blind date. Thanks for eleven years." *Robert Plant*

"I'm considering them in a contemporary perspective, finding them not awkward or flatulent at all but in lots of ways exciting. In fact, I'm saying Zeppelin deserve some respect. When Zeppelin play rock 'n' roll I can see why people call them the greatest. Led Zeppelin at Knebworth was A Triumph." *Paul Morley, NME*

"From the first few bars, Pagey leapt around the stage like a madman, never standing still for more than a second throughout the whole show, cutting an image somewhere between Chuck Berry and AC/DC's Angus Young! Led Zeppelin, more than anything, were enjoying themselves and the true spirit of the band, somewhat lost by the showcase element of Knebworth, had returned." *Steve Gett, Melody Maker*

"I'd be lying if I wasn't drunk on the whole event. If we had the preparation that other people did we might have be able to hold our head up. But I was still very charged with the whole effect of it all. The whole idea of playing 'Stairway To Heaven' with two drummers while Duran Duran cried on the side of the stage - there was something really quite surreal about that. I thought 'Are we supposed to be Sinatra? Is this 'My Way'?" *Robert Plant*

"What happened? I can't tell you. I have no idea. But a lot of people thought they saw something great. The crazy thing is, at the soundcheck, it was spectacular." *Robert Plant*

"Page and I had our usual touchy, vibration filled moment when I didn't want to sing 'Stairway To Heaven', and he said it was a necessity for the Western world and I said that I didn't think it was that important. So, the rehearsing was good, the soundcheck was good, the previous night was good.... and the gig was foul." *Robert Plant*

"They didn't play 'Stairway To Heaven', but then it wasn't that sort of a reunion. Having sensibly resisted the temptation to call themselves Led Zeppelin, Robert Plant and Jimmy Page were in no mood to treat their first joint venture in 14 years like a fan club outing for the faithful, or some elderly headbangers ball. The finale was a magnificent overwrought account of 'Kashmir', Zeppelin's great late hippie nod to all things Eastern. From Plant's hoarse muezzin wail at the opening to the inspired improvisations of the Egyptian contingent that brought it to a thunderous close 10 mintes later, this was surprisingly risky stuff. Perhaps progressive rock, as such epic meandering used to be called, isn't dead. When Page and Plant take their remarkable show on the road in the new year, we shall find out." *Robert Sandall, The Sunday Times*

"This is no by-the-numbers Eagles-type reprise. The music of Page/Plant still has vision and places to go. As the songs have held up, so have the men. Still flailing their hair and bodies long after nearly all of their peers have ceased to rock, they did their generation proud." *David Zimmerman, USA Today*

ANDY ADAMS AND DAVE LEWIS PRESENT THE LED ZEPPELIN UK CONVENTION

Led Zeppelin
Celebration Days

THE UK LED ZEPPELIN CONVENTION
LED ZEPPELIN: CELEBRATION DAYS:

PROGRESS REPORT: APRIL 22 1992

TICKET DISTRIBUTION:
* Selected outlets selling tickets in the UK include Birmingham's Reddington Records. Mail order direct from Celebration Days as advertised.

* American distribution is going through Rick Barrett's Collector's catalogue. Much interest already shown from the US. Travellers also due from all parts of Europe and as far away as Hong Kong.

* Hotel accommodation avaialable separately from The Royal National Hotel and a variety of surrounding hotels.

PRESS COVERAGE:
Already attained;
*Half page advert in April issue of Record Collector.

*News item coverage in Record Collector,Raw,Kerrang,Vox, Q, Melody Maker, Birmingham Evening Mail,Brum Beat, Yorkshire Post,South Wales Newspapers/North Wales Newspapers.

* More key provincial newspaper coverage under consideration.

* Further coverage under consideration from Time Out, City Limits, Music Week, NME, Sunday Times, Evening Standard and other national dailies.

* Follow up articles due in Raw (also running a competition), Kerrang and Rock Power.

RADIO COVERAGE:

*Over 25 local radio stations targeted throughout the UK with competition tie ins - including major Rock shows on Metro/Radio 210/Mercia Sound/Signal/Radio Forth/Radio Clyde/BRMB/Radio Aire/Devon Air/Piccadilly/Red Dragon/ etc.

* Confirmed interview on Steve Krusher Joule's Rock Show on GLR/London for Sunday May 18.

* All major Radio One Rock DJ's also targeted.

TELEVISION COVERAGE:

* News items confirmed from Raw Power and MTV. Both stations are also considering attending the event to film additional

THE UK LED ZEPPELIN CONVENTION
LED ZEPPELIN: CELEBRATION DAYS:

PROGRESS REPORT: APRIL 22 1992

TICKET DISTRIBUTION:
* Selected outlets selling tickets in the UK include Birmingham's Reddington Records. Mail order direct from Celebration Days as advertised.

* American distribution is going through Rick Barrett's Collector's catalogue. Much interest already shown from the US. Travellers also due from all parts of Europe and as far away as Hong Kong.

* Hotel accommodation avaialable separately from The Royal National Hotel and a variety of surrounding hotels.

PRESS COVERAGE:
Already attained;
*Half page advert in April issue of Record Collector.

*News item coverage in Record Collector,Raw,Kerrang,Vox, Q, Melody Maker, Birmingham Evening Mail,Brum Beat, Yorkshire Post,South Wales Newspapers/North Wales Newspapers.

* More key provincial newspaper coverage under consideration.

* Further coverage under consideration from Time Out, City Limits, Music Week, NME, Sunday Times, Evening Standard and other national dailies.

* Follow up articles due in Raw (also running a competition), Kerrang and Rock Power.

RADIO COVERAGE:

*Over 25 local radio stations targeted throughout the UK with competition tie ins - including major Rock shows on Metro/Radio 210/Mercia Sound/Signal/Radio Forth/Radio Clyde/BRMB/Radio Aire/Devon Air/Piccadilly/Red Dragon/ etc.

* Confirmed interview on Steve Krusher Joule's Rock Show on GLR/London for Sunday May 18.

* All major Radio One Rock DJ's also targeted.

TELEVISION COVERAGE:

* News items confirmed from Raw Power and MTV. Both stations are also considering attending the event to film additional footage.

* MTV Producer Mike Kausmann who put together the 1990 MTV Zepp Rockumentary has shown much interest in the event.

The Led Zep Scrapbook Volume One

17 YEARS ON....

MARCH 15, 1975

ZEPPELIN'S MAY DAZE!

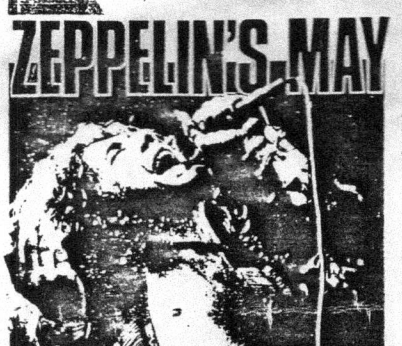

"A LOT of reverence" and a good deal of "staid Englishness" is predicted, perhaps surprisingly, for the first UK Led Zeppelin Fan Convention on May 23 and 24 in London. The event is organised by renowned Zep author Dave Lewis and Early Days And Latter Days magazine editor Andy Adams.

LED ZEPPELIN: CELEBRATION DAYS ARE HERE AGAIN!

"CELEBRATION DAYS", the first ever UK Led Zeppelin fan Convention is being staged in London on May 23 and 24 at The Royal National Hotel Exhibition Halls, Russell Square, London WC1.

The convention is being organised by well-known Zep-head Dave Lewis (former editor of Zep 'zine 'Tight But Loose' and author of 'Led Zeppelin: A Celebration' printed last year by Omnibus) and Andy Adams (editor of Zep collector's mag 'Early Days And Latter Days') and will feature a a number of events that include exhibitions of Zep memorabilia, rare video screenings, quizzes, a charity auction in aid of the Nordoff Robbins Music Therapy Charity.

Tickets are available now priced at £15.50 for both days, or £10.50 for Saturday and £8.50 for the Sunday. Write directly to Celebration Days, 14 Totnes Close, Bedford, MK40 3AX. All cheques should be made payable to 'Celebration Days' and an SAE should be enclosed.

UNIQUE ZEPP CELEBRATION PLANNED

A weekend gathering of Led Zeppelin enthusiasts planned for the spring promises to set new standards for the much-maligned fan convention.

Organisers **Dave Lewis** and **Andy Adams** are still finalising the plans, but the event is expected to include:

* The **Led Zeppelin Exhibition** — with every worldwide rarity on display.
* **Led Zeppelin In Vision** — rotating video screens running throughout the weekend.
* **Led Zeppelin In Sound** — A carefully sequenced unfolding of the band's musical career from 1963 to the present.

Other attractions planned include collectors' stalls manned by key Zeppelin dealers, a charity auction, guest speaker forum and the Ultimate Zeppelin Quiz.

Dave Lewis is also planning to revamp his 'Tight But Loose' Zep-zine to coincide, but it's doubtful whether the proposed Jimmy Page/David Coverdale collaboration will be out in time!

THE first ever UK Led Zeppelin convention is to be held in London over the weekend, May 23 and 24. "Celebration Days" will feature a Led Zeppelin exhibition including every conceivable rarity on display, Led Zeppelin In Vision — a rotation video with rare footage running throughout the weekend — and Led Zeppelin For Sale — stalls offering rarities from around the world. There will also be a guest forum featuring people very closely associated with the Zeppelin legend. The event has been put together by Zep fanzine "Tight But Loose" editor Dave Lewis and takes place at The Royal National Hotel, Exhibition Halls, Russell Square, London WC1. Tickets are £15.50 in advance for the whole weekend or £10.50 and £8.50 on the respective days.

RCA are launching the new ANNIE LENNOX album with a £300,000 marketing campaign ■ Celebration Days, the first ever UK LED ZEP Fan Convention, is being staged in London on May 23 and 24 at The Royal National Hotel Exhibition Halls, Russell Square, WC1. The weekend line-up of events includes an exhibition of Zep memorabilia, guest speakers, a charity auction in aid of Music Therapy, rare video screenings and book signings. Tickets are available now (priced £15.50 for both days, or £10.50 for Saturday and £8.50 for Sunday) direct from Celebration Days, 14 Totnes Close, Bedford MK40 3AX. Cheques made payable to Celebration Days (please enclose an SAE) ■ Spare a thought for THOMAS

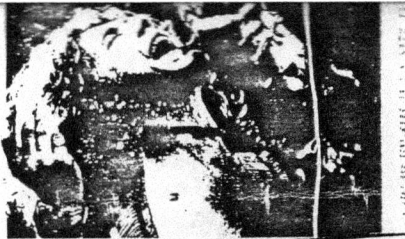

"A LOT of reverence" and a good deal of "staid Englishness" is predicted, perhaps surprisingly, for the first UK Led Zeppelin Fan Convention on May 23 and 24 in London. The event is organised by renowned Zep author Dave Lewis and Early Days And Latter Days magazine editor Andy Adams.

LED ZEPPELIN: CELEBRATION DAYS ARE HERE AGAIN!

"CELEBRATION DAYS", the first ever UK Led Zeppelin fan Convention is being staged in London on May 23 and 24 at The Royal National Hotel Exhibition Halls, Russell Square, London WC1.

The convention is being organised by well-known Zep-head Dave Lewis (former editor of Zep 'zine 'Tight But Loose' and author of 'Led Zeppelin: A Celebration' printed last year by Omnibus) and Andy Adams (editor of Zep collector's mag 'Early Days And Latter Days') and will feature a a number of events that include exhibitions of Zep memorabilia, rare video screenings, quizzes, a charity auction in aid of the Nordoff Robbins Music Therapy Charity.

Tickets are available now priced at £15.50 for both days, or £10.50 for Saturday and £8.50 for the Sunday. Write directly to Celebration Days, 14 Totnes Close, Bedford, MK40 3AX. All cheques should be made payable to 'Celebration Days' and an SAE should be enclosed.

UNIQUE ZEPP CELEBRATION PLANNED

A weekend gathering of **Led Zeppelin** enthusiasts planned for the spring promises to set new standards for the much-maligned fan convention.

Organisers **Dave Lewis** and **Andy Adams** are still finalising the plans, but the event is expected to include:

* **The Led Zeppelin Exhibition** — with every worldwide rarity on display.
* **Led Zeppelin In Vision** — rotating video screens running throughout the weekend.
* **Led Zeppelin In Sound** — A carefully sequenced unfolding of the band's musical career from 1963 to the present.

Other attractions planned include collectors' stalls manned by key Zeppelin dealers, a charity auction, guest speaker forum and the Ultimate Zeppelin Quiz.

Dave Lewis is also planning to revamp his 'Tight But Loose' Zep-zine to coincide, but it's doubtful whether the proposed **Jimmy Page/David Coverdale** collaboration will be out in time!

THE first ever UK Led Zeppelin convention is to be held in London over the weekend, May 23 and 24. "Celebration Days" will feature a Led Zeppelin exhibition including every conceivable rarity on display, Led Zeppelin In Vision – a rotation video with rare footage running throughout the weekend – and Led Zeppelin For Sale – stalls offering rarities from around the world. There will also be a guest forum featuring people very closely associated with the Zeppelin legend. The event has been put together by Zep fanzine "Tight But Loose" editor Dave Lewis and takes place at The Royal National Hotel, Exhibition Halls, Russell Square, London WC1. Tickets are £15.50 in advance for the whole weekend or £10.50 and £8.50 on the respective days.

RCA are launching the new ANNIE LENNOX album with a £300,000 marketing campaign ■ Celebration Days, the first ever UK LED ZEP Fan Convention, is being staged in London on May 23 and 24 at The Royal National Hotel Exhibition Halls, Russell Square, WC1. The weekend line-up of events includes an exhibition of Zep memorabilia, guest speakers, a charity auction in aid of Music Therapy, rare video screenings and book signings. Tickets are available now (priced £15.50 for both days, or £10.50 for Saturday and £8.50 for Sunday) direct from Celebration Days, 14 Totnes Close, Bedford MK40 3AX. Cheques made payable to Celebration Days (please enclose an SAE) ■ Spare a thought for THOMAS DOLBY, who signed...

...THE CELEBRATION CONTINUES
MAY 23/24 1992

ANDY ADAMS AND DAVE LEWIS PRESENT THE LED ZEPPELIN UK CONVENTION

Led Zeppelin Celebration Days

EVENT PROGRESS REPORT:

GUEST FORUM:

* Noted journalists Chris Welch and Chris Charlesworth who both covered Zeppelin extensively in the 70's, are confirmed for an hour long forum during which Chris Welch hopes to show cine footage of his travels with Zeppelin on their 1970 tour of Germany.

* Appearances by former Zepp touring personnel Mick Hinton and Phil Carlo confirmed.

* Collectors Forum confirmed for the Sunday, with appearances from key Zepp collectors and authors includng Robert Godwin, Andy Adams, Howard Mylett and Luis Rey.

* Appearances still under negotiation for the guest forum include DJ Alan Freeman, former Yardbirds Chris Dreja and Jim McCarty, and Kevyn Gammond who worked with Robert Plant in the Band Of Joy.
Other Radio One DJ's are also being approached. Former Zepp personel including Phil Carson and recording engineer Stuart Epps have been approached to attend. Peter Grant has been invited to attend as Guest of Honour.
* All three ex Led Zeppelin members and their management have been kept up to date with the progress of the event. Official invitations will be distributed to them prior to the launch. Jason Bonham is also being sought.

DJ FORUM:
* Appearances confirmed for DJ guest slots for GLR's Steve Krusher Joule on the Saturday and Radio 210's Brian Pithers on the Sunday.
Other names being sought.

LED ZEPPELIN EXHIBITION:
* Negotiations continuing with major memorabilia collectors worldwide to ensure the most comprehensive display of Zepp material is on show. Many rare items already confirmed.

LED ZEPPELIN IN VISION:
* Rotation footage will be screened on an 8 x 6 centrepiece video screen.
* Cine film from various private collections has been donated.
* Clearance being sought from MTV to show their 1990 Rockumentary.

** We also plan to be able to present a series of video and audio exclusives throughout the two days. These will be confirmed nearer the event.

EVENT PROGRESS REPORT:

GUEST FORUM:

* Noted journalists Chris Welch and Chris Charlesworth who both covered Zeppelin extensively in the 70's, are confirmed for an hour long forum during which Chris Welch hopes to show cine footage of his travels with Zeppelin on their 1970 tour of Germany.

* Appearances by former Zepp touring personnel Mick Hinton and Phil Carlo confirmed.

* Collectors Forum confirmed for the Sunday, with appearances from key Zepp collectors and authors includng Robert Godwin, Andy Adams, Howard Mylett and Luis Rey.

* Appearances still under negotiation for the guest forum include DJ Alan Freeman, former Yardbirds Chris Dreja and Jim McCarty, and Kevyn Gammond who worked with Robert Plant in the Band Of Joy.
Other Radio One DJ's are also being approached. Former Zepp personel including Phil Carson and recording engineer Stuart Epps have been approached to attend. Peter Grant has been invited to attend as Guest of Honour.
* All three ex Led Zeppelin members and their management have been kept up to date with the progress of the event. Official invitations will be distributed to them prior to the launch. Jason Bonham is also being sought.

DJ FORUM:
* Appearances confirmed for DJ guest slots for GLR's Steve Krusher Joule on the Saturday and Radio 210's Brian Pithers on the Sunday.
Other names being sought.

LED ZEPPELIN EXHIBITION:
* Negotiations continuing with major memorabilia collectors worldwide to ensure the most comprehensive display of Zepp material is on show. Many rare items already confirmed.

LED ZEPPELIN IN VISION:
* Rotation footage will be screened on an 8 x 6 centrepiece video screen.
* Cine film from various private collections has been donated.
* Clearance being sought from MTV to show their 1990 Rockumentary.

** We also plan to be able to present a series of video and audio exclusives throughout the two days. These will be confirmed nearer the event.

ANDY ADAMS AND DAVE LEWIS PRESENT THE LED ZEPPELIN UK CONVENTION

Led Zeppelin
Celebration Days

LED ZEPPELIN FOR SALE:
* Over 25 stalls already booked. This area should provide collectors old and new with the opportunity to purhase the widest choice of Zepp collectables ever assembled in one location.

*Leading US collector Rick Barrett will be showcasing his catalogue over three stalls.
Stalls also confirmed for the following : Robert Godwin seeling his Collectors Guide book,
Luis Rey with his Led Zeppelin Live book - Howard Mylett with his new From The Archive book - * The Tight But Loose Celebration Update Issue -* Omnibus Press with a comprehensive selection of their Zepp related titles,
*representation from Yardbirds World - *plus stalls from a variety of Zepp fanzines worldwide including Wearing And Tearing/Early Days, Italy's Oh Jimmy and US publications such as Nirvana and Electric Magic.

* An official souvenir T. Shirt and Programme at very reasonable cost will also be made available in a limited run at the event. The official programme will include a full guide to the weekend timetable, plus collecting tips and other relevent details to ensure full enjoyment of the weekend events.

BOOK SIGNINGS:
There will be book signing sessions from various Zepp authors throughout the two days.

QUIZ EVENT:
Participation in the Ultimate Zepp Quiz event will be drawn from entry forms available on the Saturday. Entry forms will cost 50p with all proceeds going to Music Therapy. The quiz will run over two days.

CHARITY AUCTION:
The Charity Auction - with all proceeds going to Music Therapy will run on both days. Items are now being collated for the auction.

THE NORDOFF ROBBINS MUSIC THERAPY CHARITY:

* Audrey Balfour the appeals organiser of the above charity has gratefully acknowledged our commitment to donating monies raised from the Quiz/Auction events to Music Therapy. We will also be displaying collection boxes over the weekend to further enhance the total collected. A feature on Music Therapy is also planned for the official programme.

* A Music Therapy representative (possibly chairman Andrew Cameron Miller) will be presented with a cheque for the total collected on the Sunday afternoon of the Convention.

OFFICIAL LAUNCH SHOWCASE:

*Leading US collector Rick Barrett will be showcasing his catalogue over three stalls.
Stalls also confirmed for the following : Robert Godwin seeling his Collectors Guide book,
Luis Rey with his Led Zeppelin Live book - Howard Mylett with his new From The Archive book - * The Tight But Loose Celebration Update Issue -* Omnibus Press with a comprehensive selection of their Zepp related titles,
*representation from Yardbirds World - *plus stalls from a variety of Zepp fanzines worldwide including Wearing And Tearing/Early Days, Italy's Oh Jimmy and US publications such as Nirvana and Electric Magic.

* An official souvenir T. Shirt and Programme at very reasonable cost will also be made available in a limited run at the event. The official programme will include a full guide to the weekend timetable, plus collecting tips and other relevent details to ensure full enjoyment of the weekend events.

BOOK SIGNINGS:
There will be book signing sessions from various Zepp authors throughout the two days.

QUIZ EVENT:
Participation in the Ultimate Zepp Quiz event will be drawn from entry forms available on the Saturday. Entry forms will cost 50p with all proceeds going to Music Therapy. The quiz will run over two days.

CHARITY AUCTION:
The Charity Auction - with all proceeds going to Music Therapy will run on both days. Items are now being collated for the auction.

THE NORDOFF ROBBINS MUSIC THERAPY CHARITY:

* Audrey Balfour the appeals organiser of the above charity has gratefully acknowledged our commitment to donating monies raised from the Quiz/Auction events to Music Therapy. We will also be displaying collection boxes over the weekend to further enhance the total collected. A feature on Music Therapy is also planned for the official programme.

* A Music Therapy representative (possibly chairman Andrew Cameron Miller) will be presented with a cheque for the total collected on the Sunday afternoon of the Convention.

OFFICIAL LAUNCH SHOWCASE:
* Celebration Days will be officially showcased to the press and media on Friday May 22 from 8.30 pm. Invitations and passes will be distributed during early May.

ANDY ADAMS AND DAVE LEWIS PRESENT **THE LED ZEPPELIN UK CONVENTION**

Led Zeppelin
Celebration Days

CELEBRATION DAYS: TENTATIVE WEEKEND SCHEDULE

* This is a brief outline of the timetable - which at this early stage is of course subject to change:

* The lay out of the Exhibition Halls allow for three seperate functioning rooms - each with ajoining access. There will also be a licenced bar within the Convention area. Food facilities are available on site at the hotel refreshment areas.

*Information Desk: An information desk will be open throughout the weekend with details of the event timetable and advice on how to best enjoy the weekend line up.

**** The Stalls/Dealer room and the Exhibition room will be open continuously from 10 am to 6pm both days.

* Additionally the main centre room will be used for the DJ/Video and Guest Speaker forums: Tentative line up reads:

SATURDAY MAY 23:

10am to 11am : Official Opening/ DJ Playback

11 am to 1pm: Video Playback/Book Signings

2pm to 3pm : Guest Speaker Forum

3pm to 4pm : Video Playback

4pm to 5pm: Guest Speaker Forum

5pm to 6pm: Video Playback

6pm to 7pm : Ultimate Quiz Part One

7.15 to 8.15: Charity Auction

8.15 to late: Video/DJ Playback with guest DJ's - The Celebration Days Party.

ANDY ADAMS AND DAVE LEWIS PRESENT THE LED ZEPPELIN UK CONVENTION

Led Zeppelin Celebration Days

17 YEARS ON....

SUNDAY MAY 24:

10 am to 11 am : DJ Playback

11am to 12 : Video Playback /Book Signings.

12 to 1 pm : Charity Auction

1pm to 2pm: DJ/Video Playback with Guest DJ's.

2pm to 3pm: Guest Speaker Forum - Collectors Forum

3pm to 4pm : Ultimate Quiz - The Final

4pm to 5pm: Official presentation of Music Therapy cheque/ Guest Speaker Forum

5pm to 7pm: Video/DJ Playback - Official Closing of Convention.

SUMMARY:

Celebration Days is shaping up to fulfill it's intentions to celebrate the musical legacy of Led Zeppelin with an inspiring and entertaining line up of weekend events for Zeppelin enthusiasts old and new. In doing so, we hope to provide a unique platform of communication for all those in attendance.

*More details to follow as they are confirmed.
DAVE LEWIS/ANDY ADAMS 22/4/92:

THE CELEBRATION CONTINUES

Jacket design for LED ZEPPELIN: HEAVEN AND HELL
by Charles R. Cross and Erik Flannigan
photographs by Neal Preston
Published by Harmony Books, 1991.

HARMONY NEWS

FOR IMMEDIATE RELEASE   Contact: Fiona Watt 212-572-2542

**HARMONY BOOKS PUBLISHES MAJOR LED ZEPPELIN BIO
ON 20TH ANNIVERSARY OF "STAIRWAY TO HEAVEN," SEPTEMBER 1991**

**LED ZEPPELIN: HEAVEN AND HELL
by Charles R. Cross and Erik Flannigan
with photographs by Neal Preston**

On November 8, 1971, Led Zeppelin's untitled fourth album, containing "Stairway to Heaven," was released in the United States. Since then Led Zeppelin has reigned supreme as the most popular heavy metal group of all time. Last year fans bought more than a million copies of the Zeppelin CD box set, but never before has the electric energy of the band been captured in print with such verve. Jimmy Page once said that the way to understand the myth of Led Zeppelin was to see them live. Well, here's the next best thing--**LED ZEPPELIN: HEAVEN AND HELL**, the LOUDEST book ever about the LOUDEST band ever!

The photographs are astonishing--capturing Jimmy Page, Robert Plant, John Paul Jones, and Bonzo in moments of musical frenzy, casual surprise, and calm intensity. Most of the 150 full-color and duotone black-and-white photographs by Neal Preston, Jim Marshall, and other great rock photographers have never before been published.

LED ZEPPELIN: HEAVEN AND HELL is a fact-packed volume that delves into the roots of Zep's music, reprints in its entirety the best interview Jimmy Page ever gave (The Trouser Press, 1977), explores the phenomenon of Led Zeppelin collectibles, reviews and analyzes all bootleg material, gives a song-by-song analysis with the details behind the writing and recording of every Led Zeppelin song released on record, and provides an annotated listing of more than four hundred concerts performed between 1968 and 1990.

Charles R. Cross is the author of BACKSTREETS: SPRINGSTEEN--THE MAN AND HIS MUSIC (Harmony Books, 1989), editor of The Rocket, and has written for Esquire, The Seattle Times, Record, Creem and Goldmine. He lives in Seattle, Washington.

Erik Flannigan, co-editor of BACKSTREETS and a contributing editor of The Rocket, also lives in Seattle and is a journalist and one of the foremost authorities on record collecting in the United States.

FOR IMMEDIATE RELEASE   Contact: Fiona Watt 212-572-2542

**HARMONY BOOKS PUBLISHES MAJOR LED ZEPPELIN BIO
ON 20TH ANNIVERSARY OF "STAIRWAY TO HEAVEN," SEPTEMBER 1991**

**LED ZEPPELIN: HEAVEN AND HELL
by Charles R. Cross and Erik Flannigan
with photographs by Neal Preston**

On November 8, 1971, Led Zeppelin's untitled fourth album, containing "Stairway to Heaven," was released in the United States. Since then Led Zeppelin has reigned supreme as the most popular heavy metal group of all time. Last year fans bought more than a million copies of the Zeppelin CD box set, but never before has the electric energy of the band been captured in print with such verve. Jimmy Page once said that the way to understand the myth of Led Zeppelin was to see them live. Well, here's the next best thing--**LED ZEPPELIN: HEAVEN AND HELL**, the LOUDEST book ever about the LOUDEST band ever!

The photographs are astonishing--capturing Jimmy Page, Robert Plant, John Paul Jones, and Bonzo in moments of musical frenzy, casual surprise, and calm intensity. Most of the 150 full-color and duotone black-and-white photographs by Neal Preston, Jim Marshall, and other great rock photographers have never before been published.

LED ZEPPELIN: HEAVEN AND HELL is a fact-packed volume that delves into the roots of Zep's music, reprints in its entirety the best interview Jimmy Page ever gave (The Trouser Press, 1977), explores the phenomenon of Led Zeppelin collectibles, reviews and analyzes all bootleg material, gives a song-by-song analysis with the details behind the writing and recording of every Led Zeppelin song released on record, and provides an annotated listing of more than four hundred concerts performed between 1968 and 1990.

Charles R. Cross is the author of BACKSTREETS: SPRINGSTEEN--THE MAN AND HIS MUSIC (Harmony Books, 1989), editor of The Rocket, and has written for Esquire, The Seattle Times, Record, Creem and Goldmine. He lives in Seattle, Washington.

Erik Flannigan, co-editor of BACKSTREETS and a contributing editor of The Rocket, also lives in Seattle and is a journalist and one of the foremost authorities on record collecting in the United States.

Neal Preston served as the official tour photographer for Led Zeppelin and published a book of his work, LED ZEPPELIN PORTRAITS. Preston's photographs have been featured on album covers and on the covers of hundreds of magazines, including Rolling Stone, People, and Time.

LED ZEPPELIN: HEAVEN AND HELL   ISBN: 0-517-58308-9
by Charles R. Cross and Erik Flannigan   Price: $25.00
Publication date: October 4, 1991   Pages: 208

HARMONY BOOKS, A DIVISION OF CROWN PUBLISHERS, INC. 201 EAST 50TH STREET, NEW YORK, NEW YORK 10022 212 572-2537

The Led Zep Scrapbook Volume One

Robert Plant — Jimmy Page

  PolyGram

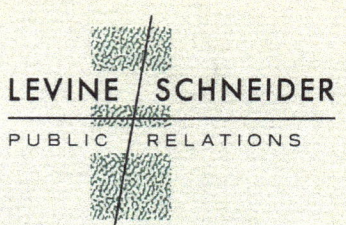

DATE: JANUARY 23, 1990

FROM: MITCHELL SCHNEIDER

PHOTO CAPTION:

It was a truly legendary rock star summit when Robert Plant showed up at one of **AEROSMITH**'s three sold-out London show as part of their recent European concert trek. Might Plant turn up onstage at one of AEROSMITH's concerts in the U.S., where they're now touring?

Pictured backstage at London's Hammersmith Odeon: AEROSMITH's Joey Kramer, Joe Perry; Robert Plant; the band's Steven Tyler, Tom Hamilton and Brad Whitford.

###

See M2M Live in Concert on the Disney Channel on April 29th at 6 PM!

M2M
Shades of Purple

WWW.M2MMUSIC.COM
WWW.M2MONLINE.COM

Selection #: 83258
Release Date: In Stores Now

Their Atlantic debut, SHADES OF PURPLE, features the GOLD single "Don't Say You Love Me" (which was also featured on the *Pokémon* soundtrack). They write, they sing, they play their own instruments and they're storming America's airwaves!

Check out the video for their new single "Mirror Mirror" on MTV!

Selection #: 83327
Release Date: June 6, 2000

Look out for her self-titled debut album this spring featuring:
"PICTURE PERFECT"

With the release of Atlantic Records' hotly anticipated soundtrack to Pokémon: The First Movie came the debut appearance of Angela Vía, one of pop music's freshest new voices. From the first melodic moments of the soundtrack's rhythmic "Catch Me If You Can" to the Latin-influenced groove of her first single, "Picture Perfect," it's clear that this energetic seventeen-year-old singer/songwriter has a lot to offer. Written and produced with Steve Kipner and David Frank, the team behind such smash hits as 98°'s "The Hardest Thing" and Christina Aguilera's "Genie In A Bottle."   **WWW.ANGELAVIA.COM**

Reacting at:
Hot 97 and KTU (NYC), KIIS FM (LA), KRBE (Houston), WDRQ (Detroit), WIOQ (Philly), WXKS (Boston) and WPLC (DC)

LED ZEPPELIN
LATTER DAYS:
The Best of Led Zeppelin Volume Two

LATTER DAYS: THE BEST OF LED ZEPPELIN VOLUME TWO, is the second of two single disc collections of Led Zeppelin's finest moments, as selected by Jimmy Page himself. VOLUME TWO serves as an ideal introduction for new fans, as well as an indispensable collection for longtime Zep-heads. Packed with 10 guaranteed classics taken from the legendary albums HOUSES OF THE HOLY, PHYSICAL GRAFFITI, PRESENCE and IN THROUGH THE OUT DOOR, the CD is enhanced with never-before-seen performance footage of "Kashmir," filmed at London's legendary Earl's Court back in 1975.

Selection #: 83278
Release Date: In Stores Now

JIMMY PAGE & ROBERT PLANT
Walking Into Clarksdale

On the heels of the smash success of Led Zeppelin's BBC SESSIONS comes the first new music from the legendary duo of Jimmy Page & Robert Plant since 1994's platinum NO QUARTER (which included vital, re-worked versions of Led Zeppelin songs as well as newly written material) and their first collaborative collection of all-new compositions since Led Zeppelin. The album sees Page & Plant taking their special blend of classic hard rock and eastern-influenced music to the brink of the millenium. As ever with these two great artists, listeners are well advised to expect the unexpected...

CATALOGUE # 83092
Call the Atlantic Marketing Dept.
For More Information or P.O.P.
@ 212.707.2042

STREET DATE: APRIL 21

Tue- 5/19/98	Pensacola, FL
Wed- 5/20/98	Tampa, FL
Fri- 5/22/98	Miami, FL
Sat- 5/23/98	Jacksonville, FL
Tue- 5/26/98	Charlotte, NC
Fri- 5/29/98	Atlanta, GA
Mon- 6/1/98	Birmingham, AL
Tue- 6/2/98	Nashville, TN
Thu- 6/4/98	Oklahoma City, OK
Sat- 6/6/98	Kansas City, MO
Sun- 6/7/98	St. Louis, MO
Tue- 6/9/98	Indianapolis, IN
Wed- 6/10/98	Milwaukee, WI
Fri- 6/12/98	Minneapolis, MN
Sat- 6/13/98	Fargo, SD
Mon- 6/15/98	Chicago, IL
Fri- 6/26/98	Detroit, MI
Mon- 6/29/98	Grand Rapids, MI

*More Dates To Follow.

* Atlantic Developing Artist
Lili Hayden Opening Thru 6/16

www.atlantic-records.com

UPCOMING RELEASES...

February 3, 1998
- Full On The Mouth (#92781) Pioneer
- MTV 120 Minutes (#83052)
- Randy Crawford (#92785) Bluemoon

February 17, 1998
- B-Tribe (#83080)
- Dimitri From Paris (#83081)
- Atlantic 50th Anniversary (#83088)

March 3, 1998
- Clannad (#83083)

March 17, 1998
- Marc Cohn (#82909)
- Page & Plant Studio Album (#83089)
- Rumors Tribute Album (#83054)
- Scott Weiland (#83084)

March 24, 1998
- Stevie Nicks Box Set (#83093)

April 7, 1998
- Athenaeum (#83071)
- CIV (#83073)
- Road Rash Soundtrack (#83096)
- Jody Watley (#83087)

Grammy Nominees!
- Jewel - Best Female Pop Vocal Performance ("Foolish Games")
- Matchbox 20 - Best Rock Performance by a Duo/Group with Vocal ("Push")
- Duncan Sheik - Best Male Pop Vocal Performance ("Barely Breathing")
- Lil' Kim - Best Rap Performance By a Duo/Group ("Not Tonight")
- Ry Cooder - Best Tropical Latin Performance (Buena Vista Social Club)
- Afro-Cuban All Stars - Best Tropical Latin Performance (A Toda Cuba Le Gusta)

Plus many more! Watch the Grammys Wednesday, Feb. 25th via CBS!

TORI AMOS

Yes, it's true. A new album from Tori Amos is scheduled for release early this spring! Stay tuned for more details - including news of a U.S. tour! In the meantime, be sure to check out her new singles, "Siren" and "Finn" from the soundtrack to the new Fox feature film, "Great Expectations" (opening in theaters January 30th). The Great Expectations Movie Score also features a new song from Tori Amos, "Paradiso Perduto." Fans will be interested to know these are the first songs Tori has written specifically for an outside project, and released before they were commercially available on a solo album. Tori's upcoming album will not include "Siren" among its tracks, so the only place you'll find that song is on the Great Expectations Soundtrack album.

Advances for the new Tori Amos recording will be available soon. Please call us **now** to reserve your copy, as quantities will be **very** limited.

P.O.P. and In-Store Play HOTLINE!
1-212-707-2042

Anni Ivil
137 East 19th Street
New York, New York 10003

Contact: Leona Faber
(212) 289-9384
(212) 477-7504

"THE BIOGRAPHY OF LED ZEPPELIN" BY RITCHIE YORKE

"It's only natural that Ritchie Yorke would write this book - he's the only journalist Zeppelin has continued to talk with through the years." Zep have maintained a unique mystique which is unrivalled among their contemporaries. Unlike most rock groups who clamor for media attention and adulation, Zep flourished without it and have traditionally maintained a low profile. The only member of the media to whom they regularly granted interviews during the first five years of their career was Ritchie Yorke, the author of the just published book, "The Led Zeppelin Biography."

Accordingly, "The Led Zeppelin Biography" is a fascinating and personalized account of Zep's flight to the top, written by the only journalist who has been along on most of the ride. It tells the inside story of a rock band which has zealously protected its privacy, and has avoided most of the media glory in which so many rock stars are all too delighted to bask. The book is likely to answer all of the questions which conceivably could be raised by a typical Led Zep fan.

"The Led Zeppelin Biography" does not back away from the steaming controversy surrounding Zep's success. Did the band and their manager somehow "conspire" to become the ultimate format hard rock group, as some detractors have alleged? Was their stunning international acceptance the result of a carefully-conceived grandslam plan to fill the vacuum arising from the demise of Cream and Hendrix? Or was their success simply the natural reaction to the outstanding musical creations of four extremely talented young British musicians?

This book traces the evolution of each Zep member from early musical influence up until the present time. Comprehensive coverage is accorded the Yardbirds, a British-blues band which has been described as the forerunners of Led Zeppelin. Many exclusive pictures serve to focus on the dynamic energy of Zep on the concert stage.

Led Zeppelin represent probably the prime pop paradox of our times. Their stupendous success came about against all the conventional rules of rock - they made it without hit singles, without TV exposure, and with virtually no critical praise or approval. Their success has baffled music industry executives and observers alike. But it certainly has not baffled the vast record-buying and concert-going audience around the world. To this day, Led Zep hold the all-time one act attendance record in the United States (Tampa in 1973 when they drew 56,800 paying fans). As if to imply absurdity (the Zeppelin airship was described as one of the worst mistakes in the history of aviation), Led Zep have smashed box office records around the globe.

"The Led Zeppelin Biography" is being published simultaneously in Canada and the United States, and a Japanese language edition is already in print. The book will undoubtedly

More...

Annie Feil
137 East 19th Street
New York, New York 10003

BIO-RITCHIE YORKE (2)

as "the patron saint of Canadian rock music." Yorke's first book "Axes Chops and Hot Licks - The Canadian Rock Music Scene" (published by Hurtig, 1971) with foreword by former CRTC chairman Pierre Juneau, remains the only work on the subject. By this time, Yorke had become - in the words of the Toronto Star's Marci McDonald - "undoubtedly the most powerful writer in Canadian music, the columnist most loved and hated, feared and fawned over by musicians, fans and record-makers alike."

From a non-writing point of view, Yorke drew much media attention with a host of other activities which included: - initiating Procol Harum's historic gold album recording with the Edmonton Symphony in 1971: discovering the Spanish youth anthem by Miquel Rios, "A Song of Joy" on the Bicentennial of Beethoven's birth; working with John and Yoko Lennon on their War Is Over (If You Want It) peace campaign, organizing their meeting with Prime Minister Trudeau in Ottawa, and taking the Lennon's anti-war message around the world including one headline-making confrontation at the Red China border in 1970; and initiating and organizing on a voluntary basis the Maple Music Junket, which Billboard magazine described as "the largest music promotion ever conducted by a single nation."

In 1973, Yorke cut back on his assorted journalist and broadcast activities to concentrate on the book field. He moved back to London to work with members and friends of Led Zeppelin on their first biography. Yorke had in fact been the first media person to predict the U.S. superstar success of Zep, at the time when most critics were panning them. That was in January 1969, and for the next five years, Yorke maintained an extremely tight relationship with grateful members of Zep. He accompanied them on tour and wrote more words about the band than any writer anywhere.

Completing "The Led Zeppelin Biography", Yorke moved to Wengen Switzerland, to write a biography of the celebrated Irish singer/songwriter, Van Morrison. "Into the Music" was published in Europe in July '75 and the New Musical Express described it as "a balanced and praiseworthy account of Van Morrison and his career to date."

After serving on the Committee of Honor at the 8th Montreux International Festival, Yorke returned to Toronto in the Fall of '74. Since then he has been working on a comprehensive history of rock music, and his first novel, entitled "Off the Road."

Yorke lists among his favorite authors Patrick White, Thomas Mann, Voltaire, Kurt Vonnegt Jr., William Blake, Marcus Aurelius, D.H. Lawrence and Rachel Carson.

* * * * * * * * *

L to R: JOHN SMITHSON, bass & fiddle, JASON BONHAM, drums, DANIEL MacMASTER, lead vocals, IAN HATTON, guitar

©1992 Sony Music Permission to reproduce this photography is limited to editorial uses in regular issues of newspapers and other regularly published periodicals and television news programming.

Jason Bonham	drums
Ian Hatton	guitars
Daniel MacMaster	lead vocals
John Smithson	bass, keyboards, violin, backing vocals

There's a hard-rock tornado cutting across the heavy metal front, and its name is **BONHAM**. Heirs apparent to the hammer of the gods, the boys of **Bonham** sliced a swath through the sphere of rock with their debut album, The Disregard Of Timekeeping, which struck gold in the U.S. and sold one million copies worldwide. Now, after more than 200 live gigs and some serious writing and studio work, **Bonham** is back with their new WTG album, MADHATTER.

"With no disrespect to Disregard," says drummer and founder Jason Bonham, "I believe this album will go out a lot further. We were actually playing like a band!" Over the course of MADHATTER's eleven tracks, **Bonham** shifts musical gears through influences as diverse as Delta blues, spaghetti westerns, r&b vamps, and symphonic climaxes. "Change Of A Season," "Good With The Bad," "Madhatter," "Los Locos" and more--all of it crunching together in the fully-developed trademark sound of **Bonham**.

As most of the Western world must know by now, Jason Bonham is the son of the legendary John Bonham of Led Zeppelin. "He was my main man, really," says Jason. "He was the one who taught me how to play drums. But I don't think he was responsible for the fact that I'm in the music industry. It wasn't until he died that I thought I wanted to get into this business."

That was in 1980, when Jason was fourteen years old. He paid his dues with '80s hard rock bands like Air Race and Virginia Woolf. In 1988, Jason filled his father's drum seat for Led Zeppelin's set at the Atlantic Records 40th anniversary celebration at New York's Madison Square Garden.

It was former Led Zep manager Peter Grant who introduced Jason to John Smithson, a multi-talented young player from Sussex, England. John, the son of a concert pianist, claims to have gotten his show-business start performing "playing to old ladies on a disappearing organ in Blackpool." John later played in "several hundred bands, or at least three," but avows that **"Bonham's** the best thing I've ever done."

Media Relations, P.O. Box 4450, New York, NY 10101-4450/(212)445-5051
1801 Century Park West, Los Angeles, CA 90067/(213) 556-4870

In _his_ previous incarnations, Ian played in "lots of r&b bands and reggae bands--that's where I came from, and those are the songs I learned first." Pre-**Bonham**, Ian also played with Robert Plant's Honeydrippers. Jason and Ian still keep "a little r&b thing going" as a side project of **Bonham**.

A native of Barrie, Ontario, singer Daniel MacMaster was brought to Jason's attention by Brian Howe of Bad Company, who'd heard Daniel's demo tape while doing a radio interview in Toronto. "Before Daniel came into the room to audition," Jason recalls, "we all said 'No matter how good he is, let's not just jump in and say he's got the gig.' He sang about three notes and we all screamed 'You've got the gig!'"

Bonham released its WTG debut, The Disregard Of Timekeeping, in July, 1989. Boosted by steady sales and the radio success of "Wait For You," **Bonham** commenced many months live gigs both as club headliners and as support to the likes of Motley Crue and the Cult. "A lot of **Bonham** fans came to see us," Jason recalls. "The others...well, by the end of the evening, they _knew_ who we were!"

In the making of MADHATTER, **Bonham** set out to create an album that would capture the soaring dynamic range and kinetic energy of their live performances. The album's fierce opening track, "Bing," had been road-tested during the Motley Crue tour. "It went over so well," says John Smithson, "that we knew we were going in the right direction."

The band retired to the isle of Ibiza, off the coast of Spain, to write the bulk of MADHATTER without the distractions of (in Jason's words) "any outside influence of music at all." The majority of the tracks were recorded in Brighton, England with producer Tony Platt, whose many credits include AC/DC, Free, and Buddy Guy. "Tony's of the old school," says Ian approvingly. "That's why we wanted him. He's into the engineering side of production--he knows how to get a _real_ drum sound." Three additional songs--"Hold On," "Running Out The Backdoor," and "Secrets"--were produced by Ron St. Germain.

MADHATTER marks a watershed in the life of **Bonham**. "When I first heard it," says Jason of the final playback, "a tear ran down my eye. I thought, 'Where's my father? I wish he were here to hear this.' Then I thought, 'We've done it!'"

##9206##

The Led Zep Scrapbook Volume One

L to R: JASON BONHAM, Drums; DANIEL MacMASTER, Lead Vocalist; IAN HATTON, Guitar; JOHN SMITHSON, Bass/Keyboards

Ian Hatton, guitar; Daniel MacMaster, lead vocalist; Jason Bonham, drums; John Smithson, bass/keyboards

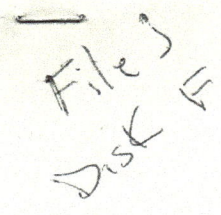

Bonham

"Most fathers give their four year old children train sets, toy cars or tricycles --- mine gave me a scaled down Ludwig drum kit," states Bonham founder and drummer Jason Bonham.

Jason was not quite four when his father John Bonham, the legendary Led Zeppelin powerhouse drummer, gave him his first drum kit. The set was an exact replica of the kit used by his father and was to be the first of many as Jason grew to become a highly talented and dedicated musician.

After serving his apprenticeship in two bands, he went on to record and tour with Jimmy Page and play with Led Zeppelin at the Atlantic 40th Anniversary celebration at New York's Madison Square Garden in 1988. Anyone who saw that show could not help but sense the emotion and spirit with which Jason energized Led Zeppelin's performance.

It was clear that Jason at the age of 22 was now ready to form his own band. His collaboration with guitarist Ian Hatton, vocalist Daniel MacMaster and keyboard/bassist John Smithson has resulted in Bonham.

The band:

Guitarist Ian Hatton (26) comes from Kidderminster, England. He toured with Robert Plant in the original incarnation of the Honeydrippers, and having been a close friend of Jason's for four years was a natural to join the band.

The search for the right vocalist ended in Barrie, Ontario, Canada with Daniel MacMaster. The 21-year-old singer was brought to the attention of Jason by Brian Howe of Bad Company who had heard his tape while doing a radio interview in Toronto.

Keyboards and bass are the domain of John Smithson (26) who comes from Sussex in southern England. Jason met John through former Led Zeppelin manager Peter Grant, who was managing the band John was in at that time. His father being a concert pianist, John has always been surrounded by various types of music and his wide range of influences blend well with Bonham's chivalrous approach to song writing. Combining these forces together, Bonham, the band, set out to write a collection of songs with passion, energy and emotion as well as technical integrity.

PRESS AND PUBLIC INFORMATION
1801 CENTURY PARK WEST, LOS ANGELES, CA 90067 (213) 556-4870
51 W. 52ND STREET, NEW YORK, NY 10019 (212) 975-5051

The album:

The Disregard Of Time Keeping is the groups WTG/CBS debut and is slated for a September release. Recorded in Los Angeles between March and July and produced by the highly acclaimed Bob Ezrin (Alice Cooper, Pink Floyd), the LP is a canvas of contrasts, both modern and traditional. The Disregard Of Time Keeping is outgoing and subtle, but yet has a strong feeling of power and style.

From the first single "Wait For You," to the addictive "Guilty," Bonham's music is flavored with a wide variety of styles from the blues, to various influential electric guitarists of the 70s and 80s to, of course, Led Zeppelin.

"That comes from me, it's in my blood and it's the only way I know how to play. After all, my father taught me all I know," said Jason.

This influence is strongly audible on the LP, but with their abundance of talent, Bonham make a sound distinctly their own. The songs show exceptional depth and plenty of versatility. The album title itself is a reaction to today's monotone way of recording pop music with loads of drum machines - and indeed there are no such to be found on the Bonham record.

As for the name Bonham..."First we were going to call it Jason Bonham, but then I thought simply Bonham - because this is a band," insists Jason. "We are all good friends, we play and work like a band, but Bonham is a name I am obviously proud of."

Bonham is indeed a real group. The collective talents are even greater that the individual parts in which all the members stand out. Witness them on The Disregard For Time Keeping, an album that speaks volumes for itself on WTG/CBS Records.

8907

MUTE CORPORATION

DIAMANDA GALÁS
with JOHN PAUL JONES
The Sporting Life

<u>The Sporting Life</u> is -- in the parlance of the pimp, the hustler, the trick, the john, the whore -- the place where affection is a commodity, where greasy twenties glitter sharper than gold, where clothes make the man, where the only love that's neither tainted nor for sale is the pure seething of obsession. Burning white hot and bubbling under the skin, criss-cross hieroglyphic votives stitched like mandala prayer-cloths into the back of eyelids so all you can see is the face of <u>the one</u>: the beloved, the flame, the completion of self, the target.

Ours is a zeitgeist, so degenerate that even sadism is defiled, debased, co-opted, assimilated, diluted, commodified. The Marquis de Sade is at this moment puking in some fetid corner of hell at the sight of children led by their metallic-booger-nose-rings into the pit of commerce, cartoon fetish magazines dappling 7-11's and Super Americas, animatronic rock-stars selling serial killers as bonus cuts, his vision of absolute negation washing through B. Daltons morphed into the kewpie-doll aerobics of Madonna Sex, faces of gore in every strip-mall, nine inch nails in the house of Tate, animal autopsies on MTV. How must he feel knowing that it's all been reduced to show-biz? That the brutal S&M hierarchy of nature has -- in a free market -- become so pathetically <u>consenual</u>?

Miscegenation has always been the double-edged sword of Damocles, In biology, it portends mutation, promotes the flourishing of the genetically dominant, twists DNA into a spiral of madness. In music, it's the convulsive trigger of the dance infernal, the wiggle of Christ-On-The-Cross shimmying down through the hymns of the church warbling field hollers in the plantation picking up some of that black back cat-scratching mama heartbeat thomp along the way, squeeze it one way, you got jazz, squeeze it another,

New York	London	Los Angeles
140 W. 22nd Street, Suite 10A		345 North Maple Drive, Suite #123
New York, NY 10011		Beverly Hills, CA 90210
Tel: (212) 255-7670 Fax: (212) 255-5056		Tel: (310) 276-2508, Fax: (310) 276-3480

you got rock 'n' roll. Problem being all that squeezing is just another psycho doing windshields down on Houston Street boombox thumping Snoop Dogg and that's why they call it the blues.

In **Diamanda Galás** there is the authentic sadomasochism of the primordial, the oracular nightmare of the ancients bearing strange fruit not so much in the culture, but in the individual psyche, As she's said, **The Sporting Life** isn't suicidal, but homicidal. Love hurts, love mars, love wounds and scars, but best of all, love kills and never has the topic been laid out with such harrowing derangement as on this new .45 magnum opus. **The Sporting Life** is the psychological-emotional equivalent of the Hellfire Club, the real one, not some chi-chi pierced nipple trend zone proffering amino acid spritzers, but of our own founding fathers -- religious zealots and crazed politicos -- linked up with the old inbred blue-blood aristocrats zipping through the streets on horseback banging the heads offa beggars with polo mallets. For sport.

The Sporting Life is obsessive-compulsive love seen from the interior outward and one senses in nearly every track the utter conviction and total dedication to the Sadean Ideal. And, an Ideal it is in the mind of the beholder, the object of affectation has no right to argue or protest....

But we jump ahead....

Diamanda Galás ... has since the release of her "Litanies of Satan" b/w "Wild Women With Steak Knives" in 1982...been pursuing these larynx clotting truths armed with the multi-timbral and multi-octave voices of the dammed. Hers is an art most easily approached from the temple of aesthetic distance.

John Paul Jones on the other claw, is a different story. As a full quarter of one of the most successful and formidable rock bands in history, he carved out some of the most enduring columns of the AOR monolith. But, to truly understand his full contribution to Led Zeppelin, a listen to **The Sporting Life** is more than instructive...it's shocking.

Diamanda Galás has...on **The Sporting Life**...created the undeniable rock record people have secretly feared she was capable of. In this new music, which is simultaneously her most accessible and most difficult, **Galás** fronts a power trio -- with her voice functioning as lead singer and scorching lead player- blasting and squiggling beyond the back of the brain into something even scarier, the place where Eros and Thanatos are grafted together in an embrace that reaches from the cradle to the grave.

Underneath the fearsome gravity of her maniacal chansons' throbs the heaviest gut-bucket Promethian blues-screech since...(to invoke comparison at this point would be heresy). **John Paul Jones** brandishes an eight string bass for the occasion while jackhammer-through-the-heart rhythms fly off the skins of the Attractions' drummer **Pete Thomas**.

The record opens with *"Skotosene"* (literally "Kill Me" in Greek) and within seconds, the symbiotic relationship between classic rock and Greek tragedy is so palpable, the room begins to spin. This is not a trumped-up whim-based *"meeting of the superstars from divergent worlds" hypefest*, it most certainly not some horrid *"experimental fusion"* of seemingly disparate sensibilities. It is a finely calibrated extension of the music of both these individuals, a collaboration in the truest sense.

A collaboration that started, in fact, when **John Paul Jones** first heard "Wild Women With Steak Knives" some twelve years ago. Though best known for his work with Led Zeppelin, **Jones** has one of the most jaw-dropping rezzes in rock. He began as a church organist as a teenager (as, in fact, **Galás** first sang in her local parish) and moonlit in various weenie rock bands. In 1963 he joined Jet Harris and Tony Meehan (the remnants of Cliff Richard's band) and had 3 #1 records in England. (*"The Beatles took our spot in the Helen Shapiro tour,"* he remembers). He became the musical director for Andrew Loog Oldham, Robert Stigwood, and Mickie Most and, among other things, cut Nico's first demo (a version of "Blowin' in the Wind") and hired John McLaughlin as a guitarist for some Herman's Hermits hits. He wrote the arrangements for hits as divergent as Lulu's "To Sir With Love" and Donovan's "Hurdy Gurdy Man." He's played with artists ranging from Tom Jones to Paul McCartney to Marianne Faithful, Bo Diddley, and the New York Dolls. Most recently, he's arranged, produced and/or performed on Peter Gabriel's <u>Us</u>, R.E.M.'s <u>Automatic for the People</u>, the Butthole Surfers' <u>Independent Worm Saloon</u>, Brian Eno's <u>Nerve Net</u>, the latest Raging Slab album, and appeared with Lenny Kravitz on the MTV Music Awards.

It wasn't until 1989 that **Jones** finally saw **Diamanda Galás** perform. That was a New Year's Day performance at the Queen Elizabeth Hall is England. It was an event that solidified **Jones'** longtime desire to work with **Galás**.

The pair met and began sending tapes of musical ideas back and forth across the Atlantic. In February 1994, **Galás** traveled to Bath, England, where she, **Jones**, and **Thomas** worked for two months to create **<u>The Sporting Life.</u>**

Much of **Galás'** work since 1984 has centered around her <u>Plague Mass</u>, an ongoing work dedicated *"to people who are HIV positive, PWArcs and PWA's who fight to stay alive in a hostile environment that offers disgusting pity and pacifying lies to persuade the diseased man to desist from fighting and participate instead in his own burial; that offers the constant threat of mandatory testing, reporting and quarantine; and that offers slow torture and a continuing design of death, or genocide, through a failure to react responsibly in a medical emergency."* Her <u>Masque of the Red Death</u> trilogy has been documented on a series of albums for Mute Records (1986, 87, 88), while a live recording of the <u>Plague Mass</u> was released in 1991.

In 1992, she recorded <u>The Singer</u>, and album of blues, gospel, and spiritual music. In 1993, Mute Records released <u>Vena Cava</u>, a piece that had its world premiere at The Kitchen in New York City in February 1992.

"There's nothing lugubrious about this record," she says of **The Sporting Life**. "It's not self pitying by any means, it's not 'oh I'm going to hang myself because I'm so miserable.' there's no self-pity in any of these songs. It's totally not the morbid funeral dirge of the last ten years. There's equal parts sarcasm and black humor."

There is in **The Sporting Life** the sheer perversity of mirth and maniacal glee that is the flipside of claustrophobia and obsession. Granted, no one is going to mistake **The Sporting Life** for a comedy album, but anyone who's ever wandered the streets insomniac and anorexic hunting down a lover will find a rather strange comfort in Galas' highly personalized reveries on love's most hideous secrets. *"Do You Take This Man?"* plays on stock and pillory wedding vows, turning romance into holy padlock. The man is trapped, imprisoned, desperately tries to escape, but she, at every turn, is puzzled by his desire to leave, there is nowhere to go and his only salvation, as sick as it seems, is to simply submit, finally and totally.

"Dark End of the Street" is a heart piercing interpretation of a song whose best known version is by Percy Sledge. In it, **Diamanda Galás** finds the haunted, delusional, compulsive horror that lies at the root of pop and soul. The kind of love banalized by the radio is the driving wheel of nature. And it stops only at death.

On *"The Sporting Life"* a group of whores decides to kill a man for the sheer thrill of it and in the course of the song, it starts to sound like a really good idea. The downside of homicidal thrill seeking comes to the surface in *"Baby's Insane,"* where the true horror of lunacy turns out to be its utterly drab and prosaic nature. Discussing the song, she says, *"Why change the sheets? Campbell's soup is fine with me & Ex-Lax 'cause I can't shit...and coffee filters...its not morbido...it's not exotic. It's as common as Shelly Winters with rollers and a flowered polyester muumuu on top of the YMCA looking down. It's nothing...we all know about it...it's as close as scabies..."*

She closes the album with *"Hex,"* a curse so terrifying that it can't be translated. On **The Sporting Life**, **Diamanda Galás** has pursued her study of madness into the marrow of her own deepest thoughts and confessions. There is, in psychology, a test called the Minnesota Multiphasic Personality Inventory, a series of 566 true-false questions designed to provide a profile of neurosis, psychosis, and other forms of mental "health" and "illness." One of the questions reads: T/F: *"I think things too horrible to talk about."* **Diamanda Galás** sings about those things. That's **The Sporting Life**....and anything else would be living a lie.

For more information, please contact:
Jennifer Gross - Director, Media & Artist Relations   212-255-7670 Ext. 237
jenngross @ mute.com

MUTE CORPORATION

ON DIAMANDA GALÁS:

" ...she 's certainly the closest equivalent we have to (Maria) Callas. Like Callas, she doesn't just use her voice as an opportunity to show off her singing technique, but to express love and loss with all the feeling that they deserve."
Interview

" Galás gave every song a ravishing ferocity and made every note a catharsis"
Misha Berson, **The Seattle Times**

" Galás delivered a wrenching solo performance that was a marvel of musical invention and sustained emotional intensity"
George Varga, **San Diego Union Tribune**

" Galás is monolithic ...an artist of power and integrity... a breathtaking variety of vocal expostulations: There's apparently no kind of sound she can't produce, within the extensive range of her voice."
Michael Feingold, **The Village Voice**

" Theatrically, Ms. Galás conjures up the spirit of the classic Greek heroine Antigone...outspoken, passionate and defiant, both on stage and off."
William Harris, **The New York Times**

" No mistaking this performer's thrilling virtuosity and terrifying artistic gifts. (*Judgment Day* is) a vision of music at its most probing and fearless."
Joshua Kosman, **San Francisco Chronicle**

" Galás actually unearths new shades of blues."
Michael Saunders, **The Boston Globe**

New York
140 W. 22nd Street, Suite 10A
New York, NY 10011
Tel: (212) 255-7670 Fax: (212) 255-6056

London

Los Angeles
345 North Maple Drive, Suite #123
Beverly Hills, CA 90210
Tel: (310) 276-2508, Fax: (310) 276-3480

DIAMANDA GALÁS DISCOGRAPHY

1982
The Litanies of Satan
(Mute)

1984
Diamanda Galás
(Mute)

1986
The Divine Punishment
(Mute)

1986
Saint of The Pit
(Mute)

1988
You Must Be Certain of the Devil
(Mute)

1988
Masque of the Red Death
(Mute)

1991
Plague Mass
(Mute)

1992
The Singer
(Mute)

1993
Vena Cava
(Mute)

1994
The Sporting Life
(Mute)

MUTE CORPORATION

JOHN PAUL JONES

1946	3rd January date of birth
1960	Organist and choirmaster (age 14) joined father's dance band
1961	Formed bands at school, played US. Airforce bases in England
1962	Turned professional, various bands touring clubs, theaters, US. bases etc.
1963	Joined JET HARRIS, TONY MEEHAN 3 no. 1 records UK. charts
1964	Musical director for ANDREW LOOG OLDHAM arranged for: 　　THE ROLLING STONES 　　P.P. ARNOLD 　　BILLY NICHOLS 　　TWICE AS MUCH 　　NICO 　　LIONEL BART 　　ANDREW OLDHAM ORCHERSTRA
1965	Musical director for ROBERT STIGWOOD arranged for 　　MIKE BERRY 　　THE OUTLAWS 　　SIMON KING
1966	Musical director for MICKEY MOST arranged for 　　HERMANS HERMITS (Kind of Hush, No Milk Today etc.) 　　DONOVAN (Mellow Yellow, Hurdy Gurdy Man etc.) 　　LULU (Boat That I Row, Film title To Sir With Love etc.)

New York	London	Los Angeles
140 W. 22nd Street, Suite 10A New York, NY 10011 Tel: (212) 255-7670 Fax: (212) 255-6056		345 North Maple Drive, Suite #123 Beverly Hills, CA 90210 Tel: (310) 276-2508, Fax: (310) 276-3480

JEFF BECK (Hi-Ho Silver Lining, Love Is Blue, Beck's Bolero, Truth album)
YARDBIRDS (Little games, Ten Little Indians etc.)
JULIE FELIX album
FRANCOISE HARDY album
GRAHAM GOULDMAN album

1966/67/68 other artists arranged for:

CLIFF RICHARD, MARC BOLAN, CAT STEVENS, THE ROLLING STONES, P.J. PROBY, DUSTY SPRINGFIELD, ANITA HARRIS, WAYNE FONTANA & THE MIND BENDERS, FREDDIE & THE DREAMERS, SHE TRINITY, AMORY KANE, FRUGAL SOUND, THE MIGHTY AVENGERS, AFFINITY, FAMILY DOGG, THE GREENBEATS, MADELINE BELL, MAGIC LANTERNS, PETER & GORDON, DOWNLINERS SECT

some artists played for:

TOM JONES, PAUL McCARTNEY, EVERLY BROTHERS, BURT BACHARACH, SAMMY DAVIS, PAUL ANKA, DEL SHANNON, ENGKEBERT HUMPERDINK, WALKER BROTHERS, MEMPHIS SLIM, ETTA JAMES, CHAMPION JACK DUPREE, PEARL BAILEY, DINAH WASHINGTON, KATHY KIRBY, JAY & THE AMERICANS, PAUL & BARRY RYAN, MARIANNE FAITHFUL, THE SUPREMES, BO DIDDLY, DETROIT SPINNERS, SHIRLEY BASSEY, SUE & SUNNY, NEW YORK DOLLS, GEORGE MARTIN + many 100's of recording and T.V. sessions.

1968	formed	LED ZEPPELIN with JIMMY PAGE
1968-1980		LED ZEPPELIN 9 albums 1 film 26 tours
1973	produced	MADELINE BELL album " COMIN'ATCHA"
1981		Set up 24 track electronic music studio Devon
1882	taught	Electronic Composition at DARLINGTON COLLEGE OF ARTS, DEVON
1983	appeared	GIVE MY REGARDS TO BROAD STREET film PAUL McCARTNEY

1984	commission	JIM FULKERSON trombone and tape for HUDDERSFIELD CONTEMPORARY MUSIC FESTIVAL
1984/85	film score	" SCREAM FOR HELP" LORIMAR
1985	produced/eng.	SCREAM FOR HELP album (JON ANDERSON, MADELINE BELL)
1986	commission	ODYSSEUS theme music Award-winning 13 part serial B.B.C. T.V.
	commission	ELECTRO-ACOUSTIC MUSIC ASSOCIATION for ALMEDIA FESTIVAL for CHRISTOPHER BOWERS- BROADBENT organ and tape
	prod/eng.	JOHN RENBOURN/STEFAN GROSSMAN album "THREE KINGDOMS"
1986/87	produced	BEN E. KING album " SAVE THE LAST DANCE FOR ME"
1987/88	produced	THE MISSION album " CHILDREN"
1988	produced	Track for LAND album "MUSIC FOR FILMS III"
1989	commission	"AMORES PASADOS" for RED BYRD and ARTS COUNCIL for BREMEN MUSIC FESTIVAL
1990	arrangements	CINDERELLA album
1990	produced	LA FURA DELS BAUS album "NOUN"
1990	produced	JACINDA JONES album
1991		Set up 32 track digital electronic music studio near Bath
1991	composed/	One hour multimedia show MERCEDES-BENZ launch
1991	produced/ composed/ MD	One hour multimedia show MEMORY PALACE for ART FUTURA for SPANISH PAVILLION, SEVILLE EXPO 1992
1992	commission	RICARDO GALLARDO "MACONDO" steel drum and tape for SONIC ARTS.

1992	commission	REBECCA ALLEN / ANIMACA SPAIN computer animation piece
1992	commission	'THE HAPPY PRINCE" opera RED BYRD
1992	commission	MONDRIAN QUARTET string quartet "MAASTRICH TIME"for ZEALAND MUSIC FESTIVAL, THE HAGUE
1992	arranged/ performed	PETER GABRIEL album "US"
1992	performed	BRIAN ENO album "NERVE NET"
1992	arrangements	REM album " AUTOMATIC FOR THE PEOPLE"- 'everybody hurts' 'Drive', 'Nightswimming' and ' The Sidewinder Sleeps Tonite'
1992	produced	BUTTHOLE SURFERS album "INDEPENDENT WORN SALOON"
1993	film score	"RISK" dir. DEIRDRE FISHEL w/KAREN SILLAS
1993	arranged	Strings for RAGING SLAB album
1993	composed	"THE SECRET ADVENTURES OF TOM THUMB" Award winning animation
1993	performed	MTV Music Awards with LENNY KRAVITZ
1994	produced/ performed	Collaboration on the album with DIAMANDA GALÁS to be released late August followed by tour in the Autumn.

MUTE CORPORATION

BIOGRAPHY
JOHN PAUL JONES

John Paul Jones is probably best known for his 12 years with one of the world's most successful bands, Led Zeppelin, but his career both before and after Led Zeppelin has been far more varied and influential than many people realize.

John Paul Jones was an organist and choirmaster at the age of 14. From 1963 he toured with many professional bands, and was a studio musician and arranger on several hundred records, television and film sessions. He was also musical director and arranger for, among others, The Rolling Stones, Donovan, Nico, Lulu, Jeff Beck and The Yardbirds. He formed Led Zeppelin, one of the seminal supergroups of the 70's with Jimmy Page in 1968, and played bass guitar and keyboards until 1980, when the group disbanded.

Although Led Zeppelin gave him opportunities to pursue some of his interests in musical experimentation and electronics, the demands of the group meant that outside projects-production for a Madelin bell album, for example- were rare.

With the group's demise in 1980 he moved to the west country, and built a 24 track recording studio with facilities for film and television work. Since then he has written music which has more accurately reflected his diverse tastes and skills - computer composition, digital sound sampling, exotic and folk music and environmental sound- working with musicians from very different backgrounds, like trombonist Jim Fulkerson.

New York	London	Los Angeles
140 W. 22nd Street, Suite 10A		345 North Maple Drive, Suite #123
New York, NY 10011		Beverly Hills, CA 90210
Tel: (212) 255-7670 Fax: (212) 255-6056		Tel: (310) 276-2508, Fax: (310) 276-3480

In 1984 he scored the soundtrack for Michael Winner's film **Scream For Help**. It was not a perfect situation, but as John Wryly says, "I learned a bit more about the film business." He also learned the frustrations of the current pop business by working with Ben E. King single-handedly producing an album of subtle, adult modern soul with this legendary singer, only to find it swallowed by the confusion following King's surprise hit with the re-released **Stand By Me**.

John's composition over the past few years include **Showdown** for Kim Fulkerson performed at the Huddersfield Festival, **Nuc Dimittis** for Christopher Bowers-Broadbent and EMAS at the Almeda Festival, **Amores Passados** for Red Byrd and the Art Council at the Bremen International Music Festival, **Maastrich Time** for the Mondriaan String Quartet, and **Macondo** for the Sonic Art Network. His production work has included **Children** for **The Mission**, an album for Ben E. King, and the Butthole Surfers' album **Independent Worm Saloon**. String arrangements by John feature on REM's highly acclaimed album **Automatic For The People**, on the tracks **The Sidewinder Sleeps Tonite, Drive, Everybody Hurts and Nightswimming**. His playing, zurdu, bass and keyboards, can be heard on **14 Black Paintings**, on Peter Gabriel's album **US**.

John's current work includes composing the music for a forthcoming film, **Risk** (Naked Eye Films, New York) and for a bizarre and fascinating animation of '**The Secret Adventures of Tom Thumb** for the BBC.

With his production of the Mission's Children album and its subsequent success, his career came full circle. He passed on skills he learned as a teenager to musicians who grew up listening to Led Zeppelin's music-combining a knowledge of modern computer based recording techniques with a traditional feel for live ambient recording, song construction and classic pop arranging. Whatever work he does in the future, however, his attitude is consistent. " I like to be interesting." he says, " rather than another mill. It's just avoiding the industry treadmills and sort of skipping lightly from one to the other."

MUTE CORPORATION

DIAMANDA GALÁS
WITH JOHN PAUL JONES
FALL 1994 TOUR

New York City	November 10	Irving Plaza
Philadelphia, PA	November 13	Irvine Auditorium
Ann Arbor, MI	November 15	The Michigan Theater
Chicago, IL	November 17	The Vic
Madison, WI	November 18	The Barrymore Theater
Lincoln, NE	November 20	The Lied Center
Columbus, OH	November 22	Mershon Auditorium
Toronto, Ont.	November 24	The Phoenix
Washington, DC	November 26	The Lincoln Theater
Austin, TX	November 30	The Paramount
Tempe, AZ	December 2	Gammage Auditorium
Los Angeles, CA	December 4	Wadsworth Theater
San Francisco, CA	December 7	Fillmore Theater
Portland, OR	December 8	The Portland Art Museum
Seattle, WA	December 10	The Moore
Vancouver, BC	December 12	Commodore Ballroom

For more information contact: Jennifer Gross 212-255-7670

New York
140 W. 22nd Street, Suite 10A
New York, NY 10011
Tel (212) 255-7670 Fax (212) 255-6056

London

Los Angeles
345 North Maple Drive, Suite #123
Beverly Hills, CA 90210
Tel (310) 276-2508 Fax (310) 276-3480

GEFFEN RECORDS

June 15, 1988

Here's <u>OUTRIDER</u>, the long-awaited solo album by Jimmy Page. It will be in the record stores June 21.

Because there was a security ban on pre-release cassettes, this is the fastest we could get you the music. We hope the "extras" in this promo pack will help make up for the short lead time.

In July we'll be announcing the details of Page's 36-date fall tour of the U.S. In addition to the guitar hero himself, the touring band will include John Miles (vocals and keyboards), Durban Laverde (bass) and Jason Bonham (drums).

We'd love to hear what you think of <u>Outrider</u>. Since relying on our clipping service is a dismal prospect, we'd be happy to exchange a CD version for Page clippings/airchecks/whatever.

If you need photos beyond the B/W shot enclosed . . . or anything else related to Page . . . don't hesitate to call.

Bryn Bridenthal
Lori Earl
Leslie Crockett
David Purdie

(213) 285-2708

9130 Sunset Boulevard	75 Rockefeller Plaza
Los Angeles California 90069	New York New York 10019
Telephone 213 278 9010	Telephone 212 484 7170
Telex: 295854	Answerback: GEFFN

GEFFEN RECORDS

JIMMY PAGE IS COMING!

        JUNE 16 -- TO RADIO
        JUNE 21 -- TO STREET

On June 8 at 11:00 A.M. radio stations all across the U.S. began playing "Wasting My Time" -- the first song from the first side of the first Jimmy Page solo album, Outrider. A CD version is enclosed, along with an advance on bio information and a B/W photo that is not being serviced with the album.

The next package you get from Geffen Records will bear the full nine tracks of Outrider, plus audio and video interviews. Watch for it right after June 16.

If you have any questions, give us a call!

        Bryn Bridenthal
        Lori Earl
        Media & Artist Relations

        213/285-2708 (direct)

9130 Sunset Boulevard	75 Rockefeller Plaza
Los Angeles California 90069	New York New York 10019
Telephone 213 278 9010	Telephone 212 484 7170
Telex: 295854	Answerback: GEFFN

JIMMY PAGE

Photo Credit: Peter Ashworth

© 1988 The David Geffen Company/Permission to reproduce limited to editorial use in newspapers and other regularly published periodicals and television news programming.

JUNE 17, 1988

TO: BRANCH MARKETING COORDINATORS
FROM: TINA RODREQUEZ
RE: WRAP-UP

 **Geffen Records Presents...**

THE FIRST SOLO ALBUM FROM THE WORLD'S LEADING GUITAR PLAYER

JIMMY PAGE — OUTRIDER

9130 Sunset Boulevard
Los Angeles California 90069
Telephone 213 278 9010
Telex: 295854

75 Rockefeller Plaza
New York New York 10019
Telephone 212 484 7170
Answerback: GEFFN

COVER STORY
Jimmy Page

Album Network

Rock's premier guitarist returns to the solo spotlight via *Outrider*, ten action-packed songs that will ignite rock radio's frequencies and burn the bins at retail! Please see **Best New Music** for our recommended tracks, and take a look at **New Action Airplay** for radio's zealous approval of "Wasting My Time," which smacks an out of the box front page **Homer!** and debut at #12* on **Power Cuts**. Keep an eye on the mail for a very special **Jimmy Page Outrider Kit** from **Geffen** which includes: (1) an hour long CD interview custom made for rock radio with "breaks" and a script sheet; (2) a video of **Jimmy** being interviewed in England; and (3) a cassette of the entire album. Add a two-hour "special edition" of **Rockline** on Wednesday, June 22, and all the pieces are in place for **Jimmy Page** to go all the way at radio and retail as a solo artist.

JIMMY PAGE preview pack will be sent this week to key retailers.

JIMMY PAGE GHS 24188 OUTRIDER STREET DATE 6/21/88

JIMMY PAGE WILL SHIP GOLD!!!

Jimmy will be appearing on Rockline, June 22nd

Jimmy will begin touring in early September.

Merchandising materials now available.

"Wasting My Time" goes BREAKER in R&R and #1 most added.
Album Network has the track as the #1 Most Added, #3 Most Requested and #2 New Action.

Video for "Wasting My Time" now being completed.

This record will prove to be a monster. Please make sure you market is covered with Jimmy Page displays.

Featuring!

"WASTING MY TIME"—Already All Over American Radio!
(Electric Guitar-Jimmy Page • Vocals-John Miles • Bass-Tony Franklin • Drums-Jason Bonham)

"WANNA MAKE LOVE"
(Electric Guitar-Jimmy Page • Vocals-John Miles
Bass-Durban Laverde • Drums-Jason Bonham)

"THE ONLY ONE"
(Electric Guitar-Jimmy Page • Vocals-Robert Plant*
Bass-Felix Krish • Drums-Jason Bonham)
Page And Plant Together Again!

"HUMMINGBIRD"
(Electric & Synthesizer Guitars-Jimmy Page
Vocals-Chris Farlow • Bass-Durban Laverde
Drums-Jason Bonham)

"PRISON BLUES"
(Electric Guitar-Jimmy Page • Vocals-Chris Farlow
Bass-Felix Krish • Drums-Jason Bonham)

"Wasting My Time" (Geffen)
Posers, beware! The man who <u>invented</u> blues-based British hard rock is back with one smoker of a tune, "Wasting My Time." Jimmy Page's raw and raucous guitar is a welcome treat, John Miles' vocal work perfectly carries this rocker, Jason Bonham pounds the skins in the tradition of his dad and Tony Franklin keeps the bass pumped up. Page talks about "Wasting My Time:" "It's a driving riff with nothing but guitars. I'd jammed with John (Miles) in Ibiza, and when it came to the point of making the album, I knew he had a great voice. I thought it would be worth calling him up and seeing whether he'd like to come in. He's extremely versatile within his vocal approach."

THE BEST NEW MUSIC

Jimmy Page

Geffen GHS 24188

The First Solo Album From The World's Leading Guitar Player!
JIMMY PAGE   OUTRIDER
Featuring! **"WASTING MY TIME"**
* *PowerCuts*   **12** Debut! *Hornet*
Shipping Gold...**OUT NOW!** ··Album Network

HEART has just completed several weeks of touring in England and Europe in support of their Epic album, PRIVATE AUDITION. After HEART's performance at England's Milton Keynes arena, Led Zeppelin leader Robert Plant stopped by to visit with the group. HEART will be starting their U.S. tour in early July.

Pictured above are: Ann Wilson, Robert Plant, Nancy Wilson, new members Mark Andes Denny Carmassi and original HEART member Howard Leese.
photo/Chris Walter

For further information, please contact Lois Marino (212) 975-8569 or Sue Sawyer (213) 556-4870.

H E A R T

VIDEO BEAT NEA NOV. 23 'THE FIRM'

JIMMY PAGE
Outrider

Produced by Jimmy Page
GHS/M5G/2-24188

- First solo album from the legendary guitar hero (Yardbirds, Led Zeppelin, The Firm), and his first for **Geffen Records.**
- Includes **John Miles, Robert Plant** and **Chris Farlow** on vocals; **Jason Bonham** (the late Bonzo's son) and **Barrymore Barlow** on drums; **Felix Krish, Durban Laverde** and **Tony Franklin** on bass.
- Eight of the nine tracks were composed by **Page** with lyrics written by the respective vocalists; ninth track is Leon Russell's **"Hummingbird."**
- Side One emphasizes the rock 'n' roll, the fast, the hard, and the aggressive—all of the elements **Page** pioneered. Clearly, his guitar hasn't mellowed any. Fresh and powerful as he lets it all out.
- Side Two is more bluesy, but still intense and explosive as **Page** gives an appreciative nod to rock's blues roots.
- 36-date tour of the U.S. is slated for fall.
- Performance music video of first single, **"Wasting My Time,"** to be directed by **Marty Callner** for **Creem Cheese Productions.**

SIDE ONE: Wasting My Time ■ Wanna Make Love ■ Writes Of Winter ■ The Only One ■ Liquid Mercury

SIDE TWO: Hummingbird ■ Emerald Eyes ■ Prison Blues ■ Blues Anthem

GHS-24188-G	MSG-24188-G	2-24188-O	
Bar Code No.	Bar Code No.	Bar Code No.	
7599-24188-1	7599-24188-4	7599-24188-2	

IT BITES
Once Around The World

Produced by Steve Hillage and It Bites
GHS/M5G/2-24189

- Second album from this young quartet from the north of England.
- Members of the band have been playing together since they were sixteen.
- Challenging compositions and superior instrumental and arranging skills are group hallmarks.
- Key tracks include **"Kiss Like Judas," "Midnight"** and the epic title cut.
- Cassette and CD versions feature the bonus track, **"Hunting The Whale."**
- The band is becoming a UK chart fixture.
- Side one producer **Hillage** is a major figure in British progressive rock.

SIDE ONE: Midnight ■ Kiss Like Judas ■ Yellow Christian ■ Rose Marie ■ Black December

SIDE TWO: Old Man And The Angel ■ Plastic Dreamer ■ Once Around The World (also on cassette and CD: Hunting The Whale)

DISCOGRAPHY: *The Big Lad In The Windmill* (GHS/M5G 24116)

GHS/24189-D	M5G/24189-G	2-24189-G	
Bar Code No.	Bar Code No.	Bar Code No.	
7599-24189-1	7599-24189-4	7599-24189-2	

"I got 'em from the hide of a cow that died."

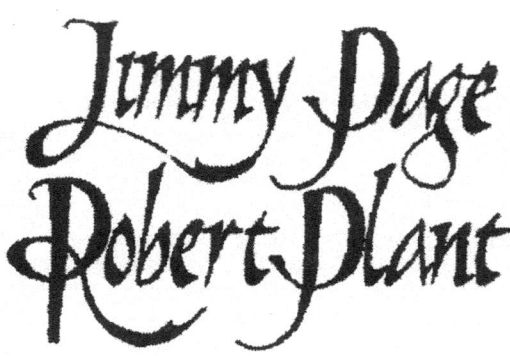

"When we first got back together, it was so immediately apparent that the two of us were just channeling the music. That's what we had always had, and it was so apparent that it was there. It was almost effortless. It was undeniable, and it was something not to be abused."
— Jimmy Page

"I'd seen so many artists from way back who had come together again, and the outcome was almost so pedestrian, almost just an excuse for leaving the house. Whatever we were to do had to be very positive, and full of intention."
— Robert Plant

When Jimmy Page and Robert Plant reunited in 1994 for their first full-blown project together since the break-up of Led Zeppelin in 1980, it was to be no mere trot 'round the block for old time's sake. It was a musical extravaganza that reinvigorated the past while blazing a trail to the future. Not only was their vision undimmed, but their artistic horizon, if anything, had broadened over the years.

Starting with a live MTV special titled <u>Unledded</u>, what might have been a tentative return to collaboration became a triumph captured both on videotape and on the RIAA platinum album, "NO QUARTER." Such Zeppelin songs as "Gallows Pole" and "Kashmir," whose original studio versions had hitherto seemed definitive, were stunningly rearranged to present a thrilling new face, while four new songs inspired by North African rhythms took a bow.

One ground-breaking world tour later — in America, the most successful of 1995 — Page & Plant cemented their reunion by going back into the studio. What emerges in the spring of 1998 is "WALKING INTO CLARKSDALE," their first collection of all-new collaborative material since 1979 and the release of Led Zeppelin's last studio album, "IN THROUGH THE OUT DOOR."

-more-

Yet at no stage was their continued reunion inevitable. Robert Plant recalls 1994's tentative first steps, when the two of them had to discover if they could still spark musically without combusting personally: "We had to decide how comfortable we could make it. There had been a lot of stuff flying around between us, and most of it was coming from my adamance not to have anything to do with a Led Zeppelin rerun. I'd missed Jimmy's playing so much that as soon as we started working, I realized that we'd wasted quite a bit of time. Working in that old room down in King's Cross, it really started sparkling again, but it took until halfway through the world tour to realize that we were really happening, and if we wanted to really enjoy ourselves musically, we had to put our backs into what we were doing."

And so it proved... Page & Plant's "reunion" was one of prodigious logistic and aesthetic ambition. On stage, Jimmy and Robert were joined by the core rhythm section of bassist Charlie Jones and drummer Michael Lee, plus Ed Shearmur (keyboards), Porl Thompson (guitar, banjo), Nigel Eaton (hurdy-gurdy), an eight-member Egyptian ensemble, and locally recruited string sections. "It was a community, with all the ups and downs a community has — 'Peyton Place' gone wild!" Robert recalls. "You really were in a small moving caravan. If we had done it as a four-piece, we probably wouldn't be here now. We really had to hone our personalities and our expectations to this creature that we'd created; there was no slouching. It was so exciting, a dream come true, which neither of us could have created without the other."

By the tour's triumphant climax and sad farewells, Jimmy and Robert were confident in their renewed relationship and raring to return to the studio as soon as possible. Further inspired by recent individual travels abroad — Jimmy to northern Brazil, Robert to the Silk Road of Central Asia — they reconvened with Jones and Lee, the rhythmic center of the live band. "After that huge extravaganza," says Page, "we really wanted to have a very honest, minimalist performance album. We wanted to get back to getting the chemistry going between the two of us, just writing songs within a band framework."

The quartet of Page, Plant, Jones, and Lee headed into London's Abbey Road Studios, whose walls have resounded over the years to some of the world's greatest music. Enter what would seem to be an unexpected wild card: Steve Albini. Famed for his work recording the likes of Nirvana, PJ Harvey, Bush, The Pixies, and his own Big Black/Rapeman/Shellac, he was perhaps a less-than-obvious collaborator for Jimmy Page, a man renowned for knowing his own mind in the studio. "The greatest problem for a band that plays organically is someone to record it," Jimmy explains. "Steve was the perfect conduit for just letting us get on with it. He really knows how to EQ using microphones, the old science of recording. Plus the three of us do meet in many, many similar pockets of musical appreciation."

The album — soon to be dubbed "WALKING INTO CLARKSDALE" — took just 35 days to record. Jimmy and Robert were keen to capture all the flavors that go into their globally eclectic songwriting style, without overcooking the actual recording process, and so losing the spirit of spontaneous invention. "We wanted to keep it fresh," says Robert. "We wanted to get a performance onto tape that sounded like a *performance* rather than a construction of ideas... It's virtually a live album."

-more-

As ever, Jimmy and Robert — who, when they first got together 30 years ago this summer, discovered a shared enthusiasm for Joan Baez and Howlin' Wolf — remain true-blue music fans. Among those on their personal playlists during the creation of "WALKING INTO CLARKSDALE" were the British world-dance outfit Transglobal Underground, the Sikh drummer troupe The Dhol Foundation, Anglo-Arabic chanteuse Natacha Atlas and the late Jeff Buckley, whom Jimmy and Robert had visited to express their admiration in the year before he died. A close listen to the album reveals a spectrum of influences, from the Santo & Johnny/Dick Dale/Ventures surf-guitar twang of "Heart In Your Hand" to the Roy Orbison's-just-met-Jerry Garcia stylings of "Please Read The Letter." Then there is Clarksdale itself, the Mississippi Delta town steeped in so much blues history. As Jimmy says, "It's all part of your musical heritage and your roots, isn't it? It's all in there, and it weaves itself around and can come through."

The next step? As always, to follow where the music takes them. Fiercely proud of their records, Page and Plant have always regarded the music that comes out of the studio as the starting point of a musical journey, not an ending. "All the way through from Zeppelin, when a song went into the set on stage, that was just the beginning," Jimmy notes. "It would change, and I'm looking forward to doing that on the new songs. That's what is so exciting about going on the road — seeing how songs evolve from their embryonic state on the record. That's the beauty of the thing."

"Now, we lean backwards as well as leaning forwards. It's got new vitality," says Robert. "We'd rather be measured by what happened two years ago or two hours ago than what happened 25 years ago."

4/98

Atlantic Recording Corporation
1290 Avenue of the Americas New York, NY 10104 212/707.2020 Fax: 405.5475
9229 Sunset Blvd. Los Angeles, CA 90069 310/205.7450 Fax: 205.5916
http://www.atlantic-records.com

BEST OF THE MONTH REVIEWS

OUR CRITICS CHOOSE THE OUTSTANDING CURRENT RELEASES

Page & Plant: Led, It Be

Heavy metal has been ridiculed, dismissed, and loved like the dickens for nigh on thirty years now. But today, this once singular genre means many things to many people. A recent feature in *The New York Times* identified no fewer than fourteen subgenres from "math metal" to "turncoat metal." And among the bands acknowledged as forerunners was Led Zeppelin, classified under the heading "folk metal." How quaint.

As guitarist, singer, and primary writers for Led Zeppelin, Jimmy Page and Robert Plant were metal's Lennon and McCartney (or, if you prefer, its Jagger and Richards). After varying success in their own careers, they restaked Zeppelin's claim with the "unledded" *No Quarter* in 1994. Then came word that they were asking alternative-rock producer Steve Albini to help them make their first all-new studio album together since the nearly twenty-years-gone *In Through the Out Door*. What would *this* sound like? Well, surprise: *Walking into Clarksdale* sounds exactly like . . . folk metal. And it is very, very good.

Yes, the billing is "Page & Plant," and, yes, all twelve songs are credited to Page, Plant, bassist Charlie Jones, and drummer Michael Lee. But in its sound and fury and intelligence, *Clarksdale* comes across like prime Zep, a work that could have fit comfortably between that band's third and fourth albums. Page and Plant produced, but I'll bet that Albini, who recorded and mixed, helped give the album its punch-rock *Physical Graffiti* feel, right down to Lee's echoes of John Bonham.

Clarksdale is not, however, an album that bashes you over the head. It begins subtly with "Shining in the Light," an acoustic rumbler with some tasteful power chords — a "Ramble On" for the Nineties. "When the World Was Young" and "Blue Train" are two long-drizzling rain songs, and "Please Read the Letter" is one of those great, angled Page–Plant creations, making the most of sly harmonies and lurking guitars. From there it's on to the saga "Most High," a masterpiece of song construction with flavorsome, exotic instrumentation. Notice how the track *slides* in and out of its rock beat. Notice, too, that Page has worked textural wonders to this point in the album without a single guitar solo. That's saved for the title track, a blues riff kicked up a notch by a teasing solo, and "Burning Up," where Page really cranks in a "Sick Again" groove. The reflections of "When I Was a Child" calm things down until, eventually, the album closes with the raucous "Sons of Freedom."

Friends, this is no retread Led. Sparked by Page's exploratory guitar and Plant's steady, clear vocals, *Walking into Clarksdale* summons the fire and finesse of old in a work that is utterly fresh. It recalls the days when heavy metal was, simply, hard rock with attitude — or, in the case of Jimmy Page and Robert Plant, with attitude and grace. *Ken Richardson*

PAGE & PLANT Walking into Clarksdale
Shining in the Light; When the World Was Young; Upon a Golden Horse; Blue Train; Please Read the Letter; Most High; Heart in Your Hand; Walking into Clarksdale; Burning Up; When I Was a Child; House of Love; Sons of Freedom
(Atlantic, 61 min)

THE ONCE AND FUTURE ZEP
RECORDINGS BY ANTHONY DeCURTIS

Jimmy Page and Robert Plant put their solo careers behind them and get the Led out

★★★♪

WALKING INTO CLARKSDALE
Jimmy Page and Robert Plant
ATLANTIC

THE ZEP LEGACY LOOMS large over the history of rock & roll, and no one is more illuminated by its white-hot glare – or clouded by its shadow – than Jimmy Page and Robert Plant. After Led Zeppelin broke up in 1980 in the wake of drummer John Bonham's death, both men alternately sought to escape and embrace their past – and each other – with mixed results, particularly in Page's case. Page and Plant finally accepted the inevitable in 1994 and reunited for an *MTV Unplugged* performance coyly titled "Unledded," an accompanying live album (*No Quarter*) and a triumphant world tour.

At that point, the process of getting the Led out was more psychological than real; that is, Page and Plant clearly needed to believe they were leaving the past behind even if they weren't. True, the duo refused the insanely lucrative prospect of getting back together as Led Zeppelin; never invited Zep bassist John Paul Jones to join the group; did not include any songs credited to the entire band as songwriters on "Unledded" and *No Quarter*; avoided redoing the most obvious Zep chestnuts on those outings; and substantially rearranged the smartly chosen Zep songs they did perform. Still, let's get real. No one watched "Unledded" or bought *No Quarter* – let alone showed up for the tour – to hear such new songs as "Yallah" or "Wah Wah." No, the excitement was all about the spectacular versions of "The Battle of Evermore," "Since I've Been Loving You" and "Kashmir" – and rightly so.

Now, on *Walking Into Clarksdale*, Page and Plant offer their first full set of new songs, and a bracingly satisfying effort it is – indisputable proof that, far from strolling merrily to the bank, they are taking their joint venture dead seriously. Anyone led by the album's title to expect a return to Zep's bludgeoning, epic blues – Clarksdale is located in the Mississippi Delta and holds a resonant place in the music's lore – will not find what he's looking for. Just for old-times' sake, the title track does lift a rhythmic motif from Bo Diddley's "I'm a Man," but that's about it.

Of course, the ghost of Led Zeppelin still lingers. More specifically, *Clarksdale* resounds with rich echoes from the band's aesthetically ambitious midperiod – primarily *Houses of the Holy* (1973) and *Physical Graffiti* (1975). Sometimes the references are explicit, as in the way the softly strummed opening of "When the World Was Young" recalls the similarly atmospheric beginning of "The Rain Song."

Often, however, the reminders simply reside in how ingeniously these twelve songs are constructed – that is, with a vision that sets these men leagues apart from their innumerable imitators. Page is in excellent form, effortlessly summoning the spirits of light and dark that his extraordinary playing has always sought to embody. Bassist Charlie Jones and drummer Michael Lee from the "Unledded" band are back, and they have forgotten none of the lessons they learned. Bruising riffs start, slam to a halt, then kick in again. Quiet acoustic-guitar parts disappear within storms of thunderous electric chords. Strings provide a strange, celestial elegance to crashing rhythms and unsettling time signatures. Folk-rock melodies deliver warmth and humanity to arrangements that might otherwise be daunting in their architectural scale. The album's surging first single, "Most High," blends Anglo-Celtic mysticism and Middle Eastern fervor in the finest Zep tradition. The much-bruited presence of studio brat Steve Albini, who has worked with Nirvana, PJ Harvey, the Pixies and Bush, lends raw, contemporary force to this meticulous re-creation of Led Zeppelin's classic sound.

The images that govern Plant's definitive Zeppelin lyrics return as well. "Love's true flame dies without the warmth of your sun," he intimates in "Blue Train," an expression of his conviction that as fiercely as erotic desires burn, they are part of a larger natural world that subsumes all things. It is essentially a pagan belief, and virtually every song on *Clarksdale* shimmers with symbols drawn from the elements of earth, air, fire and water. And as always, Plant's voice whirls urgently from a whisper to a scream. If on the wistful "When I Was a Child" he is an aging hippie looking back in wide-eyed wonder as though awakened from a dream, on "Sons of Freedom" he is a wailing celebrant at a Bacchic rite.

What Page and Plant must have meant by their title is the notion of revisiting a mythic past – in this case their own ecstatic dancing days. Can these two warriors go home again? Well, like all journeys back, this one lacks the pure shock, the wild revelation, of discovery. But even visceral pleasure comes in many forms, and *Walking Into Clarksdale* brims with the thrilling awareness of how much mystery still lives in what you think you already know. ◆

Billboard

APRIL 18, 1998

IN MUSIC NEWS

Atlantic Pulling Out All Stops For New Page/Plant Album

PAGE 9

Page, Plant Keep 'Walking'
Atlantic Set Fueled By Live Work

■ BY ED CHRISTMAN

NEW YORK—Jimmy Page and Robert Plant, whose music has been described as "the hammer of the gods," are about to present the faithful with their first new album of musical offerings in almost 20 years. "Walking Into Clarksdale" hits U.S. stores April 21 on Atlantic Records.

Mercury, to which Page and Plant are signed for the world outside North America, will release the set internationally April 20.

Produced by Page and Plant and recorded and mixed by noted indie rock producer Steve Albini, the album simultaneously evokes the classic sound they created with Led Zeppelin while breaking new musical ground for the duo. Since the breakup of their trendsetting band in 1980, the two had been making solo albums until they reunited in mid-1994 to record the live "No Quarter" album.

Initially, with the exception of "Most High," which is destined to be recognized as a Page and Plant classic, the bulk of "Walking Into Clarksdale" appears to eschew their trademark riff-built songs in favor of more melodic and softer compositions. But after repeated plays, the songs, which are mainly electric guitar-based, ultimately reveal a series of musical signatures Page and Plant created and are identifiably theirs.

Val Azzoli, co-chairman/co-CEO (U.S.) of the Atlantic Group, says the label has high hopes for the album. "Not only is it a great record, they are not resting on their laurels," he says. "It's not a Led Zeppelin album; it's a Jimmy and Robert album. As they have done throughout their career, they are pushing the envelope yet again."

Atlantic itself is looking to break new ground in marketing the album. In addition to traditional promotional tools—including aggressive print advertising, a strong buy-in deal for merchants, and a planned generous dispersal of co-op advertising funds—the company has made a deal with Ticketmaster to upsell the album to customers who call in to order tickets to the duo's upcoming tour. Ticketmaster order takers will make customers aware that the duo has a new album in stores and give them the chance to order the album at its $16.98 list price at the same time they purchase tickets to the concerts.

The tour kicks off May 19 in Pensacola, Fla., with the first leg ending in mid-July in New York, according to Bill Curbishley, principal of London-based Trinifold Management, who booked the tour himself instead of using a booking agency. After a break, the tour picks up in early September, starting in Vancouver, and makes its way through the West to Texas; it finishes in October in New Orleans. Page and Plant close out 1998 by touring Europe and in February 1999 resume touring in Australia and Japan before heading to South America in March to finish up the tour.

In addition to Page and Plant, the band includes Charlie Jones on bass and Michael Lee on drums, both of whom were part of the platinum "No Quarter" project and who share songwriting credits on the album. On keyboards for the tour is Phil Andrews, who did not play on the album.

PAGE & PLANT

In the U.S., the tour will be sponsored exclusively by Best Buy, which plans to support it with a "massive multimillion-dollar TV campaign," according to Vicky Germaise, Atlantic's senior VP of marketing (U.S.).

Already, Page and Plant have toured Eastern Europe with a set that was composed largely of Led Zeppelin songs but included five new songs from the "Walking" album.

The tour will bring their younger fans "as near as they are ever going to be to seeing Led Zeppelin," while for older fans, "it is the last chance to see them before the millennium," says Curbishley.

In fact, live performances, which drove the Led Zeppelin creative engine throughout its existence, clearly were at the heart of making this album, which was recorded at Abbey Road Studios in London.

Sitting in the penthouse suite in New York's SoHo Grand Hotel, Page and Plant describe the album as perfor-
(Continued on page 85)

JIMMY PAGE, ROBERT PLANT KEEP 'WALKING'

(Continued from page 9)

mance-oriented, with many songs recorded live in the studio, and acknowledge that Page's guitar orchestration approach is barely evident.

After having toured with two orchestras on the last tour in support of "No Quarter," "what we needed to do is get back to a minimalist format," says Page. Plant adds, "We wanted to make a band album that would be a live-sounding record. We didn't want to have it overcooked. We wanted it to feel like a bit of an adventure."

Already, Plant notes that on the Eastern European tour, the band's rendition of "Most High" has "opened up," with the song evolving beyond its original framework. Spontaneity has always been a key ingredient of the musical relationship between Page and Plant, says the former. "We feed off of that, and we are very fortunate that it is still there," he says.

HYPNOTIC RIFFS

The first single, "Most High," like Led Zep's "Kashmir," takes the listener to another place, this time to North Africa, where the two mesh their pioneering use of hypnotic metallic riffs with mutations of the repetitive trance music and primal rhythms closely associated with music from that region. The traditional rock instruments of guitar, bass, drums, and keyboards are augmented by accordion and the *rhiata*, a double-reed instrument, with Plant's instantly identifiable vocals layered over the top.

The label was planning to take that song to radio April 6 but went a week earlier, after leaks starting appearing on the air. The track debuts at No. 10 on Billboard's Mainstream Rock Tracks chart this issue.

Neal Mirsky, PD of WYSP Philadelphia, describes the song as "excellent," adding, "If you saw them on the last tour when they brought the Indian orchestra with them, it's kind of got that feel."

Like the other songs on the album, "Most High" is published by Computer Chance Ltd. and administered by Succubus Music Inc., via an arrangement with Warner/Chappell.

PROPER POSITIONING

Atlantic executive VP/GM Ron Shapiro labels the music on "Walking Into Clarksdale" as "vital new recordings from great music makers" and says it is now Atlantic's job to bring the album to all the duo's fans. In order to accomplish that, the label plans to ship a half-million units into stores by street date and will make sure the record is properly positioned in-store, he reports.

Lew Garrett, VP of purchasing and merchandising at the North Canton, Ohio-based Camelot Music, says the album "should be a huge record. There still is a market for icon artists."

Bob Bell, new release music buyer at the Torrance, Calif.-based Wherehouse Entertainment, adds that "No Quarter" and "Led Zeppelin Live At The BBC" did "a good job setting up the new album, and the last tour generated a lot of excitement. Another tour this time could do the same thing."

Germaise says that in order to promote the album, the label will run TV advertising from April 17 to May 3 on VH1, MTV, Comedy Central, E!, and USA Network, which will tag various retailers. Also, there will be a full run of national print advertising from Rolling Stone to Hit Parader and the alternative press.

Germaise adds that Atlantic has made "a very substantial radio buy" at classic rock stations in the top 20 markets across the U.S. Also, she notes that Page and Plant did a whole series of interviews with a number of nationally based shows and stations, including CNN.

Shapiro says the goal of the label's marketing campaign is to ensure that "we reach as many consumers as possible. It's a great album, and we want to make sure that the whole world knows it's in the stores."

ATLANTIC RECORDS

9229 SUNSET BLVD.
LOS ANGELES, CA 90069
TELEPHONE: (310) 205-7450
FAX: (310) 205-7475

For Immediate Release
February 13, 1995

JIMMY PAGE & ROBERT PLANT TEXAS TOUR DATES

March 13	Austin, TX.	Frank Erwin Center
March 14	Houston, TX.	Summit
March 18	Dallas, TX.	Reunion Arena

For more information, ticket requests -

Bobbie Gale
310/205-5711

The Led Zep Scrapbook Volume One

John Paul Jones - ZOOMA
First solo album from legendary Led Zeppelin artist John Paul Jones

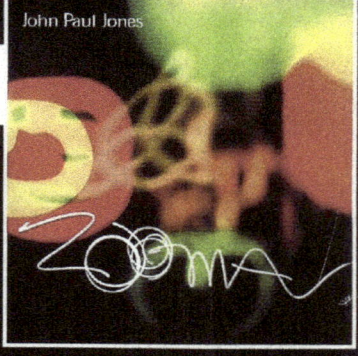

This "roaring and powerful" 9-track instrumental album features Jones playing four-string, ten-string, and 12-string basses, as well as bass lap steel, kyma, mandola, organ, and guitars, while also arranging and conducting members of the London Symphony Orchestra for one of the tracks.

John Paul Jones envisions ZOOMA as the advent of an on-going solo career. He is keen to return to touring, and a planned world tour will begin with major cities in the U.S. in the fall.

MARKETING POINTS

- Syndicated radio interviews.
- In store support.
- Mainstream advertising
  to support feature led press campaign.
- **British and US long lead features to date:**
  Mojo news piece and large feature; Guitar Magazine; Bassist (cover feature); Record Collector; Bass Player (cover); Billboard; Bassics; 20th Century Guitar (cover); Guitar World; Classic rock (cover); British Airways Highlife; Making Music; Front; Rock Sound; Sound on Sound; Total Guitar; Marie Claire; Footloose; Major broadsheet coverage
- **Touring**
  October : Selected US cities
  November : Selected European cities
  2000 : Major world tour

DGM9909
CD
Release Date: September 14, 1999
List Price: $15.98
File Under: Rock
UPC: 633367990921

1. Zooma
2. Grind
3. The Smile of Your Shadow
4. Goose
5. Bass 'n' Drums
6. B. Fingers
7. Snake Eyes
8. Nosumi Blues
9. Tidal

Discipline Global Mobile
www.disciplineglobalmobile.com
phone: 213 386 3900

Distributed by
Ryko Distribution Partners
To order, contact your sales rep

Press Contact:
Lois Najarian / Susan Blond, Inc.
212.333.7728 x105

For Immediate Release
August 3, 1999

LEGENDARY LED ZEPPELIN ARTIST JOHN PAUL JONES TO RELEASE FIRST SOLO ALBUM ON SEPTEMBER 14
U.S. Tour This Fall To Support *Zooma*

NEW YORK, NY – Rock n' roll legend, **John Paul Jones**, former bass and keyboardist of the ultimate rock group Led Zeppelin, is set to release his first solo album, *Zooma*, on September 14, 1999. This long-awaited instrumental album not only emphasizes John's myriad of avant-garde influences, it marks his return into solid rock territory. *Zooma* will be released on the Discipline Global Mobile label and distributed by Rykodisc. A U.S. tour in support of *Zooma* will begin in October, 1999.

As the only remaining Zeppelin member to progress and experiment with new styles and directions, John Paul Jones is now at the advent of an on-going solo career. For the last three decades, the artist has made enormous contributions to music history as a composer, arranger, producer and musician. Effectively conveying his impressive ability and musical vision, Jones composed and produced all nine tracks on his new album, and mixed several as well. He also plays a variety of instruments including four, ten and twelve string basses, bass lap steel, mandola, organ and guitars.

Most recently, John Paul Jones has collaborated with **REM** (arranging strings on *Automatic For The People*), **Diamanda Galas** (producing and performing on her 1994 release *The Sporting Life* and subsequent world tour) and with **Heart** (producing and performing on their 1994 live release). Other collaborations have been with the **Rolling Stones, Jeff Beck, Butthole Surfers, Brian Eno, Peter Gabriel** and **Lenny Kravitz**.

Discipline Global Mobile, specializing in instrumental and avant-garde rock music, was founded by King Crimson guitarist Robert Fripp. John Paul Jones chose DGM because of their unique standard trading policy; no contracts exist between the artist and the record company and artists retain the rights to their work at all times.

#

NEW YORK · LOS ANGELES
FIFTY WEST 57TH STREET NEW YORK NY 10019
212.333.7728 FAX 212.262.1373 PUBLICITY@SUSANBLONDINC.COM

For Immediate Release: September 29, 1999

Press Contacts:
Lois Najarian/Courtney Friedman
Susan Blond Inc.
212-333-7728, ext. 128

JOHN PAUL JONES EMBARKS ON FIRST EVER SOLO U.S. TOUR IN SUPPORT OF UPCOMING ZOOMA

New York, NY – John Paul Jones, the artist internationally renowned as the bass and keyboardist for the legendary Led Zeppelin, will commence a three week U.S. tour of selected dates in support of his long awaited solo album *Zooma*, referred to by *Mojo* magazine as "a bass player's album in excelsis." The tour begins on October 12th in Northampton, MA and ends in Las Vegas on November 1st. This will be John Paul Jones first ever solo tour.

Jones comments, "One of the main reasons why I felt the need to compose and record *Zooma* is so that I can get back on the stage and really rock hard."

NOW APPEARING:	
OCTOBER 21, 1999	**CABOOZE ON THE WEST BANK**
Ticket Price: $20.00 in advance	917 Cedar Avenue South
$22.00 at door	**Minneapolis**
Show Time: 9:30 p.m.	

For the last three decades, John Paul Jones has made enormous contributions to music history as a composer, arranger, producer and instrumentalist. Effectively conveying his impressive ability and personal musical vision, Jones composed and produced all nine tracks on his new album. He also plays a variety of instruments including four, ten and twelve string basses, bass lap steel, mandola, organ and guitars.

Zooma was released on September 14, 1999 on Robert Fripp's Discipline Global Mobile label and distributed by Rykodisc. John Paul Jones plans to tour the States again in the new year.

NEW YORK · LOS ANGELES
FIFTY WEST 57TH STREET NEW YORK NY 10019
212 333 7728 FAX 212 262 1474 PUBLICITY@SUSANBLONDINC.COM

Discipline Global Mobile
PO Box 1533 - Salisbury - Wiltshire - SP5 5ER - UK
tel : (44) 1722 780187 fax: (44) 1722 781042
PO Box 5282 - Beverly Hills - CA 90209 5282 - USA
tel : (1) 213 386 3900 fax: (1) 213 386 6005

photo: Amy & Tanveer

John Paul Jones

JOHN PAUL JONES
Zooma
Release date: September 14, 1999

In the soundscape of pop, amidst today's glut of mundane entertainments and predictable products, the release this Fall of *Zooma*, John Paul Jones' brilliant solo debut is a remarkable musical landmark. An event not simply for the fame and notoriety of John Paul Jones, nor even for the historical import of the first signature statement from one with so singularly rich a musical legacy, the fact is that *Zooma* is a much needed shock to the system. Internationally revered as the blistering bass half of the rocking rhythm section of the world's greatest band, Led Zeppelin, he's equally respected as an impeccable arranger, uncanny producer and immensely inventive composer within that soft white belly of the behemoth music industry and the extreme margins of the avant-garde alike. John Paul Jones has been an enduring and defining voice in contemporary music for some thirty-five plus, dauntingly prolific years. And while his quiet modesty atop the elite mountain of mass celebrity where egos run rampant with vanity and self-indulgent hubris has marked John Paul Jones as something of a mystery to his followers and more simply as a really nice ordinary guy among his fellow artists, it's safe to say that just about everyone's been a touch curious as to what he'd had to say on his own- away from the monumental classics of Zeppelin and free of the logistic restraints of making everyone else's music just that much better.

And make no mistake about it- *Zooma* is a definitive statement. You don't so much get the sense that he's waited this long to do that solo just thing because he's been so bloody busy, as a deeper impression that somehow he's been figuring out the perfect way to collect and distill a lifetime of creative fire into one absolutely incendiary blast. Forged in the hottest furnace of Rock and Roll's primal fury, *Zooma* comes out alchemically transformed, precious as a gem, sharp as a diamond and born of an intricate internal complexity so sublime as to shine with the clarity of a crystal. A potently emotive album, *Zooma* is a mesmerizing evocation of the energy and excitement John Paul Jones looks to mine from the deepest dredges of musical expression. Maintaining a steadfast belief that "little has actually changed in terms of how music works for me," Jones has approached a personal requisite of authenticity and originality with an abiding sense of that "continuity through the ages." With some deftly inscribed blasts of those emblematic bass lines his fans crave, and a constantly shifting clever pastiche of ideas and sensibilities he's helped to shape over his career, the haunting refrain of John Paul Jones' immense sonic lexicon is never far away, but always somewhere at a distance off, like some vaguely familiar landscape subsumed in a flood of new and challenging ideas. That is the essential truth to *Zooma*, that this is an artist who is captivated with the process of creation.

Largely overshadowed by his nine phenomenally successful albums with Led Zeppelin between 1969 and 1980, John Paul Jones had long before established himself as a virtuoso musician, devastating performer and consummate craftsman at the fine art of composition, providing the musical direction and arrangement for a string of hits by the likes of The Rolling Stones, Nico, Herman's Hermits, Donovan, Lulu, Jeff Beck, The Yardbirds, Francoise Hardy, Marc Bolan, Cliff Richard and Cat Stevens dating as far back as 1963, when he had already logged three number one hits in his native England by the age of

NEW YORK · LOS ANGELES
FIFTY WEST 57TH STREET NEW YORK NY 10019
212.333.7728 FAX 212.262.1373 PUBLICITY@SUSANBLONDINC.COM

seventeen. Certainly his skills and absolute understanding of the organic anatomy by which any memorable song is constructed are a major constant in everything he has touched leading up to, and including, *Zooma*. The common ground in all the work is how John Paul Jones approaches every aspect of musicianship from the compositional point of view. For him the issue that every song presents is the question of "what you need and where you need it", a totally linear approach to the basic architecture of music where sound design is a matter of finding a way to move the song and his audience from here to there, the fluid and formal dynamics of tension and release by which his primary objective of eliciting a strong reaction is achieved. What this more personal album also reveals however is the degree to which his aesthetics have evolved far beyond the tired and trite topography of popular music. Exploring the possibilities opened up by early electronic music and musique concrete, dedicating the past few years to building his own studio, availing himself of the latest computer technologies, and informed by an epic journey he has taken throughout the Eighties and Nineties on the margins of artistic expression far from the well worn path of the mainstream (including multivarious collaborative efforts with a veritable who's who of the cutting edge, from the Butthole Surfers, Diamanda Galas and La Fura Dels Baus to R.E.M., Peter Gabriel and Brian Eno), Jones makes sure that whatever familiar comforts Zooma offers are amply offset by some of the most challenging, dissonant, head-spinning audio assaults this side of our millennial dread. "Melody doesn't have to be beautiful," he reminds us, and for all the lush and lovely moments that unfold in *Zooma* be prepared for John Paul Jones own idiosyncratic and iconoclastic surprise way of giving you "a good kick in the head."

Press Contact:
Lois Najarian
Susan Blond, Inc.
212-333-7728, ext. 105

NEW YORK · LOS ANGELES
FIFTY WEST 57TH STREET NEW YORK NY 10019
212.333.7728 FAX 212.262.1373 PUBLICITY@SUSANBLONDINC.COM

SUSAN BLOND INC.

Billboard

THE INTERNATIONAL NEWSWEEKLY OF MUSIC, VIDEO, AND HOME ENTERTAINMENT

$5.95 (U.S.), $6.95 (CAN.), £4.95 (U.K.), Y2,500 (JAPAN)

AUGUST 14, 1999

Zeppelin's Jones Makes Solo Return
Instrumental 'Zooma' Set On Discipline Global Precedes Tour

BY ED CHRISTMAN

NEW YORK—Since Led Zeppelin broke up in 1980, John Paul Jones has kept himself busy as a producer, but it wasn't until his collaboration with Diamanda Galas in 1994 that a missing ingredient in his artistic life became obvious.

"When I toured with Diamanda, I realized I had been missing playing live," says Jones, who played bass and keyboards in the most influential band of the 1970s. "Once I realized it, I had to figure out how to be able to get out for live shows again. So I decided to make an album."

With the Sept. 14 release of "Zooma" on Discipline Global Mobile in North America and Europe and Pony Canyon in Japan, Jones plans to hit the road to support the album, which is one of the major thrusts in promoting it.

"In marketing the album, we will rely on a lot of word-of-mouth for a very powerful performance on-stage and on the album, which will speak for itself," says Jones' manager, Richard Chadwick of Opium Arts Ltd. in London.

JONES

The instrumental album, which was written and produced by Jones in a home studio, clearly shows—in case there were any doubts about his contributions—that he was one of the main architects of the Led Zeppelin sound. The riff-laden album is built around intricate bass/drum interplay that defines the term "Zeppelin-esque." On the record, Jones plays multiple bass guitars, including the bass lap steel, which he calls the lead instrument on the record. He also plays mandola, guitar, and organ.

Jones will hit the road in October, first coming to North America and then moving on to Europe in November and Japan through December. In the new year, there may be another go-round in the U.S. In North America, the booking agent is Steve Martin of the Agency in New York. Neil Warnock, who is with the Agency in London, handles the rest of the world.

Jones says he's still assembling the band, which will take the form of a power trio. "Nick Beggs is *(Continued on page 15)*

PUBLICITY@SUSANBLONDINC.COM
250 WEST 57TH STREET SUITE 622 | NEW YORK, NY 10107 | 212.333.7728 | FAX: 212.262.1373
14542 VENTURA BOULEVARD SUITE 210 | SHERMAN OAKS, CA 91403 | 818.788.8474 | FAX: 818.788.8551

ZEPPELIN'S JONES MAKES SOLO RETURN
(Continued from page 12)

going to be on a Chapman Stick, which is half-bass and half-guitar, so when I am playing guitar he can play bass and vice versa," he says. "The drums are not settled."

On "Zooma," drums were handled by Pete Thomas of Elvis Costello & the Attractions fame. He also manned the drum seat for Galas' "The Sporting Life," which Jones produced, co-wrote, and played on. Other musicians on "Zooma" include Trey Gunn of King Crimson on guitar; Paul Leary of the Butthole Surfers, a band produced by Jones, on guitar; and Denny Fongheiser on *djembe*. The album was written and produced by Jones; his publishing is handled by Warner/Chappell Music.

Although "Zooma" is Jones' first official solo album, he wrote and produced the 1986 soundtrack to the film "Scream For Help." Jones also played the majority of the music on that Atlantic set.

Jones started recording for "Zooma" a little more than two years ago, with the rhythm tracks taking about a month. After that, Jones did "a lot of programming and overdubs," he says. "I took my time since I had my own studio; I did some experimenting."

In describing the track "B. Fingers," Jones says, "I just like the excitement that [John] Bonham and I used to get. I wrote all the drum parts, especially the kick and the snare drum. That's the powerhouse that generates the excitement here, as it did with Zeppelin."

He adds, "One thing this album isn't ... is democratic. I let [Thomas] do his own fills, but it's my beat."

After completing the album, Jones decided to sign to Robert Fripp's label, since the two share the same manager, Chadwick.

"I was considering what label to bring the album to. I wasn't overly enthusiastic with being on a major," Jones relates. "[Chadwick] told me about [Fripp's] label, which has no contract and the artist retains ownership of the master. And I thought, 'This is where I want to be.'"

With the album in hand, David Singleton, label manager for the Solsbury, England-based Discipline Global, says that in addition to press and word-of-mouth, the company plans to use the Internet to market the album.

"Anything without vocals is difficult to get radio play for, so in terms of helping people hear the album, the Web will be a major tool," Singleton says. "But John's very nervous about making the whole track available, so we will have one-minute edits. We are considering online chats, but that will be much nearer to the release date."

Singleton says the label also plans to promote the album through retail. Ryko Distribution Partners, the U.S. distributor, will have co-op advertising funds available for the shops, he says. Listening parties are also planned.

Chadwick says that Jones' legacy will help with the marketing. "The name is big enough to do quite enough for us, we think," he says.

Bob Douglas, director of music merchandising at Amazon.com, based in Seattle, says that Jones' name may help market the album to the press, but he's not so sure it will result in sales. "There is a thin slice of the Zeppelin audience," he says. "But beyond that, it stands on his own merits. [Jones] is a great musician and great arranger."

One of the tracks that displays Jones' arranging skill is "Snake Eyes," in which a heavy riff ends majestically with a prolonged string passage played by the London Symphony Orchestra. When the suggestion is made that that would have been a good song with which to end the album, Jones responds, "I like the way the album ends, with 'Tidal.' It ends on a note of desperation."

> *'I had to figure out how to be able to get out for live shows again. So I decided to make an album'*
>
> *– JOHN PAUL JONES –*

BILLBOARD AUGUST 14, 1999

SUSAN BLOND, INC.
250 WEST 57TH STREET SUITE 622
NEW YORK, NY 10107-0622
212.333.7728 FAX 262.1373

ul Jones

"You'll need the volume about there," says an obviously happy John Paul Jones from the control room of his London home studio. After more than a decade with a highly innovative and successful rock band, and after a decade of producing, arranging, and guesting with numerous other successful acts, the former Led Zeppelin bassist is ready to press PLAY on his first-ever solo project. Featuring drummer Pete Thomas and guest appearances by Butthole Surfers guitarist Paul Leary, bassist/Stick player Trey Gunn, and session drummer Denny Fongheiser, *Zooma* combines awesome bass

Zooms Ahead

By Adrian Ashton
Photographs By James Cumpsty

John Paul Jones continued

technique, Zep-style power riffs, and melodic lines played on a variety of bass instruments. Like *The Sporting Life*, Jones's 1994 collaboration with avant-garde vocalist Diamanda Galás, the new disc pushes bass playing to its sonic limits. JPJ has signed with Discipline Global Mobile, a label set up by King Crimson guitarist Robert Fripp that allows artists to retain copyright. "I really support the ethic behind this," says John Paul—and when you listen to *Zooma* you realize the label's different approach perfectly matches the record's unique style.

What inspired you to come up with such a varied album?

I had a lot of fun doing the Sporting Life tour; it was so enjoyable I wanted to do it again. Diamanda reasons that if you're going to put that much effort into playing music, it might as well be your own. The way for me to continue to do that was to record an album and take it out on the road.

How will it work live?

Well, there aren't as many overdubs as you might think. I did a lot of it using my custom Manson basses, which are wired in stereo. [*See sidebar.*] I can put the bridge pickup through a guitar amp together with some processing, leaving the neck pickup for the straight bass sound. For example, the bridge part in the title track is my bridge pickup only through a patch on a T.C. Electronic G Force. That can all be reproduced live. There's no need for extra guitar, even though it sounds like there's one coming in. Plus, since it's a 10-string bass, it actually sounds as if there are four of us playing! I did double the part very quietly with an electric mandola just to bring it out a little bit, though.

The other sounds all come from the Kyma system, which I'll be taking on tour. The Kyma is a software program that can manipulate any sound—it can listen to the bass audio and either react to it or process it. For example, you can hit a note and it will trigger some other sound. It's a very flexible design, so I can make it do what I want. On "Goose," a ghost bass appears the second time around and seems to be playing harmony—it's not! That's actually the Kyma system listening to the bass, doing a frequency analysis, and then re-synthesizing it and playing it back within certain restricted parameters. And it's doing it all live.

I can use the program to create sounds I hear in my head, but sometimes you end up with happy accidents—if you're there to pick out the good stuff.

What other instruments do you use to inspire ideas?

I've just had a doubleneck lap-steel bass made.

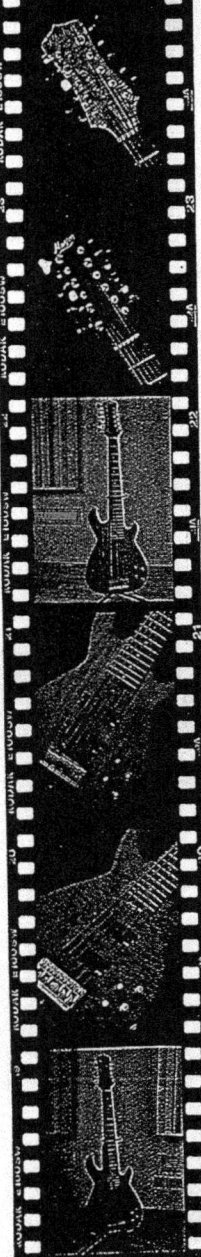

Whole Lotta Gear

Beautifully displayed at his studio complex, John Paul Jones's favorite instruments are close at hand: his '63 Fender Jazz Bass, '52 Fender Precision, Fender Bass VI, and a tripleneck acoustic built by U.K. luthier Andy Manson. (See November '94.) On the studio floor is a unique Manson Guitars doubleneck lap-steel bass. Andy's brother Hugh Manson, JPJ's tech and builder of all his electric custom instruments, explains the instrument's history: "The first lap steel I made for him is an 8-string ranging from a .135 bass string to a .010 guitar gauge. It has a Hipshot Trilogy Bridge system and D Tuners for a huge variety of tuning options." The pickup is a custom-made EMG. The instrument appears on several *Zooma* tracks. On the lap-steel bass, one neck is tuned to open *E* and the other to *A*. A custom stand featuring JPJ's *Led Zeppelin IV* runic symbol makes a neat finishing touch. Although the instrument was built after *Zooma* was finished, you'll be able to hear it on the tour.

The incredible *Zooma* bass sounds come from three doubled-string basses. "John's first doubled-string bass was his 8-string," Hugh elaborates, "which he took on tour with Diamanda Galás. Naturally he wanted to take that further, so I built a 12-string—not a 4 with two octave strings, but a 6 with an octave or doubling string above. This was quite heavy due to the steel neck-reinforcement rods, so I made a much lighter 10-string tuned *EADGC*." The 10 has a quilted-maple top and EMG pickups and circuitry, each pickup having its own output. "In the studio we fed the neck pickup into an SWR SM-900, Big Ben 1x18, or Goliath 4x10, while the bridge pickup went into a Matchless or Soldano Decatone guitar amp. We're trying out Fender Tone Masters for the live work. John liked LEDs in his basses with Zeppelin so he could see where he had to go onstage, and he's gone one further by having color-coordinated Sims LEDs in his 10-string. I then made a lighter 12-string that uses graphite neck reinforcement. But we just had to go one step further, so I fitted blue Sims LEDs, and I added a circuit so whenever John plays a note the lights go on but switch off when he stops!" And it doesn't stop there. After producing some sessions with Heart, JPJ asked Hugh to build a Precision Bass with a Jazz neck. Strung with Rotosound flatwounds, bridge and pickup covers in place, and finished in a vintage salmon pink, it's the ideal Motown instrument. Hugh continues, "There's an *f*-hole archtop mandolin and matching mandola, a regular mandola, an electric solid mandola [used on the *Zooma* title track], and an 8-string acoustic bass all made by my brother Andy. I've recently made a bass mandola tuned *GDAE* and a 4-string electric mandolin. Then there's all the repair and renovation work as well. The '63 Jazz has just gotten a new neck, and I've restored a Framus electric mandolin."

Tucked away in a separate room are more vintage instruments: Jimmy Page's white Fender Stratocaster, a Gibson SG, Fender Bass V, a pair of sunburst fretted and fretless '70s Precisions, '80s Manson Kestrel bass, Manson 4-string bass (named "Eric"), plus another quilted-top 4-string ("That's Son of Eric," says Hugh). Even the great basses of the Zeppelin days are kept in working order, including the custom Alembics, Hagstrom 8-string, and Gibson EB-1, with only the 8-string Alembic forced into retirement due to neck warping. MIT Ripcords provide the instrument-to-amp connections, and MIT GAS Terminators provide amp-to-speaker links.

John Paul Jones *continued*

I immediately knew what I wanted it for—but at the same time I started discovering other ideas and sounds on it. With the doubled-string basses I noticed early on that you can do things like play narrow intervals, such as minor seconds, which you just couldn't get away with on a 4-string because it would just rumble away. But with a 10-string your ear tends to follow the octave string rather than the fundamental, and the higher string helps define the fundamental in more than just the obvious ways. So it really increases the instrument's musical range.

Do you ever play them with the strings sounding separately?

I usually play both together, but with the 8-string bass on the Diamanda tour I actually began to separate the strings. There's one instance where I would start a line on just the octave strings and then bring in the lower strings.

What's the live lineup going to be?

I'm using drummer Geoff Dugmore and Stick player Nick Beggs. When I'm playing lap steel Nick can play bass, and when I'm on bass he can go up the other end on the Stick or play pad parts. I tried playing Stick myself for a while, but it felt

"This is my band, so I'm in charge."

Richard Patterson
Bassist past and present with:
Miles Davis
David Sanborn
Boz Scaggs
Roberta Flack

LAKLAND
2044 N. Dominick, Chicago, IL 60614 773.871.9684
www.lakland.com

John Paul Jones continued

like playing bass backwards—and I just thought life was too short to get into that! Trey Gunn will also be playing touch guitar, which is like a Stick but with a different string arrangement. I went with Trey for that sound partly, but my main reason is the way he plays and his musicianship. Good Stick players are remarkable.

How do you approach writing for an album?

I usually write away from an instrument. I can't write in the studio. I may just go for a walk and take a manuscript book so I can jot down ideas; then I'll go back and find the instrument I want to play the part on. I first wrote the *Zooma* title track while producing a band called Elephant Ride at a studio near Zuma Beach. I had the riff in my head and played it on my acoustic 8-string bass.

Actually, the oldest track is "B. Fingers," which I wrote at the end of the Diamanda sessions. I wrote it, tried it out, but couldn't play it—it was too hard.

Does "B. Fingers" stand for bass fingers or bleeding fingers?

Broken fingers—no, all of them! [*Laughs.*] I dug it out again and practiced it until I could play it. I'll probably have to practice it some more for the tour. The bridge is just great to jam on. "B. Fingers" reminds me of the fun Bonzo [Zeppelin drummer John Bonham] and I used to have playing the middle section to "Dazed and Confused." We would do lots of different phrasings, and it almost became a rhythm section soloing together.

You take that to an extreme on "Drum 'n' Bass."

I was in Los Angeles doing a djembe overdub with Denny Fongheiser [who drummed on the Galás tour], and I said, "Why not bring your kit along?" I rented a vintage Jazz Bass, and that's what came out in the studio. It was a lot of fun and has its own charm. You can hear the drummer laughing at the end.

It's very percussive, as if your strings are slapping against the fingerboard.

I've always played like that. I'm actually a very noisy player. I have to be careful when I'm in the studio playing fingerstyle, because I make all sorts of rattles and noises, even though I don't

Nice chops: steering the mighty Zeppelin, 1974.

actually ever play in the slapping style. Again, I decided life was too short to get into that! In my very first band the last person to join was the drummer; we went for a while as two guitars and bass, so I had to make up for it by making a lot of noise.

You play a lot of lap steel on Zooma. *Where do your slide influences come from?*

When I toured with Zeppelin I used to take a Gibson lap steel with me as my hotel instrument, although I never played it onstage. Diamanda spotted it in the studio, made me plug it in, and then made me do a number on it! I really like it now; it gives a real contrast to all the low end that's going on. Now of course I have a lap-steel bass as well. I mean, I can't go out with a normal instrument—that would be letting the side down!

Has 4-string bass reached its limits?

Oh, no. There are always things to do. Sometimes you can go back and revisit eras and find fresh ways of looking at an instrument. I used my old Fender Jazz for all the 4-string parts. The Precision stayed on the wall, though.

How did you feel about the Led Zeppelin BBC radio sessions that have been released?

I was pleased and quite surprised, really. It's a very cocky young band knowing they're good and showing off. There's some good stuff on there.

During those sessions you were introduced as John Paul Jones, arranger and producer, but you quickly pointed out you were arranger and bass player. Is that how you view yourself today?

I'd like to think it's John Paul Jones, musician. On *Zooma* I thought I'd like some strings, so I arranged some string parts and then conducted an orchestra.

> "We were more funky than other rock bands at that time."

How did you record the bass?

Direct and miked. I used about five tracks for the bass, taking the low end from one pickup into the SWR and the high end into a Matchless HC 30 guitar amp. Then I would just use what sounded best. I use very little EQ—I like to get the sound of the amp.

"Nosumi Blues" has a real Zeppelin feel to it. Is that era and early blues still an influence?

I wasn't into the early blues as much as Plant and Page were; a lot of that came after Zeppelin. I was into R&B and jazz. Certainly the high-power electric blues was newer to me, but I had played in a blues band. In a way, a song like "You Shook Me" was a slightly different style, which we helped create. So yes, that influence is going to come through.

Do you think Zeppelin would have remained an electric blues band had you not joined?

The band would have been different with any

A Selected Discography

Solo album: *Zooma*, Discipline Global Mobile. **With Diamanda Galás:** *The Sporting Life*, Mute. **With Led Zeppelin:** (all on Atlantic) *BBC Sessions; Coda; In Through the Out Door; Presence; The Song Remains the Same; Physical Graffiti; Houses of the Holy; Led Zeppelin IV; Led Zeppelin III; Led Zeppelin II; Led Zeppelin*. **With Peter Gabriel:** *Us*, Geffen. **With Paul McCartney:** (both on Capitol) *Give My Regards to Broad Street; Back to the Egg*. **Soundtracks:** *Music from the Film Scream for Help*, out of print.

change of member, really. You could say I widened the influences a bit and reinforced others. Bonzo helped reinforce the soul/R&B element because he was into that, too.

You were almost a funk influence.

Yes—we both were. We used to love it; we were more funky than other rock bands at that time, and we were both huge James Brown and Motown fans. Bonzo could sing all the Motown classics—he would start going into "Tracks of My Tears" while playing drums! We'd incorporate that element into the live shows and on the records. I have jazz influences, but you can't say that's a jazz line or that's a blues line. "B. Fingers"

Continued on page 81
See music, pages 48 and 50

John Paul Jones
continued from page 47

is like a bebop line. It's almost rock-jazz—because jazz-rock is the worst of both worlds! The line is jazzy, but there's nothing polite about it. We're almost throwing down a challenge with some of these lines—play me if you can!

I'm not sure where rock is going these days. I like the intensity of metal—the tensions and the sound—but I'd like to see more diversity.

Do you think Led Zeppelin created heavy metal?

I'd like to think so—that we did something really destructive [*laughs*]. But we weren't heavy metal, because the music was too varied. A lot of bands listen to the same type of music, and consequently they never go out of their circle. You should listen to everything, no matter what you play, because you always get answers to musical questions from other music styles. We were very varied, so maybe it's more truthful to say a couple of Zeppelin tracks invented heavy metal, although even "Black Dog" and "Whole Lotta Love" haven't been copied in any way. Sampled and imitated, perhaps. I was asked during the last tour if Diamanda's album was Zeppelin-influenced, and Diamanda quipped, "Don't you think Zeppelin was JPJ-influenced?"

You played "Communication Breakdown" on Diamanda's tour. Will you play any Zeppelin during the new one?

I may! I shall mainly be playing the whole of *Zooma*, but there could be one or two other things.

What are the tour plans?

We'll be in the States for October and then back to Europe and the U.K. during November. There may be a revisit to the States later before going on to Australia and Japan.

How have you filled your time since the Diamanda tour?

I moved to London and built a new studio in my home. I took a lot of time mixing the album and had the time to experiment. Engineering was new to me, even though I learned a lot through production work. Recording live drums was new, but I persevered and am really pleased with the results. I always kept overdubs to a minimum, though, because it was in the back of my mind to perform the material live.

Was drummer Pete Thomas your first choice?

Yes. I'm very fussy with drum parts. I write out the parts and do demos on drum machines, because the bass part has to be very exact as well. Regarding fills—everything above the waist was completely free! A bass drum beat here and a bass drum beat there makes so much difference in a riff; you've really got to lock together and reinforce each other. That's what Bonzo and I did so well.

How long did it take you to forge that special rhythm-section link with Bonzo?

He was very confident and cocky when we started, and I realized he knew what he was doing, so I could immediately work on slotting in. Suddenly he looked up and thought, Hang on—here's someone else who knows what he's doing. As you know, bassists and drummers recognize each other, and when that happens you know that if you try something the other will be listening and will support. The whole point is to make the band sound good, so it happened pretty damn quick with Bonzo and me. I would listen to the kick and either reinforce what was going on or stop, damp the bass, and just let the beat come through alone. On my solo work I let that happen with the snare drum: I'll write riffs where I stop to allow the snare alone to come through. It's really effective; it gives character and life to the riff.

It's a discipline to leave space.

Yes—but it's the simplest way to bring something to life. The bass is best for that. Hip-hop people have discovered that effect—they just take out the bass for a couple of bars, and it's so effective when it comes back in again.

Is there any possibility of a Led Zeppelin reunion?

No. Or, in two words, No ... no! They're doing their thing, and I'm doing mine. Plus, this is my band, so I'm in charge. We met up for the Diamond Album Awards [for record sales over ten million] and played for the Rock & Roll Hall of Fame—but Zeppelin was all done a long time ago, and I want to look forward. ♪

BP Recommends
continued from page 66

DEEP RUMBA
This Night Becomes a Rumba [Justin Time/American Clave]
Bassist: Andy Gonzalez
Instrument: 50-year-old German plywood acoustic
Raw, riveting traditional rumba with Gonzalez's bass surrounded by ten percussionists and some notable guest vocalists, including Rubén Blades. High points include Andy leading the charge on the standard "I Wish You Love" and a conga-fied cover of Cream's "Sunshine of Your Love." (CJ)

DAYS OF THE NEW
2 [Outpost/Universal]
Bassist: Travis Meeks
Instrument: Spector 4-string
Acoustic guitar ace Travis Meeks has forged ahead with a sophomore album without bassist Jesse Vest and his other bandmates. Even so, Meeks's able bass parts provide power and grit under strong pop compositions and intricate guitar work. (BL) ♪

JOHN PAUL JONES, ROBERT PLANT AND JIMMY PAGE OF LED ZEPPELIN

Inter-Office Memo

 ATLANTIC RECORDING CORPORATION

To	All Concerned	From	Judy Libow
Subject	ROBERT PLANT - ROCKLINE		
Date	October 18, 1990	Copies to	D. Morris, M. Schulman

This is to inform you that Robert Plant, and his entire band, will be the special guests on Rockline, Monday evening, October 29 live from Los Angeles.

Please tune in!

PRESS RELEASE ATLANTIC RECORDS PUBLICITY 75 ROCKEFELLER PLAZA, NY 10019 (212) 275-2035

FOR IMMEDIATE RELEASE

AUGUST 17, 1992

"LED ZEPPELIN" BOXED SET GARNERS RIAA MULTI-PLATINUM CERTS

"LED ZEPPELIN," the Atlantic 4-CD/4-cassette/5-LP boxed set, has been simultaneously certified double and triple platinum by the RIAA for U.S. sales in excess of 500,000 and 750,000 units respectively. The announcement was made by Atlantic Senior Vice President/General Manager Val Azzoli, who noted that the set is rapidly approaching the quadruple platinum mark at retail.

Released in October of 1990, "LED ZEPPELIN" is the best-selling historical boxed set to date. It includes selections from each of the band's nine studio albums, all produced Jimmy Page, plus two previously-unreleased tracks. The retrospective contains 54 tracks personally selected and sequenced by Jimmy Page, Robert Plant, and John Paul Jones.

In addition, "LED ZEPPELIN II," released in October of 1969, has been certified sextuple platinum by the RIAA for U.S. sales in excess of 6,000,000 units.

ATLANTIC RECORDS 9229 SUNSET BLVD. LOS ANGELES, CA 90069

PRESS RELEASE ATLANTIC RECORDS PUBLICITY 75 ROCKEFELLER PLAZA, NY 10019 (212) 275-2035

FOR IMMEDIATE RELEASE

APRIL 26, 1993

LED ZEPPELIN BOXED SET SOARS TO QUADRUPLE PLATINUM

"LED ZEPPELIN," the 4-CD/4-cassette boxed set retrospective, has been certified quadruple platinum by the RIAA for U.S. sales in excess of one million units. The announcement was made by Atlantic Senior Vice President/General Manager Val Azzoli, who noted that "LED ZEPPELIN" is the best-selling historical boxed set to date.

Released in October 1990, "LED ZEPPELIN" contains 54 tracks personally selected and sequenced by Jimmy Page, Robert Plant, and John Paul Jones, and digitally remastered by Jimmy Page and engineer George Marino at Sterling sound in New York City.

ATLANTIC RECORDS 9229 SUNSET BLVD. LOS ANGELES, CA 90069

ATLANTIC
RECORDING
CORPORATION

75
ROCKEFELLER
PLAZA
NEW YORK,
NY 10019
TELEPHONE:
(212) 275-2000

FOR IMMEDIATE RELEASE
MARCH 14, 1995

"ENCOMIUM: A TRIBUTE TO LED ZEPPELIN"

Atlantic Records has announced the release of "ENCOMIUM: A TRIBUTE TO LED ZEPPELIN," the highly-anticipated tribute to the songs of Jimmy Page, Robert Plant, John Paul Jones, and John Bonham. Due in stores on March 21st, the 12-track collection features performances by an array of notable artists: 4 Non Blondes; Big Head Todd And The Monsters; Blind Melon; Cracker; Sheryl Crow; Duran Duran; Helmet With David Yow (of The Jesus Lizard); Atlantic recording group Hootie & The Blowfish; new Atlantic recording group Never The Bride; Atlantic recording artists Robert Plant and Tori Amos; Rollins Band; and Atlantic recording group Stone Temple Pilots. The album's Executive Producers are Jolene Cherry; Page/Plant manager Bill Curbishley; and Atlantic A&R rep Kevin Williamson.

Due to the consistently high quality of the album's performances, "ENCOMIUM" has been serviced in its entirety to pop, AOR, alternative, and triple A outlets nationwide; many of the album's tracks are already receiving airplay. In addition, Atlantic is servicing an Interactive Press Kit (IPK) about the project, available on floppy disk for both the Macintosh and Windows formats. The IPK can also be downloaded from zoso.com, Jimmy Page & Robert Plant's World Wide Web site. The address is: **http://www.atlantic-records.com/zoso/**.

A complete track listing follows on the next page.

- more -

Following is the complete track listing of "ENCOMIUM":

Misty Moutain Hop -- 4 Non Blondes
Hey Hey What Can I Do -- Hootie & The Blowfish
D'yer Mak'er -- Sheryl Crow
Dancing Days -- Stone Temple Pilots
Tangerine -- Big Head Todd and the Monsters
Thank You -- Duran Duran
Out On The Tiles -- Blind Melon
Good Times Bad Times -- Cracker
Custard Pie -- Helmet with David Yow
Four Sticks -- Rollins Band
Going To California -- Never The Bride
Down By The Seaside -- Robert Plant and Tori Amos

encomium: glowing and warmly enthusiastic praise

# # #

PRESS RELEASE ATLANTIC RECORDS PUBLICITY 75 ROCKEFELLER PLAZA, NY 10019 (212) 275-2035

FOR IMMEDIATE RELEASE
MAY 10, 1993

ROBERT PLANT'S "CALLING TO YOU" EXPLODES AT RADIO; ALBUM READY

In its first week of release, Robert Plant's new single, "Calling To You," has exploded at album radio outlets across the country. Far and away the #1 most-added track of the week, the song debuted on over 200 stations, and it immediately became one of the top five hottest songs at AOR radio nationwide. The companion video clip, directed by Peter Christopherson, had its World Premiere on MTV on May 8th.

"Calling To You" is the first track to be released from Plant's forthcoming Es Paranza/Atlantic album, "FATE OF NATIONS," which is due in retail stores on May 25th. Written by Plant and Chris Blackwell, "Calling To You" features Robert's new guitarists, Kevin Scott MacMichael & Francis Dunnery, along with long-time mate Charlie Jones on bass and drummer Pete Thompson. The song also features a very special guest performance by acclaimed, renegade classical violinist Nigel Kennedy, who also appears in the video.

In its Single Review of "Calling To You," <u>Billboard</u> commented: "Rich, splendidly resounding opening salvo from Plant's exceptional 'FATE OF NATIONS' album, the pealing vocalist eclipses

- more -

ATLANTIC RECORDS 9229 SUNSET BLVD. LOS ANGELES, CA 90069

- 2 -

all emulators... This is drama, sinew, and sonic pow as only a seasoned evergreen could invent."

"FATE OF NATIONS," Robert Plant's first solo album in three years, was produced by Chris Hughes and Robert, with mixing by Tim Palmer. All the songs but one were co-written by Plant, the exception being a rendition of the Tim Hardin classic, "If I Were A Carpenter." In addition to the aforementioned Nigel Kennedy, other special guests on the album include Clannad's Máire Brennan, guitarist Richard Thompson, Maartin Allcock on mandolin, and a trio of Indian musicians.

Coinciding with the release of "FATE OF NATIONS," Plant embarks on major world tour at the end of this month. The itinerary begins with an extensive series of shows throughout Europe, including a series of dates with Lenny Kravitz.

On stage, Plant will be joined by new guitarists Kevin Scott MacMichael & Francis Dunnery, keyboardist/guitarist Phil Johnstone, bassist Charlie Jones, and new drummer Michael Lee.

# # #

PRESS RELEASE ATLANTIC RECORDS PUBLICITY 75 ROCKEFELLER PLAZA, NY 10019 (212) 275-2035

FOR IMMEDIATE RELEASE

MAY 10, 1993

ROBERT PLANT IS "CALLING TO YOU" FROM WNEW-FM --

While in New York City for an extensive series of media interviews, Es Paranza/Atlantic recording artist Robert Plant stopped by radio station WNEW-FM for a live on-the-air interview with Carol Miller. During his visit to the station, Plant premiered "Calling To You," the first radio track from his forthcoming album, "FATE OF NATIONS." In its first week of release, "Calling To You" was far and away the #1 most-added song at album radio nationwide.

ATLANTIC RECORDS 9229 SUNSET BLVD. LOS ANGELES, CA 90069

PRESS RELEASE ATLANTIC RECORDS PUBLICITY 75 ROCKEFELLER PLAZA, NY 10019 (212) 275-2035

FOR IMMEDIATE RELEASE
MAY 17, 1993

ROBERT PLANT: "FATE OF NATIONS"

"FATE OF NATIONS," the new solo album from Es Paranza/Atlantic recording artist Robert Plant, is set to hit the nation's retail stores on Tuesday, May 25th. Plant's first solo album in three years, it was produced by Chris Hughes and Robert, with mixing by Tim Palmer. All the songs but one were co-written by Plant, the exception being a rendition of the Tim Hardin classic, "If I Were A Carpenter."

In its first week of release, the album's first single, "Calling To You," exploded at album radio outlets across the country. Far and away the #1 most-added track, the song debuted on over 200 stations and is currently one of the top five hottest songs at AOR radio nationwide. The companion video clip, directed by Peter Christopherson, had its World Premiere on MTV on May 8th. Both the song and the video feature a very special guest appearance by acclaimed, renegade classical violinist Nigel Kennedy.

The core band on "FATE OF NATIONS" consists of Plant's new guitarists, Kevin Scott MacMichael & Francis Dunnery, along with

- more -

ATLANTIC RECORDS 9229 SUNSET BLVD. LOS ANGELES, CA 90069

long-time mates Phil Johnstone (keyboards) and Charlie Jones (bass). The drum duties were shared by producer Chris Hughes, Pete Thompson, and new recruit Michael Lee - now a member of Plant's touring band.

In addition to Nigel Kennedy, other special guests on the album include Clannad's Máire Brennan, guitarist Richard Thompson, Maartin Allcock on mandolin, and a trio of Indian musicians.

Coinciding with the release of "FATE OF NATIONS," Plant embarks on a major world tour at the end of this month. The itinerary begins with an extensive series of shows throughout Europe, including a string of dates with Lenny Kravitz. Plant and company are scheduled to reach North America on October 1st.

The complete track listing of "FATE OF NATIONS" is: **Calling To You * Down To The Sea * Come Into My Life * I Believe * 29 Palms * Memory Song (Hello Hello) * If I Were A Carpenter * Promised Land * The Greatest Gift * Great Spirit * Network News.**

Plant's previous solo albums include: PICTURES AT ELEVEN (1982), THE PRINCIPLE OF MOMENTS (1983), SHAKEN 'N STIRRED (1985), NOW AND ZEN (1988), and MANIC NIRVANA (1990).

# # #

ATLANTIC RECORDING CORPORATION

75 ROCKEFELLER PLAZA
NEW YORK, NY 10019
TELEPHONE:
(212) 275-2000

FOR IMMEDIATE RELEASE

DECEMBER 13, 1993

ROBERT PLANT'S "FATE OF NATIONS" WINS RIAA GOLD;
RAVE-GATHERING NORTH AMERICAN TOUR COMPLETED

Robert Plant's "FATE OF NATIONS," the Es Paranza/Atlantic recording artist's sixth solo album, has been certified gold by the RIAA for U.S. sales in excess of 500,000 units. The announcement was made by Atlantic Executive Vice President/ General Manager Val Azzoli. Produced by Chris Hughes and Robert Plant, the album was released in May.

Plant is currently in the midst of his marathon 1993-94 "FATE OF NATIONS" world tour, which opened in Europe nearly seven months ago. Every show on the global trek has yielded unqualified rave reviews from fans and critics alike, who are acclaiming the concerts as the best live performances of Plant's solo career. The North America leg of the itinerary began in mid-September and wound up earlier this month with two shows at New York City's Paramount Theater.

On stage, Plant is joined by: guitarist Francis Dunnery - whose own debut Atlantic album will be released in 1994, guitarist/keyboardist Phil Johnstone, bassist Charlie Jones, drummer Michael Lee, and guitarist Innes Sibun.

- more -

- 2 -

"Calling To You," the first single from "FATE OF NATIONS," hit #1 on the national album radio charts. The two subsequent singles, "29 Palms" and "I Believe," were also top 5 album radio hits. "Promised Land," the just-released fourth track from "FATE OF NATIONS," is steadily climbing the national AOR radio listings at this writing.

All of the songs on "FATE OF NATIONS" are Plant originals, with the sole exception being a rendition of the Tim Hardin classic, "If I Were A Carpenter."

# # #

ATLANTIC RECORDING CORPORATION

1290 AVENUE OF THE AMERICAS NEW YORK, NY 10104
TELEPHONE: (212)707-2000

FOR IMMEDIATE RELEASE
JUNE 30, 1997

<u>RAINER PTÁCEK SHINES BRIGHTLY ON "THE INNER FLAME";
ROBERT PLANT, HOWE GELB HELM BENEFIT TRIBUTE TO GUITARIST</u>

Atlantic Records has announced the July 8th release of a truly unique tribute album. "THE INNER FLAME" brings an accomplished and remarkably diverse group of talents together to acknowledge the inspirational work of cult blues guitarist Rainer Ptácek. Highlighted by all-new recordings from such artists as Robert Plant & Jimmy Page, Emmylou Harris, Evan Dando, PJ Harvey, Madeleine Peyroux, Victoria Williams, and Giant Sand, "THE INNER FLAME" was conceived to raise funds to assist Ptácek with medical costs stemming from his battle with brain cancer.

Executive produced by longtime Rainer fans/friends Robert Plant and Giant Sand-man Howe Gelb, the tale of "THE INNER FLAME" begins with Plant, who met Ptácek during sessions for Robert's 1993 "FATE OF NATIONS" album. The two hit it off and collaborated on five songs that subsequently appeared on various "...NATIONS" single releases.

In assembling the tracks for "THE INNER FLAME," Plant and Gelb enlisted a wide array of contributors. Giant Sand — Gelb, bassist Joey Burns, and

- more -

drummer John Convertino — and Rainer himself serve as the backup band for a number of tracks on the album, including Austin, Texas blues singer Kris McKay's "One Man Crusade" and Buffalo Tom mainman Bill Janovitz's explosive "Powder Keg."

Other highlights include: Robert Plant and Jimmy Page's "Rude World," the duo's first new recording since 1995's RIAA platinum "NO QUARTER"; Rainer's duet with Giant Sand on the extraordinary and emotional title track; Emmylou Harris' "The Good Book," featuring guitars by both Ptácek and Gelb; "Something's Gotta Be Done" by Victoria Williams and her husband (ex-Jayhawk) Mark Olson; and 22-year-old vocal sensation Madeleine Peyroux, who joins Rainer on "Life Is Fine," a song that pairs Ptácek's music with a 1959 poem by Langston Hughes.

* * * * *

Born of Czech descent in East Germany, raised on the Southside of Chicago, Ptácek has resided in Tucson, Arizona since the 1970s. There he developed a sensual desert blues sound, dominated by a masterful inventiveness on the National steel and Dobro guitars, that can be found on his five import-only albums. In 1996, Ptácek was diagnosed with brain cancer, leaving the uninsured musician with mounting medical bills. Portions of the proceeds stemming from the sale of "THE INNER FLAME" will go to Charitable Fund for Rainer Ptácek (P.O. Box 13719, Tucson, AZ, 85732-3719).

#

The Inner Flame

How's your inner flame? Does it still burn a lot?
Do you still complain when it's way too hot?
— *Rainer Ptácek, 1997*

A truly special compilation, "THE INNER FLAME" brings an accomplished and remarkably diverse group of talents together to acknowledge the inspirational work of cult blues guitarist Rainer Ptácek. As eclectic as it is fascinating, the album is highlighted by all-new recordings from such top artists as Robert Plant & Jimmy Page, Emmylou Harris, Evan Dando, PJ Harvey, Madeleine Peyroux, Victoria Williams, and Giant Sand.

Conceived under much of the same sense of philanthropy and artistic appreciation as the acclaimed "SWEET RELIEF" albums for Victoria Williams and Vic Chesnutt, "THE INNER FLAME" is both a tribute and a benefit album. A portion of the album's proceeds will go towards helping Ptácek cope with mounting medical bills related to ongoing treatments for cancer, now thankfully in remission.

For those not in the know, Rainer (as he's known to family, friends and fans) is a sonic innovator with roots that place him in any number of locales. Born of Czech descent in East Germany, raised in the Southside of Chicago, Ptácek has resided among the canyons, cactus flowers and Colossal Caves of Tucson, Arizona since the 1970s. There he not only started a family — Rainer and wife Patty have three children — but developed his sensual desert blues sound dominated by his masterful inventiveness on the National steel and Dobro guitars.

Over the course of five import-only albums, and collaborations with a mixed bag of divergent artists that include Tucson country punks Naked Prey and the ambient/techno ensemble, the Grid — not to mention the aforementioned Plant, Williams and Giant Sand — Rainer has established himself as an instinctive, honest songwriter and a singularly gifted musician.

"I was just blown away by the way he could create so much tension and atmosphere in a sort of non-physical delivery," Robert Plant says, recalling the first time he saw Rainer performing in a London club. "He wasn't standing up and jumping around and pulling faces and doing all the usual blues stuff, he was just playing and capturing some of his better riffs with a sample pedal and building on them to make this great meld of sound, which is really beautiful. I was really refreshed by the kind of contemporary approach to music within the blues idiom."

"We're mutually in love with the same music," Ptácek says of Plant. "He comes from a very old blues kind of a place."

* * * * *

-more-

In February 1996, Ptácek was diagnosed with a brain tumor the "size of a fist," according to the guitarist. "I saw the MRI," Rainer says with a wry grin, "and it was big! Interestingly enough, it was in the heart of the brain — it's called the inner brain — which is why they couldn't do any real surgery on it. It had to be treated from the inside. That also saved me from it's attaching itself to other parts of my body. The outer brain doesn't let things in or out."

Ptácek underwent intensive chemotherapy within months of being diagnosed. By summer's end, the cancer had gone into remission. But while the immediate threat to his life had passed, Ptácek still faced an intense period of rehabilitation. Ptácek was healthy, but nearly buried under the weight of a staggering pile of medical bills.

Which is where "THE INNER FLAME" comes in. After the news of Rainer's illness struck, Ptácek's close friend Howe Gelb, of Tucson's freewheeling psychedelic-country-rock pioneers, Giant Sand, began trying to put together some way of raising a few dollars to offset Rainer's medical costs. He reached out to Victoria Williams, herself the recipient of other musicians' goodwill and "SWEET RELIEF" after being diagnosed with multiple sclerosis. John Parish, PJ Harvey's frequent collaborator and a big Rainer fan, also offered up his services. But it was Robert Plant who truly lit the spark for "THE INNER FLAME."

Plant had worked with Ptácek during the sessions for his 1993 "FATE OF NATIONS" album, collaborating on five songs that later appeared on various singles. Well-known for his love of blues music and for helping to bring blues to the forefront of popular rock 'n' roll expression as part of the mighty Led Zeppelin, Plant is unbridled in his admiration for Ptácek's songwriting and guitar playing. Upon hearing of Ptácek's plight, the legendary singer offered his invaluable assistance in getting the project underway.

"Robert had been in contact with Rainer and he wanted to do anything he could," Gelb says. "He's the guy that brought it all home. He gave it a home at Atlantic and was so cool. He was a sort of gatekeeper. He understood what we were trying to do and all about the gravitational flow of Rainer."

"Rainer told me that he and Howe had been discussing getting some people to play on the album," says Plant, tracing the genesis of his involvement with "THE INNER FLAME." "It just seemed a very obvious thing to do. He is not a particularly well-known artist, but he's got some very strong music and it's nice to be able to actually get it out on a broader stage. There's lots of great writers around and a lot of great music goes unheard, so this is a fantastic way of illuminating his craft."

Together, Plant and Gelb chose to emulate the "SWEET RELIEF" records in gathering together artists to pay homage to a little-known songwriter while at the same time raising money to support that songwriter in a time of need. They enlisted a wide array of contributors — including both avowed Ptácek fans and those likely musicians with an instinctive ear for such genius. The heart-felt renditions of Ptácek songs found on "THE INNER FLAME" reveal strength and artistic unity in their interpretative wide berth and openness to fresh approaches.

-more-

Rainer and Giant Sand kick off the proceedings with the extraordinary and emotional title track, emblematic for its focus on Ptácek's ardent, atmospheric National steel and Gelb's spaced-out stinging guitar. The one song on the album that was written after Rainer's illness, "The Inner Flame" is remarkably also one of Ptácek's best. "Concentrating on trying to get my skills back gave me a different focus than I had before," he says proudly.

For his friend Howe, there was a palpable sense of relief upon hearing Ptácek's new material. "I realized that Rainer had not only come back to true form, but had actually progressed," he recalls. "I said, 'Listen, this song is really good and it might be important to do something brand new to show where you're at.' The next day we were in the studio."

Perhaps the most startling track on "THE INNER FLAME" is Robert Plant and Jimmy Page's "Rude World," the duo's first new recording since 1994's "NO QUARTER." Over a mechanized rhythm track and swirling Wurlitzer organ, Plant lets loose his unearthly and unmistakable voice as Page wrings a wrenching wash of phased noise out of his six-string. As ever, the pair create some of the most mesmerizing modern blues imaginable.

"It was great to work on it," Plant says of "Rude World." "We had some help from Charlie Jones and Phil Andrews, who produced the track down in Bristol, the land of Portishead and Tricky. They created all the backing tracks and rhythm tracks and the drum loops. Jimmy and I just played on top of it, and it sounds pretty hot."

Heat is in no short supply on "THE INNER FLAME." The record is fraught with Ptácek's brand of bluesy slowburn, with any number of incandescent moments. Among the searing highlights are:

- Austin, Texas blues singer Kris McKay's "One Man Crusade" and Buffalo Tom mainman Bill Janovitz's explosive "Powder Keg," both featuring the backing of Rainer and the great Giant Sand core trio — Gelb, bassist Joey Burns, and drummer John Convertino
- Plant and Ranier's "21 Years," originally recorded during the "FATE OF NATIONS" sessions
- Emmylou Harris' "The Good Book," featuring guitars by Ptácek and Gelb on electric piano
- Chicago indie-blues group, the Drovers' jammy take on "Worried Spirits"
- The haunting "Losin' Ground" by Polly Jean Harvey, John Parish and ex-Captain Beefheart sideman-turned-producer Eric Drew Feldman
- "Something's Gotta Be Done" by Victoria Williams and her husband, ex-Jayhawk Mark Olson
- LK, the UK-based combo featuring former members of EMF, rocking out on "I Am A Sinner"
- Jonathan Richman's instrumental version of "Broken Promises"
- 22-year-old vocal sensation Madeleine Peyroux and Rainer's "Life Is Fine," which pairs Ptácek's music with the 1959 poem by Langston Hughes

"The main thing about Rainer is that he picks up the vibe or hears that little voice," Howe Gelb says admiringly of Ptácek's gifts as a songwriter, explaining why so many artists were touched enough to take part in "THE INNER FLAME." "He has always had that indescribable something that is just gravitational."

* * * * *

-more-

"Everybody needs some help some time or another," Robert Plant says, "and Rainer had helped me way back and contributed to my record, and it was time for me to lend him a hand. The dramatics of it are kind of secondary to the gesture in as much as I wanted to help him.

"His improvement has been phenomenal," he adds, noting Rainer's recovery. "It's been great. Every day is a new day, and if anybody truly appreciates life, of all the people I know, it must be him — he savors every moment."

Despite the sad events that set it in motion, "THE INNER FLAME" is a remarkably life-affirming work. For Rainer, the positive vibrations generated by the well-wishes of his fans, friends and family may well be the secret behind his current good health.

"It makes me feel really grateful," Rainer Ptácek, the man with the Inner Flame, says. "I really do believe that the power of love played a large part in my healing. I know it did, to the point of my saying that's what healed me. The doctors had their part in it, but the sympathy and love that I felt from everybody, that's what really healed me. And here I am. The scenario could have been totally different."

7/97

Atlantic Recording Corporation
1290 Ave. of the Americas New York, NY 10104 212/707.2020 fax: 405.5475
9229 Sunset Blvd. Los Angeles, CA 90069 310/205.7450 fax: 205.5916

Howe Gelb

Rainer Ptáček

Rainer & Emmylou Harris

Robert Plant

The Inner Flame

PRESS RELEASE ATLANTIC RECORDS PUBLICITY 75 ROCKEFELLER PLAZA, NY 10019 (212) 484-8210

FOR IMMEDIATE RELEASE
JANUARY 7, 1991

LED ZEPPELIN BOXED SET IGNITES CATALOGUE SALES

Coinciding with the success "LED ZEPPELIN," the retrospective boxed set, which was simultaneously certified gold and platinum by the RIAA for U.S. sales in excess of 250,000 and 500,000 units respectively, the legendary group's catalogue has been selling briskly. Documenting this sales surge are the latest series of RIAA certifications, which include: quadruple platinum for 1969's "LED ZEPPELIN," double platinum for 1969's "LED ZEPPELIN II," double platinum for 1970's "LED ZEPPELIN III," deca-platinum for 1971's "LED ZEPPELIN," quintuple platinum for 1973's "HOUSES OF THE HOLY," quadruple platinum for 1975's "PHYSICAL GRAFFITI," double platinum for 1976's "PRESENCE," and quintuple platinum for 1979's "IN THROUGH THE OUT DOOR."

The video from "Over The Hills & Far Away," one of the songs included in the "LED ZEPPELIN" boxed set, is currently in Active rotation on MTV.

ATLANTIC RECORDS 9229 SUNSET BLVD. LOS ANGELES, CA 90069

GEFFEN RECORDS

FOR IMMEDIATE RELEASE   April 28, 1988

JIMMY PAGE'S FIRST SOLO ALBUM
TO RELEASE ON GEFFEN WORLDWIDE

<u>Outrider</u>, the first solo album by legendary guitarist Jimmy Page, will be released worldwide on Geffen Records June 21. All nine tracks were produced by Page and recorded at his own studio in England.

"I wanted to do a guitar album, but not an entirely instrumental one," Page commented. "Not being a singer myself, that presents a problem. If you have only one singer, people automatically get an impression in their mind what they're going to hear . . . and this album is going to be quite different, I'm sure, from what people might expect. Even though it's a small cast, there are a number of singers on it to give different textures."

One side of <u>Outrider</u> features rock-oriented tracks, while the other side is based in the blues.

"It's definitely a Jimmy Page album, there's no two ways about that," he added. "I put even <u>more</u> guitars on that I originally thought I was going to. I've taken care of what is virtually an army of guitars." John Miles, Robert Plant and Chris Farlow are the <u>Outrider</u> vocalists. The album also includes Jason Bonham and Barrymore Barlow on drums; Felix Krish, Durban Laverde and Tony Franklin on bass.

The advance single from the album will be "Wasting My Time," written by Page and Miles. A performance music video, directed by Marty Callner of Creem Cheese Productions, is planned to support the track.

A 36-date U.S. tour is slated to begin in the fall.

# # #

Contacts: Bryn Bridenthal
Lori Earl
Leslie Crockett
213/285-2708

9130 Sunset Boulevard	75 Rockefeller Plaza
Los Angeles California 90069	New York New York 10019
Telephone 213 278 9010	Telephone 212 484 7170
Telex: 295854	Answerback: GEFFN

JIMMY PAGE

©1988 The David Geffen Company/Permission to reproduce limited to editorial use in newspapers and other regularly published periodicals and television news programming.

Photo Credit: Peter Ashworth

© 1988 The David Geffen Company/Permission to reproduce limited to editorial use in newspapers and other regularly published periodicals and television news programming.

PRESS RELEASE ATLANTIC RECORDS PUBLICITY 75 ROCKEFELLER PLAZA, NY 10019 (212) 484-6210

FOR IMMEDIATE RELEASE
June 25, 1990

contact: Maria C. Malta
(212)484-8149

ROBERT PLANT SETS OUT ON "MANIC NIRVANA" U.S. TOUR

Es Paranza/Atlantic recording artist Robert Plant has finalized plans for the first U.S. leg of his "MANIC NIRVANA" world tour. Scheduled to begin on July 5 in Albany, New York, the itinerary runs through mid-August, hitting 23 cities across the country. The opening act on all U.S. dates will be Atlantic recording artist Alannah Myles. The "MANIC NIRVANA" tour commenced in Europe on May 1.

The upcoming Stateside shows mark Plant's first North American concerts since the highly successful "Non Stop Go" tour of 1988. The latter tour, in support of the "NOW AND ZEN" album, introduced the new Robert Plant band: Chris Blackwell (drums, some guitars), Doug Boyle (master guitars), Phil Johnstone (keyboards, some guitars), Charlie Jones (bass), and Robert Plant (vocals).

The announcement of Plant's U.S. tour coincides with the great success of the "MANIC NIRVANA" album, which has been #1 at album radio nationwide for many weeks and is rapidly nearing the platinum mark in U.S. sales. A new track from the album, "Your Ma Said You Cried In Your Sleep Last Night" has been released to radio.

ROBERT PLANT "MANIC NIRVANA" U.S. TOUR 1990

July	5	Albany, NY	Knickerbocker Arena
"	7	Philadelphia, PA	Spectrum
"	8	Binghamton, NY	Broome County Arena
"	10-11	Mansfield, MA	Great Woods
"	13	Portland, ME	Cumberland City Civic Center
"	14	Hartford, CT	Civic Center
"	16	Landover, MD	Capital Centre
"	17	Wantaugh, NY	Jones Beach Theatre
"	19	E. Rutherford, NJ	Meadowlands Arena
"	20	Rochester, NY	War Memorial Arena
"	22	Pittsburgh, PA	Star Lake Amphitheatre
"	23	Cuyahoga Falls, OH	Blossom Music Center
"	25	Clarkston, MI	Pine Knob Music Theatre
"	26	Noblesville, In	Deer Creek Music Center

continued...

Robert Plant Tour 1990
Continued...

July	28	East Troy, WI	Alpine Valley Theatre
"	29	Cincinnati, OH	Riverbend Music Theatre
August	1	Atlanta, GA	Omni
"	3	Houston , TX	Summit
"	4	Dallas, TX	Reunion Arena
"	6	Tucson, AZ	Tucson Community Center Arena
"	7	Phoenix, AZ	Veterans Memorial Coliseum
"	9	San Diego, CA	Sports Arena
"	10-11	Laguna Hills, CA	Irvine Meadows Amphitheatre
"	13	Mountain View, CA	Shoreline Amphitheatre
"	14	Sacramento, CA	Cal Expo Amphitheatre

more to come...

CATCH ROBERT PLANT IN A TOWN NEAR YOU!!!

The Led Zep Scrapbook Volume One

CHRIS BLACKWELL   CHARLIE JONES
DOUG BOYLE   ROBERT PLANT   PHIL JOHNSTONE

 **ROBERT PLANT**

The Led Zep Scrapbook Volume One

ROBERT PLANT

PHOTO CREDIT: DAVID GAHR

 **ROBERT PLANT**

 **ROBERT PLANT**

CHRIS BLACKWELL

ROBERT PLANT

DOUG BOYLE

CHARLIE JONES

PHIL JOHNSTONE

Since the release of his first solo album in 1982, Robert Plant has explored diverse, often unexpected terrain, continually stretching musical boundaries. Unflinchingly establishing a new identity for a new era, his work has embraced a remarkable range of sounds and emotions. With Led Zeppelin, Robert set a standard against which others continue to be judged. With that unit's demise, he could have rested on his proverbial laurels, as so many of his peers have done. Instead, he has chosen to move forward, meet new challenges, and set new standards.

"Success breeds many, many things in a person," Robert comments. "The one most obvious thing I see is the desire to maintain success by repetition–to get some kind of idea that's good, that works, and then hang on to it for ever and ever. It's like drudgery. In that case, you might as well be an accountant, rather than keep repeating yourself on a really well-established thread of success. I started out to be an accountant. Now I'm more of an emotional accountant than a financial one."

1988 was a watershed year for Plant. With the release of his fourth solo album, "NOW AND ZEN," he entered a vibrant new phase of his musical life. As *Rolling Stone* stated: "This record is some kind of stylistic event: a seamless pop fusion of hard guitar rock, gorgeous computerization and sharp startling songcraft....The nine tracks on 'NOW AND ZEN' don't simply sound contemporary; they point to new ways to transmute roots-rock verities of swing and harmony amid the technological conventions of late-Eighties pop."

A commercial and critical triumph, "NOW AND ZEN" also introduced Robert's remarkable new band, a crew of fresh players who quickly became one of the hottest propositions in rock and roll. Following the album's release, Plant, drummer Chris Blackwell, guitarist Doug Boyle, keyboardist Phil Johnstone, and bassist Charlie Jones embarked on the hugely successful "Non Stop Go" tour, an exhilarating experience for all. "This fragile unit was turning and facing circumstances that they were never prepared for," Plant notes. "But I'm a ludicrous optimist, and the anxiety was funny anxiety. Even so, I didn't know it would be as good as it was; it was tremendous. It maintained the child in me."

So strong was the bond between the members of the new band, so high the energy level, that a mere six weeks after the conclusion of the "Non Stop Go" tour, the group reconvened to begin work on the music that would become "MANIC NIRVANA." "It had been so good," Robert recalls, "that I was still feeling it bump in there, you know?....There is no cynicism, no well-tried and tested bullshit. Here I'm a working guy with a big, broad grin. They've allowed me to continue to be crazy. It's become all-encompassing, because it's so much fun, so new, and so fresh. It's a *band*, and the band gives me fire, and I give them fire, and we're selling fire."

The result is music which celebrates possibility in an all-encompassing sonic embrace. In the world of "MANIC NIRVANA," everything is possible and no restraints are imposed. "I think 'NOW AND ZEN' was in many respects a little cagey, a little safe," says Robert. "Personality-wise, we were getting to know each other. If you don't know how far the extremes can be pushed, then middle ground is where you can end up. I think I took a couple of options which were a bit soft. 'MANIC NIRVANA' now reverses those decisions."

"On 'MANIC NIRVANA,'" Robert continues, "the whole shooting match is there for all to behold. It's wild, but there's humor there still. We're starting to kick the gas pedal down. We're all there: everybody's opening up, stretching out, laughing, looking at each other. Every time we achieve one higher stage, then the band becomes bigger within itself, and much more confident. It's a great experience."

Recorded at Olympic Studios in London (where, ironically, the first Led Zeppelin album was recorded in 1968), "MANIC NIRVANA" was produced by Plant and bandmate Phil Johnstone, and co-produced and engineered by Mark Stent. It is an album of mesmerizing intensity. "I tried to create something sonically that is seductive, that feels like just before the first touch," Robert notes. "You know that you've got the facility to use high-tech equipment, but at the same time you've got to ride the wild beat. I want to keep that raunchy, edgy side."

Throughout the album, Robert pulls no punches as he re-invents himself once again for a new decade. From the opening high-energy burst of "Hurting Kind (I've Got My Eyes On You)" to the churning electricity of the final track, "Watching You" (with voices by Siddi Makain Mushkin), the album draws on an array of musical reference points in forging a thoroughly unique musical vision. From James Brown to Woodstock, everything is fair game in the "fast bliss" of "MANIC NIRVANA."

All but one of the songs on the album were penned by Robert and members of the band. That lone exception is a cover of "Your Ma Said You Cried In Your Sleep Last Night," an early-60's gem written by Schlaks/Glazer and originally recorded by Kenny Dino. The "unavoidable" surface noise on the track comes direct from Robert's personal copy of the single, which was sampled for its bass drum sound–clicks, crackle, and all. (And for the benefit of true Zep followers, a special last verse is included.)

The dense, multi-layered feel of much of "MANIC NIRVANA" is contrasted by the simple voice-with-acoustic guitar approach of "Liars Dance." Robert comments: "Acoustic songs take the heat out of the thing for awhile, and they are crucial to the balance. It's also crucial for our growing as a band. It's an area of guitar-playing that Doug hadn't had very much experience in. So I suggested that he listen to Buffalo Springfield, the Youngbloods, people like that."

On "MANIC NIRVANA," Robert's voice sounds better than ever. "I'm singing with more confidence, and I pushed my vocal range so I could use all the high notes I wanted. At the same time, I wanted to be intimate. You've got to be able to get right in and be in somebody's ear....The lyrics are also very important, much more intense and much more focused than in the past."

"MANIC NIRVANA" finds Robert Plant on fertile musical ground, in the company of a band boasting sizable musical gifts. His enthusiasm is understandably unbounded: "This really could be something in years to come that could be counted as a very special contribution to contemporary pop music. Especially as it is a little left of center, it doesn't take itself that seriously, and it's a bit frantic. If nothing else, we're developing our own little thread, our own little chink of light."

* * * * * * * * *

Robert Anthony Plant was born on August 20, 1948 in Bromwich, Staffordshire, England. The son of a civil engineer, he may very well have become a chartered accountant if it hadn't been for the lure of the blues. By the mid-60's, Plant had become one of two vocal prodigies on the Birmingham music scene, the other being one Stevie Winwood. Known locally at "The Wild Man of Blues from the Black Country," Robert paid his dues in a string of outfits, among them The Delta Blues Band, The New Memphis Bluesbreakers, Black Snake Moan, Banned, and The Crawling King Snakes.

In 1966, Robert was asked to join The Tennessee Teens who, after changing their name to Listen, released a single entitled "You Better Run." At the age of 18, Robert cut two solo singles, "Our Song" and "Long Time Coming," which were issued through CBS and have long since become rare collector's items. Most notable among his early associations was the group known as the Band of Joy (which also included John Bonham). When that group split up, Plant sang with a unit called Hobbstweedle and also worked briefly with Alexis Korner, the legendary "founding father" of the British blues movement.

Robert had given himself until the age of 20 to make it as a rock singer, and in early 1968, that self-imposed deadline was rapidly approaching. Enter Jimmy Page, already a renowned guitarist, who (upon the recommendation of vocalist Terry Reid) invited Plant to be part of a new group. Page, Plant, John Paul Jones, and John Bonham first converged in a small London rehearsal hall, initially calling themselves The New Yardbirds (after Page's previous group). The chemistry was immediate. By year's end, they had changed their name to Led Zeppelin, recording their self-titled debut album in just 36 hours. Released by Atlantic Records in January 1969, it quickly established Zeppelin as a ground-breaking new force in rock. The rest, as they say, is hysteria.

Between 1969 and 1979, Led Zeppelin released nine massively successful albums (a tenth, "CODA," was released posthumously in 1982), while playing a series of record-shattering global tours. Throughout their career, the group drew on a remarkable variety of musical ideas, refusing to limit their creativity. As one critic commented: "There is no more exhilarating experience in rock than Plant and Page pushing their considerable talents towards the dizzying outer limits of the genre they more or less created."

At the turn of the decade, Robert could look back on ten turbulent years marked by professional triumph and marred by personal tragedy. In 1980, a year after the release of Zeppelin's "IN THROUGH THE OUT DOOR," John Bonham's untimely death put the band's fate beyond doubt. They broke up, and so began the struggle by each former member to successfully move out from under a colossal shadow, not only of a legendary group, but of an inspirational creative partnership.

For Robert Plant, this did not mean debasing the coinage of the performing style he had originally minted. On the contrary, the idea was to fuse the two seemingly contrasting elements that had fired Led Zeppelin and had long inspired his personal approach–the primal rebel yelp of Sun-era Elvis and the exotic, pastoral, and mysterious head-music he'd been turned on to in the late-60's via such West Coast groups as Love, Moby Grape, and Kaleidoscope.

Robert's post-Zeppelin solo career grew out of his involvement with a group called The Honeydrippers, a collection of local musicians who got together to play the blues. In early 1981, Plant made a number of low-key club appearances with the band, in a very real sense getting back to his roots. By the following fall, he had begun recording his debut solo album at Rockfield Studios in Wales.

In June 1982, Robert Plant released "PICTURES AT ELEVEN." It was an album of firsts. Foremost, it was the first full-scale recording of Robert Plant on his own, while marking his first studio work in three years. It was his first outing as a producer, as well as the first album of Plant compositions to be performed outside Led Zeppelin. A worldwide success, "PICTURES AT ELEVEN" was a triumphant return to active duty.

A year later, Robert returned with his second solo effort, "THE PRINCIPLE OF MOMENTS," the first album to be released on Plant's own Es Paranza label (distributed by Atlantic). Very much an album of contrasts, it demonstrated Robert's ongoing desire to explore fresh musical/lyrical ground. Topping charts around the world, it earned RIAA platinum certification in the U.S., solidly confirming Plant's increasing success in establishing a new musical identity. In August 1983, Robert embarked on his debut concert tour as a solo artist, garnering rave reviews from fans and critics alike.

In 1984, Plant's travels led him down an unusual side path–one which took many by surprise, but actually revealed a long-standing aspect of his musical persona. An avid and knowledgeable collector of vintage R&B and rock 'n' roll classics, Robert had for some time harbored the notion of paying tribute to his influences by recording some of his favorite tunes from the 40's, 50's, and 60's. That desire finally became reality with the release of a five-song mini-LP entitled "THE HONEYDRIPPERS, VOLUME ONE" (reviving the name adopted for those first post-Zep gigs in '81).

The whirlwind Honeydrippers sessions in New York and London were overseen by Atlantic Records founder and Chairman Ahmet Ertegun, credited on the album by his 50's songwriting pseudonym, Nugetre. The anonymity of the project extended to all the musicians involved, as the focus was on the music and not on personalities. Despite the low-key approach, "THE HONEY-DRIPPERS" struck a major chord with the public, moving into the upper reaches of the charts and earning RIAA platinum. As Ertegun commented: "It's clear that if you do any style very well, there will be an audience for it. Robert sings these songs with love."

Despite the success of The Honeydrippers, it was but a sideline to Robert's ongoing musical development. That fact was reconfirmed with the 1985 release of the third solo album, "SHAKEN 'N STIRRED." Plant's most adventurous work up to that time, it offered richly-inventive, forward-thinking rock. Another successful world tour followed. In July '85, the North American leg of the itinerary was interrupted for a reunion of former Zepmen Plant, Jimmy Page, and John Paul Jones (joined by drummers Phil Collins and Tony Thompson) at the landmark Live Aid concert in Philadelphia.

By the conclusion of the "SHAKEN 'N STIRRED" tour, Robert felt that the time had come to end phase one of his solo career. "There was anxiety, anger, and frustration. Personnel-wise it wasn't happening anymore; a kind of complacency had set in. When the tour finally ground to a halt, I knew I had to regroup." To reinvigorate his musical life, Robert began to look for new partners. As noted above, the talent search led to the recruitment of Phil Johnstone (via a demo tape which included the song "Heaven Knows"), Doug Boyle, and Chris Blackwell, along with bassist Phil Scragg (later replaced by Charlie Jones).

Released in February 1988, the first album by the new unit, "NOW AND ZEN," became Plant's most successful solo work to date. Spurred on by such radio favorites as "Heaven Knows," "Tall Cool One," and "Ship Of Fools," the album hit the top ten on U.S. charts and soared past the RIAA platinum mark. The "Non Stop Go" tour marked Robert's first North American concert performances in three years, as well as Charlie Jones's debut with the band. On May 14, 1988, Plant made two appearances at the historic Atlantic Records 40th Anniversary concert held at New York's Madison Square Garden: with his new band and as part of the Led Zeppelin reunion performance (with Jason Bonham on drums).

And now here we are in 1990 with "MANIC NIRVANA," the next stop on Robert Plant's musical odyssey. "Rock and roll comes screaming out of the back alleys of distaste and dislike and frustration," Plant muses. "It begins as an angst-ridden adolescent expression machine. However, there are those who perpetuate that and take it on through the years, focusing even finer and finer on the detail of the scream, the scream that made them want to do it in the first place. Today, I'm not just having a scream for a scream's sake, but I'm trying to mold and sculpt the scream."

3/90

The Led Zep Scrapbook Volume One

PRESS RELEASE ATLANTIC RECORDS PUBLICITY 75 ROCKEFELLER PLAZA, NY 10019 (212) 275-2035

FOR IMMEDIATE RELEASE

MARCH 2, 1992

LED ZEPPELIN "REMASTERS" COMPILATION RELEASED

Atlantic Records has announced the release this week of "REMASTERS," a special three-CD/three-cassette Led Zeppelin anthology. Produced by Jimmy Page, this retrospective contains 26 tracks digitally remastered by guitarist Jimmy Page and engineer George Marino. In addition, the set includes "PROFILED" - an hour's worth of interviews with Jimmy Page, vocalist Robert Plant, and bassist/keyboardist John Paul Jones.

In the fall of 1990, Atlantic released "LED ZEPPELIN," the four-CD/four-cassette/six-LP retrospective that is the best-selling historical boxed set to date. "REMASTERS" includes 25 Led Zeppelin tracks culled from the boxed set, plus the additional track, "Good Times Bad Times."

The three-CD "REMASTERS" set is packaged in a special 6 x 12 digibinder and includes two lavish eight-page booklets. The three cassettes are set in a 6 x 12 tray housed in an outer binder like that of the CD set. All three cassettes are packaged with deluxe, photo-packed J-cards.

The complete song listing of "REMASTERS" is as follows: Communication Breakdown * Babe I'm Gonna Leave You * Good Times

- more -

- 2 -

Bad Times * Dazed And Confused * Whole Lotta Love * Heartbreaker * Ramble On * Immigrant Song * Celebration Day * Since I've Been Loving You * Black Dog * Rock And Roll * The Battle Of Evermore * Misty Mountain Hop * Stairway To Heaven * The Song Remains The Same * The Rain Song * D!yer Mak'er * No Quarter * Houses Of The Holy * Kashmir * Trampled Underfoot * Nobody's Fault But Mine * Achilles Last Stand * All My Love * In The Evening.

ATLANTIC RECORDING CORPORATION

75 ROCKEFELLER PLAZA
NEW YORK, NY 10019
TELEPHONE:
(212) 275-2000

FOR IMMEDIATE RELEASE
NOVEMBER 1, 1994

"NO QUARTER" TAKEN IN PREPARATION FOR PAGE/PLANT ALBUM; FERVENT ANTICIPATION WHETTED VIA RADIO, RETAIL, AND THE INTERNET

On the heels of Jimmy Page & Robert Plant's "Unledded," the highest-rated MTV Unplugged show in the music network's history, a flurry of activity is surrounding the November 8th release by Atlantic Records of the companion "NO QUARTER" album. With "Gallows Pole," the first single from the album, a top track at rock outlets nationwide and in Stress rotation at MTV, the anticipation for the full album is reaching near fever-pitch. In order to satisfy this demand, Atlantic has released a second single - Page & Plant's radical re-working of the classic Led Zeppelin tune "Nobody's Fault But Mine" - to rock radio in advance of the album's release.

In the retail world, "NO QUARTER" is shaping up to be one of the biggest releases of the year. As part of its comprehensive marketing campaign, Atlantic is sponsoring a series of "Midnight Madness" sales nationwide on the night of November 7th, giving die-hards the opportunity to beat the release-day rush. In addition to putting the album on sale the moment the clock strikes midnight, many of the participating retail outlets will tune in to MTV's re-airing of "Unledded" (which takes place 10:00 PM EST).

Curious fans have several opportunities to hear the "NO QUARTER" album - and learn more about it - prior to November 8th. Atlantic Records has

- more -

established a dedicated World Wide Web site on the internet for Jimmy Page & Robert Plant, which features exclusive photos, graphics, location reports from the recording of the album, video clips, and sound clips of every tune. Cyber surfers can also leave questions and comments about the project; these will be forwarded to Page and Plant, and their responses will be posted on the site. The site - which will be frequently updated with the latest Page/Plant information as well as additional exclusive content - can be found at the following address: http://mosaic.echonyc.com/unled/.

In addition, on November 5th, lunch-time patrons at the House Of Blues in Los Angeles, CA, Cambridge, MA, and New Orleans, LA will be able to hear "NO QUARTER" in its entirety, days before the album hits stores. This marks the first such promotion for the blues bar.

# # #

PRESS RELEASE ATLANTIC RECORDS PUBLICITY 75 ROCKEFELLER PLAZA, NY 10019 (212) 484-8210

FOR IMMEDIATE RELEASE
OCTOBER 14, 1991

ATLANTIC RELAUNCHES LED ZEPPELIN BOXED SET

Atlantic Records is launching a special marketing campaign this week for "LED ZEPPELIN," the ultra-successful boxed set released a year ago this month. The campaign for this four-CD/four-cassette retrospective, with a running time of nearly five hours, will include extensive media advertising and in-store support.

The best-selling boxed set to date, "LED ZEPPELIN" has been certified platinum by the RIAA and is rapidly nearing the double platinum mark. The set contains 54 tracks personally selected and sequenced by Jimmy Page, Robert Plant, and John Paul Jones, and digitally remastered by Jimmy Page and engineer George Marino at Sterling Sound in New York City.

This compilation includes selections from each of the band's nine studio albums, all produced by Jimmy Page, plus two previously-unreleased tracks: "Travelling Riverside Blues" and "White Summer/Black Mountain Side" - both culled from 1969 BBC broadcasts.

- more -

ATLANTIC RECORDS 9229 SUNSET BLVD. LOS ANGELES, CA 90069

- 2 -

The boxed set's deluxe packaging includes a 36-page, four-color booklet featuring numerous photographs; new essays by noted rock journalists Cameron Crowe, Kurt Loder, and Robert Palmer; complete track-by-track credits; and a discography. Production of the boxed set was overseen by Atlantic Director of Catalogue Development Yves Beauvais.

PRESS RELEASE ATLANTIC RECORDS PUBLICITY 75 ROCKEFELLER PLAZA, NY 10019 (212) 484-8200

FOR IMMEDIATE RELEASE
FROM: BOB KAUS
MAY 13, 1985

<u>ROBERT PLANT: "SHAKEN 'N STIRRED"</u>

Es Paranza/Atlantic recording artist Robert Plant releases his third solo album this week, entitled "SHAKEN 'N STIRRED." Produced by Robert Plant, Benji Lefevre and Tim Palmer, the LP includes the first single, "Little By Little." The latter was the #1 most-added record at album radio stations from coast to coast upon its release.

"SHAKEN 'N STIRRED" is comprised of nine new songs written by Plant in collaboration with members of his band - Robbie Blunt (guitars and synthesised guitars), Paul Martinez (bass and guitar), Jezz Woodroffe (keyboards), and Ritchie Hayward (drums). The album also features additional vocals by Toni Halliday.

Following the release of "SHAKEN 'N STIRRED," Robert Plant and company will embark on an extensive world tour. The North American portion of the itinerary will commence on June 10th, with more details to be announced in the near future.

Robert Plant released his first solo album, "PICTURES AT ELEVEN," in June 1982. This was followed in July 1983 by the RIAA platinum "THE PRINCIPLE OF MOMENTS." That same year, Plant embarked on his triumphant debut tour as a solo artist. In 1984, Robert's career took an unusual side path with the release of the mini-LP, "THE HONEYDRIPPERS, VOLUME ONE." A collection of rhythm & blues classics from the 40's, 50's & 60's, it also earned RIAA platinum certification.

ATLANTIC RECORDS 9229 SUNSET BLVD. LOS ANGELES, CA 90069

PRESS RELEASE ATLANTIC RECORDS PUBLICITY 75 ROCKEFELLER PLAZA, NY 10019 (212) 484-8200

FOR IMMEDIATE RELEASE
FROM: BOB KAUS
MAY 13, 1985

WAKSCHAL NAMED ATLANTIC VICE PRESIDENT OF FOREIGN & MECHANICAL ROYALTIES

Fran Wakschal has been promoted to the newly-created position of Vice President of Foreign & Mechanical Royalties for Atlantic Records, based at the company's New York headquarters. The announcement was made this week by Atlantic Vice Chairman Sheldon Vogel, who commented: "In her 36 years with the Atlantic family, Fran has been an invaluable participant in the company's development from a small, independent label into a major international firm. Her numerous contributions have been instrumental to our growth, and her devotion to the company has been extraordinary. I am very pleased to announce this much-deserved promotion."

Fran Wakschal is the senior employee of Atlantic Records, having joined the label in 1949, just two years after its inception. Starting out as the label's first bookkeeper, she was then promoted to Office Manager. Between 1960 and 1969, she worked part-time for the company, while raising a family. Returning to Atlantic full-time, she was promoted to Foreign & Mechanical Royalties Manager; and in 1975, she was named Director of Foreign & Mechanical Royalties. Immediately prior to her promotion to Vice President, Ms. Wakschal had served as Atlantic/Elektra Assistant Vice President of Foreign & Mechanical Royalties since June 1983.

(PHOTO ATTACHED)

ATLANTIC RECORDS 9229 SUNSET BLVD. LOS ANGELES, CA 90069

FOR IMMEDIATE RELEASE
AUGUST 4, 1998

ATLANTIC
RECORDS

9229
SUNSET
BLVD.
LOS ANGELES,
CA 90069
TELEPHONE:
(310) 205-7450

PAGE & PLANT WALKING BACK INTO AMERICA; CELEBRATED TOUR RESUMES SEPTEMBER 5th

Atlantic recording artists Jimmy Page & Robert Plant have announced the second leg of their acclaimed "Walking Into Everywhere" tour of North America. The concert series, which coincides with the recent release of the duo's RIAA gold album, "WALKING INTO CLARKSDALE," is being presented by Best Buy.

The upcoming itinerary kicks off on September 5th at the G.M. Place in Vancouver, British Columbia. The October 1st date at the Lakefront Arena in New Orleans, Louisiana will be broadcast live by the Westwood One radio network on over 125 affiliates across North America. Page & Plant and their band — bassist Charlie Jones and drummer Michael Lee, plus keyboardist Phil Andrews — are currently headlining a number of European festivals, including the opening night of England's legendary Reading Festival on August 28th.

The first leg of the "Walking Into Everywhere" tour drew rave reviews across the country. The group's sold-out July 16th date at New York City's Madison Square Garden was hailed by all three major daily newspapers. The New York Post's Dan Aquilante, calling the tour "one not to miss," stated: "It isn't often that men manage to live up to their legends, but Robert Plant and

- more -

Jimmy Page did just that... It was living raucous rock that had hammer-of-the-gods excitement to it." In her New York Times review, Ann Powers noted that Plant's "wails shattered the air as he hit every high note... he deftly juxtaposed urgency with weariness, tenderness with rage," and pointed out that Page remains "a fervent experimentalist" whose "riffs dazzled." The New York Daily News' Jim Farber declared the duo to be in "glorious shape," stating that "a special fury marked Page's solos. He tore away at his frets like a shark tasting blood in the water." Farber went on to praise Plant, whose "charisma remains unblemished, matching the rough sex of the music."

* * * * *

The eagerly anticipated "WALKING INTO CLARKSDALE" debuted at #8 (with a bullet) on the Billboard 200 album chart. The album is Page & Plant's first offering since 1994's RIAA platinum "NO QUARTER," and their first collection of all-new collaborative material since Led Zeppelin's last studio album, "IN THROUGH THE OUT DOOR," in 1979.

"WALKING INTO CLARKSDALE" has received enormous critical acclaim from the likes of Rolling Stone, Time, Details, Entertainment Weekly (which gave it an "A-"), The Village Voice, Los Angeles Times, GQ, Atlantic Monthly, and Time Out New York.

"...CLARKSDALE" has thus far yielded two top-charting smashes at rock radio nationwide: "Most High" and the current "Shining In The Light."

(TOUR ITINERARY ATTACHED)

JIMMY PAGE & ROBERT PLANT
WALKING INTO EVERYWHERE — SEPTEMBER/OCTOBER '98

September

5	Vancouver, British Columbia	G.M. Place
6	Quincy, Washington	The Gorge
8	Portland, Oregon	The Rose Garden
11	Concord, California	Concorde Pavillion
12	Mountain View, California	Shoreline Amphitheatre
15	Salt Lake City, Utah	The E Centre
16	Denver, Colorado	Red Rocks
18	Laguna Hills, California	Irvine Meadows
19	Los Angeles, California	Hollywood Bowl
21	San Diego, California	Cox Arena
23	Las Vegas, Nevada	MGM Grand
24	Phoenix, Arizona	America West Arena
26	San Antonio, Texas	The Alamo Dome
27	Dallas, Texas	Reunion Arena
30	Houston, Texas	Woodlands Pavillion

October

1	New Orleans, Louisiana	Lakefront Arena
2	Memphis, Tennessee	Pyramid Arena

#

For additional information, please see The Atlantic Group website at
www.atlantic-records.com.

ROBERT PLANT AND THE STRANGE SENSATION

Robert Plant's new album, *Mighty Rearranger* out May 10th, is an extraordinary accomplishment from one of the most inventive, consistently daring and talented figures in contemporary music. **Plant's** band **The Strange Sensation** who worked with him on 2002's Grammy nominated, *Dreamland*, have been vital in the development of what looks set to be one of this year's most talked about albums.

Robert Plant and The Strange Sensation formed in 2001. The band draws together talent from across a broad spectrum of contemporary musicians: Clive Deamer (drums) from Portishead and Roni Size projects; John Baggott (bass) of Portishead and Massive Attack; Billy Fuller (bass) - from Bristol band 'Fuzz Against Junk; Skin – ambient guitar formerly of Brit Pop phenomena Cast and Justin Adams playing gimbri, darbouka and guitar, late of Sinead O'Connor, Jah Wobble and the Wayward Shakes. Their first album together, *Dreamland* was informed by **Plant's** attraction to and affection for the music of Southern Morocco, and the psychedelic indo-rock of mid to late 60's in USA.

Mighty Rearranger was written and created in Snowdonia and in the lea of Solsbury Hill. The album developed organically, arising out of joyful anarchic experimentation.

As guitarist Justin Adams says:

"It's always idiosyncratic; we're a weird bunch of characters and we all do stuff in a non standard way. Robert is an interesting person to work with. He encourages people's individual styles: he's happy for me to bring in unfamiliar North African rhythms and for John to introduce weird electronic sounds: it doesn't happen that often nowadays. Usually it's one guy at home with a computer. It wasn't like that in 60's and 70's - people were breaking rules and inventing new forms of music: we are closer to that spirit: of weird and anarchic ways."

The result is an inspired collection of songs that are raw and bristling with energy but also rich in texture and detail. The whole album is remarkably coherent, with a strong sense of unity that arises out of the unique democratic creative process and the unusual gigs the band have been playing.

Shore Fire Media
32 Court Street, Suite 1600, Brooklyn, NY 11201
718.522.7171 / fax 718.522.7242

"On this album we used computers as part of the writing process," says **Robert**." We recorded spontaneous jams and rough ideas which we've been able to manipulate while keeping our raw energy. The touring that we've done in the Arctic Circle, the Sahara Desert, Baltic States as well as the weird and difficult times we have been through while writing the album have helped us to develop a real band dynamic".

Since the end of Led Zeppelin in 1980 **Plant** has recorded many solo projects and collaborated with a host of colorful accomplices. He and Jimmy Page renewed their long-time partnership in '94 to create the **No Quarter** project – a mélange of North African, Egyptian and New Wave folk roots sounds.

In recent times, **Plant** has recorded with Afro Celt Sound System and along with Skin and Justin Adams, traveled to South Sahara, North of Timbuktu in Mali to participate in the 2nd Festival of the Desert, a gathering of African Saharan and assorted soul musicians including Oumou Sangare, Ali Farka Toure, Tinariwen and Tidawt. This project ultimately became a CD compilation to be found on the Harmonia Mundi label and was featured on DVD.

2003 saw the prestigious release of the definitive **Plant** retrospective, ***Sixty Six to Timbuktu***, which included a selection of Plant's solo work from his first recording date to his appearance in Mali.

The new album, titled ***Mighty Rearranger*** is a collection of 12 all new, all original songs due for release in May 10th 2005. Committed and powerful the album is an electrifying tour de force and takes the world music influences explored in ***Dreamland*** and uses them as a springboard for a more electric sound. ***Mighty Rearranger*** recalls the drive and passion of **Robert Plant** and Led Zeppelin's strongest work and is packed full of explosive riffs, compulsive guitar hooks as well as tender and highly expressive arrangements.

This new project also sees the return of **Plant's** Es Paranza label which is intended to be a vehicle for future projects concerning Plant and other musicians.

# # # #

For more information on Robert Plant and The Strange Sensation, please contact Nick Baily [nbaily@shorefire.com] at Shore Fire Media, 718.5252.7171 ext 36.

CHRIS BLACKWELL

DOUG BOYLE

ROBERT PLANT

CHARLIE JONES

PHIL JOHNSTONE

The Led Zep Scrapbook Volume One

Robert Plant

ROBERT PLANT

FOR IMMEDIATE RELEASE:
June 2002

**UNIVERSAL RECORDS SET TO RELEASE NEW SOLO ALBUM
FROM THE LEGENDARY ROBERT PLANT ENTITLED *DREAMLAND*
ON JULY 16
First Solo Album In Nine Years**

New York. N.Y. -- Universal Records is set to release the new solo album from the legendary Led Zeppelin frontman **ROBERT PLANT** entitled Dreamland on July 16. The first single "Darkness, Darkness," will be released to radio on June 4.

Demonstrating that classic music can always breed fresh possibilities, **PLANT** again pushes the creative envelope with *Dreamland*, which features **PLANT**'s intimate interpretations of his favorite songs as well as two new compositions, bringing together the very best of vintage folk, blues and psychedelic songs, with moody Middle Eastern scales, reflective Asian drones and foot-stomping hard rock. Once again, **PLANT**, the tumble-haired icon from the Led Zeppelin years, stands at the nexus of an eclectic musical hurricane.

From Bob Dylan's "One More Cup Of Coffee", recorded for the Desire album, to Tim Buckley's "Song To The Siren" this assorted collection of new tracks and compositions is as diverse as **PLANT**'s career itself. Not only does **PLANT** cover the classic "Hey Joe" made famous by the Jimi Hendrix Experience (first recorded by The Leaves) but also lesser known gems like "Skip's Song", an unreleased track from Skip Spence, the troubled and brilliant singer/songwriter from Moby Grape.

Also of particular interest on Dreamland is "Win My Train Fare Home", **PLANT**'s reconstruction of Arthur Crudup's "If I Ever Get Lucky". Woven into **PLANT**'s interpretation of the track are passages from Crudup's "That's Alright Mama" as well as Robert Johnson's "Milk Cows Calf Blues" and John Lee Hooker's "Crawlin' King Snake".

Dreamland was self-produced and recorded with his newly assembled band, Strange Sensation which features guitarist Porl Thompson (a former member of The Cure), guitarist Justin Adams (Jah Wobble and Sinead O'Connor), keyboardist and string arranger John Baggott (Portishead), drummer Clive Deamer (Portishead, Roni Size), and bassist Charlie Jones (Page & Plant).

Following the release of Dreamland you can catch **ROBERT PLANT** as he makes an appearance as the musical guest on *The Late Show With David Letterman* on July 18. In addition, **ROBERT PLANT** will begin select solo dates July 20 in Chippewa Falls, Wisconsin and a tour with The Who which kicks off July 26th in Boston at the Tweeter Center.

For Further information contact:
Jay Wilson
Director of Media Relations
Universal Records
212-373-0684
jay.wilson@umusic.com.

1755 BROADWAY, NEW YORK, NY 10019 TEL 212.373.0697 WWW.UNIVERSALRECORDS.COM

ROBERT PLANT

Slipping themselves into the middle of the bill at one of Roger Daltrey's Teenage Cancer Trust shows at the Albert Hall early in 2002, Robert Plant and his new band Strange Sensation offered a tantalising glimpse of the music they'd been working up for Plant's new album, <u>Dreamland</u>. Demonstrating that classic music can always breed fresh possibilities, they resurrected a selection of vintage folk, blues and psychedelic songs, then peeled them open and rebuilt them using Middle Eastern scales, Asian drones and hard rock. Plant, the tumble-haired icon from the Led Zeppelin years, stood at the centre of this eclectic dust-storm like a magician exerting mysterious control over the elements.

"You can probably hear the great future for this band lurking on the fade-outs of the tracks," he says, referring to the 10 pieces he has assembled for the new album. "For instance, the kind of improvisation at the end of Bukka White's "Funny In My Mind (I Believe I'm Fixin' To Die)", is the kind of playing you will experience in a full hour-and-30-minute show. There is a good communion of souls, there's a lot of great guitar-filigree going on, not on a blues base but in that kind of Indo-raga style of playing, somewhere between John Fahey, The Flaming Lips and The Electric Prunes."

Echoes of The Cure can be attributed to former Cure guitarist Porl Thompson, who first signed on with Plant in 1995 when Robert joined up with Jimmy Page for the No Quarter tour. That project may have helped to inspire the music Strange Sensation are currently making, since it involved Plant and Page satisfying their fans' insatiable yearnings to hear the Zeppelin catalogue again, yet in an evolved, expanded form which fired the imagination of musicians reluctant merely to repeat their past.

"It was a major moment for me, the No Quarter project," Plant recalls, "because it was incredibly stimulating and so moving, and we were able to reinvent the past without it being a creative millstone.

Plant has never lost the urge to keep exploring. He takes the view that his past achievements will always be there for anyone who wants to check them out, so now he might as well exploit the freedom his successes now afford him. He doesn't mind ripping everything up and starting again. "My music has got to be an honest reflection of where I'm coming from today."

Since the demise of Led Zeppelin in 1980, he has released a sequence of solo albums which have been frequently impressive and always interesting, not least 1990's Manic Nirvana or 1993's absorbing Fate Of Nations. His plan is for a more spontaneous, improvisatory approach. He had to find musicians who understood where he was coming from, yet also willing to pick up the ball and run with it to destinations nobody could possibly predict. The sprinkling of original pieces on the new album are credited to "Robert Plant and band", reflecting the power-sharing nature of the relationship.

In addition to Thompson and his long-serving ally Charlie Jones on bass, he recruited drummer Clive Deamer (who has run the gamut from Roni Size and Portishead to Jeff Beck and Dr John), keyboards player and string arranger John Baggott (an Emmy-winning soundtrack composer who has also put in stints with Portishead, Massive Attack and Tom Jones), and guitarist Justin Adams, whose own band The Wayward Sheikhs draws from African and blues sources – the perfect training ground for a stint with the inquisitive Plant.

"Justin takes away any chance of it being just rock for rock's sake," Plant enthuses. There's a family history of connections with the Middle East and North Africa. He plays the ghimbri on "Hey Joe" on the album, it's a three-stringed instrument which changes the whole mood and Justin knows how to play it as it's supposed to be played."

1755 BROADWAY, NEW YORK, NY 10019   TEL 212.373.0697   WWW.UNIVERSALRECORDS.COM

As for the choice of material, Plant's love of the blues has always been matched by his enthusiasm for Sixties folk-rock and the multi-coloured experimentation that was seething through the American West Coast during the psychedelic era. It was a time when an entire youth culture was up for grabs, and anything seemed possible. "You'd get amazing bills in those days," he remembers. "You'd get Pacific Gas And Electric, It's A Beautiful Day, Jefferson Airplane, Led Zeppelin, John Lee Hooker and Jerry Lee Lewis for a day. People were just lying there on the floor and we were a bit of background noise for their state of mind."

Arthur Lee and Love, Tim Buckley, Jimi Hendrix, Moby Grape, Neil Young and Crosby Stills & Nash have been part of Robert's musical landscape for 30-odd years, although you wouldn't necessarily be able to tell that from listening to the Zeppelin catalogue. However "maybe you can hear a little of it in "Down By The Seaside" or "Going To California", or "That's The Way."

For this new project, the challenge was to capture the music's original spirit and build something fresh and unexpected from it. Plant eased himself into the process gradually. Before Strange Sensation took shape, he tried out potential material with the enigmatically-named Priory of Brion. This was a band he put together with his old mate Kevyn Gammond, with whom he'd played in the Midlands-based Band Of Joy alongside drummer John Bonham in the pre-Zeppelin era. On their own magical mystery tour which took them from Tromso in Norway to the balmy air of Sardinia, they experimented with a wide range of material, from Donovan's "Season Of The Witch" to Love's "A House Is Not A Motel", Dylan's "Girl From The North Country" to Neil Young's "Southern Man."

Plant wanted to avoid huge gigs and superstar expectations. "I just wanted to take it easy. With no pressure, no road crew to speak of – and just kick back a bit and sing those songs while I could still sing."

By the time he'd assembled Strange Sensation for some American dates last year, the picture was becoming clear. US critics noted the way Plant might "engage guitarist Porl Thompson...in an Arabic-inflected duel of descending scales" on "Morning Dew", or deliver "Hey Joe" in "a dramatic funereal reading, thick with spacey electronic sounds." Somebody coined the term "cosmic jukebox" to describe their music, which Robert found pleasingly apt.

Years ago Plant first met folk singer Tim Rose, co-author of "Morning Dew", back in the Band Of Joy days, but his new version of the song seems to loom out of some prehistoric mist.

Plant isn't the first artist either to cover Tim Buckley's "Song To The Siren", but in collusion with his bandmates he has stretched it into a diaphanous mirage, hovering in perfumed slow motion. Bob Dylan's "One More Cup Of Coffee" sounds like an Old Testament lament, Plant wearily moaning the lyric as if he has a thousand miles of burning desert to cross while the musicians sound as if they're hallucinating in the heat.

If you're familiar with Jimi Hendrix's recording of "Hey Joe", you probably won't recognize Plant's version until you get to the part where the band hurriedly scribble in the Hendrix riff, just for reference. "Love did it before Hendrix" Plant points out (and, he might have added, so did The Byrds). But I think the version of "Hey Joe" that we do is so removed from all the other versions that it's got its own life."

And there had to be some blues, though this bunch drag Arthur Crudup's "Win My Train Fare Home" out of the gutbucket and into a laboratory where they stick electrodes in it and subject it to experiments in modal jazz and ambient swirls.

"I guess we can go anywhere we want to go," Plant ponders. "I don't know whether there's a place for me within contemporary pop culture or if there's a place for it in my head now, but I know there's an energy about this music and a style which is worth pursuing and pushing a bit more. There's a kind of musical empathy I haven't been aware of for a long time."

Nobody can predict how far Strange Sensation might travel, but the Dreamland album suggests countless possibilities for further mystic exploration.

Tune in, and catch it while you can

ROBERT PLANT OF   LED ZEPPELIN

robert plant

robert plant

ROBERT PLANT

LED WHO? Rockin' ROBERT PLANT (left) seems unperturbed by the fact that comedian EMO PHILIPS had never heard of Plant or his former band, Led Zeppelin, until the two met backstage during EMO's recent six-night SRO engagement at Caroline's. Of course, it's only a matter of time before EMO is even bigger than Led Zeppelin. Beat the rush: Hear EMO PHILIPS and E=MO^2, his new album on Epic Records, now! (Photo: Laurie Paladino)

jimmy page   robert plant
NO QUARTER

"Ever onward" was their motto in Led Zeppelin. And it still is their motto, although fourteen years have passed and solo activities have laid diversions in the road, and Led Zeppelin itself lies over the hills and far away.

Jimmy Page and Robert Plant constitute one of rock's definitive musical double-nuclei, a partnership as emblematic in its way as those other slash-sealed marriages of talent, Lennon/McCartney and Jagger/Richards. As the creative partnership at the heart of Led Zeppelin, Page/Plant re-wrote the textbook on rock's dynamic vocabulary, having set out their stall from the start by tackling, of all things, a Joan Baez song, "Babe I'm Gonna Leave You." "I wanted to play it heavy," said Page later, laying out the fundamentals of the Zep aesthetic, "but with light and shade."

From "LED ZEPPELIN" in 1969 to Zep's final opus, "IN THROUGH THE OUT DOOR," a decade later, they explored just about every avenue open to the classic four-piece rock configuration, and some that, by rights, weren't open to anyone at all. With drummer John Bonham and bassist/keyboardist John Paul Jones, they wandered the musical hinterlands of British folk, of Indian and Arab tradition, of reggae, funk, blues, rockabilly and country. They defined musical "heaviness" for all time as a dynamic value rather than as a static one; and along the way they acquired a *nonpareil* reputation for their live work and for uncompromising independence in the face of an increasingly corporatised music industry. When the irreplaceable Bonham died in 1980, there was nowhere left for Zeppelin to go but to the wind.

But double-nuclei are notoriously difficult to separate. Over the years following Zeppelin's formal split, Page involved himself in a variety of his own projects, contributed occasionally to Plant's solo records, and popped up every once in a while, Gibson in hand, to add a secondary drama to the climax of the singer's live shows. Then there was the brace of strictly ad hoc Zep "re-unions," at Live Aid in '85 and to celebrate the 40th anniversary of Atlantic Records in '88, the latter with Bonham's son Jason at the drums. But formal restoration of the partnership did not arrive until late 1993.

"I'd been wanting to work with Robert again for a long time," says Page, "and it was a long time coming. 14 years, really. And now the time was right. But we were both agreed that if we were going to do something then it had to be new; and that if were to look at the old material, then we'd have to treat it as an old picture ready for a new frame."

(more)

Resumption of full creative relations was brought into sharper focus by MTV's timely request for a Page/Plant "unplugged" performance to showcase old material in a fresh light. *Unledded*, it would be called. A companion album, which would come to be dubbed "NO QUARTER," was slated for release by Atlantic Records.

Work on the project began early in 1994 in London's King's Cross. And old affinities found instant renewal. "We said, 'hey, let's try this,'" says Plant, "'and see how it goes.' And we found that the communion was perhaps a little more fluent now even than it was way-back-when. We found that we arrived at decisions very quickly, without much pussyfooting around... but there was never any question of us just rolling out the old barrel. It had to be new. We *had* to use our imaginations. I mean, what would be the point of us producing a middle-aged sigh of relief from round the coffee table?"

One crucial stimulus to the collective imagination arrived in the shape of prepared tape-loops of African drum patterns, sent to the duo from Paris by musical acquaintance Martin Meissonnier. The tender new "Wonderful One" is a direct product of those transactions. Then there was the partnership's abiding fascination with all things Arabic, which Zeppelin had previously addressed in songs like "Kashmir" yet never quite resolved to their absolute satisfaction.

Here was a landscape that begged deeper exploration. "Kashmir," after all, told the story of a journey made by Plant across the southern deserts of Morocco on a road without apparent end... "And by last year," he says, "I was completely obsessed with Morocco, and with the potential of working alongside another culture and another musical sensitivity." So in the spring, Page and Plant went back to Morocco and played in the central square of Marrakesh with the gnaoui.

The gnaoui, as far as can be told, are the descendants of black Africans brought to the region as slaves by migratory Arabs. The writer Paul Bowles has described them as a people who now "have both a therapeutic and propitiatory function" in Moroccan society, which they serve in practical terms with music: a hypnotic, incantatory music sung and played on plucked string instruments, cymbals, and drums in long, looping, endlessly climactic riffs, swells, and cross-currents. Page and Plant were in their element.

"Morocco is a living, pulsating entity which is changing rapidly all the time," enthuses Plant. "But there are parts of Marrakesh that carry on as they have done for a thousand years. And the music is a reflection of all of that, of all times and all religions, and of all the natural expectations and conditions of the people who live there. It's amazing, it's pumping, it's furious, it's anxious, it's happy, and it's far more real than anything you'll ever experience in a western city."

(more)

Three new songs came out of the time spent in Marrakesh: "City Don't Cry," "Yallah," and "Wah Wah." Also from the Moroccan trip came the inspiration to set familiar Zeppelin material within an Arabic frame. Robert and Jimmy quartered their back catalogue for songs that would lend themselves to penetration by Arab drums, auds, nays, and fiddles. They also considered other options.

Like Wales, for instance, the home of so much of their own past. So off they went to the misty mountains, with Robert's rhythm section from the "Fate Of Nations" tour — Charlie Jones (bass, percussion) and Michael Lee (drums, percussion) — plus ex-Cure man Porl Thompson (guitar, banjo), Jim Sutherland (bodhran, mandolin), and Nigel Eaton (hurdy-gurdy). Once again expectations were exceeded, as a new, and newly lustrous, northern light was cast on those elements of the Zep canon that evince British folk connections.

Then it was time to bring it on home to a live audience at London Studios on the South Bank — two consecutive late-August nights when Page, Plant, and company conflated a history of variants into a coherent whole: old with new, acoustic with electric, English string orchestra with Arab drum ensemble, European folk instrumentation with the ghazali vocals of Najma Akhtar, Egyptian violins with English brass, east with west, north with south, Page, at last, with Plant. In less than a year, they had arrived at the first way-station on a new itinerary. And so the journey goes. Ever onward.

9/94

Jimmy Page & Robert Plant (Unledded) debuts October 12th on MTV

"NO QUARTER — JIMMY PAGE & ROBERT PLANT"
will be released by Atlantic Records on November 8th

Atlantic Recording Corporation
75 Rockefeller Plaza New York, NY 10019 212/275.2020 Fax: 247.2303
9229 Sunset Blvd Los Angeles, CA 90069 310/205.7450 Fax: 205.7475

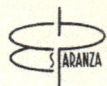

robert plant

For over a dozen years now, Robert Plant has occupied a singular role in modern music. That unmistakable voice and that charismatic presence - combined with music of undeniable creativity and energy - have placed Robert in a category wholly his own. In the eyes of many, he has created a standard against which others are judged. Now, in the 1980's, Robert Plant is revising that standard once again, as he embarks on a new phase of his remarkable musical life.

Over the past two years, Robert has recorded and released his first two solo albums - "PICTURES AT ELEVEN" and "THE PRINCIPLE OF MOMENTS." Both have offered state-of-the-art rock that is inventive, captivating, and often unexpected in its diversity of sounds and moods. Most importantly, they have clearly established that Robert is eager to move forward, to make new music for a new time.

Robert Anthony Plant was born on August 20, 1948 in Bromwich, Staffordshire, England. The son of a Birmingham civil engineer, he may very well have become a chartered accountant if it hadn't been for the lure of the blues. By the mid-60's, Plant was immersed in the Birmingham music scene, singing in a string of bands, among them The Delta Blues Band, The New Memphis Bluesbreakers, The Black Snake Moan, The Banned, and The Crawling King Snakes.

In 1966, Robert was asked to join The Tennessee Teens who, after changing their name to Listen, released a single entitled "You Better Run." At the age of 18, Robert cut two solo singles, "Our Song" and "Long Time Coming," which were issued through CBS and have long since become rare collector's items. Most notable among his early associations was the group known as the Band of Joy (which also included drummer John Bonham). When that group split up, Plant sang with a unit called Hobbstweedle and also worked briefly with Alexis Korner, the legendary "founding father" of the British Blues Movement.

In 1968, upon the recommendation of vocalist Terry Reid, guitarist Jimmy Page invited Robert Plant to be part of a new group he was putting together. Page, Plant, John Paul Jones and John Bonham first converged in a small London rehearsal hall, initially calling themselves The New Yardbirds (after Page's previous group). The chemistry was immediate and perfect. By the end of the year, they had changed their name to Led Zeppelin, recording their classic self-titled debut album in just 15 hours. Released by Atlantic Records in January 1969, that LP quickly established Led Zeppelin as a ground-breaking new force in rock.

(cont'd)

9229 SUNSET BOULEVARD, LOS ANGELES, CALIFORNIA 90069

Between 1969 and 1980, Led Zeppelin released nine multi-million-selling albums (a tenth LP, "CODA," was released posthumously in November 1982). They played a series of record-shattering global tours, reigning as the #1 band in the world. In the course of the decade, the group drew on a remarkable variety of musical ideas, refusing to limit their creativity. As their entry in the Illustrated Encyclopedia of Rock stated: "There is no more exhilarating experience in rock than Plant and Page pushing their considerable talents towards the dizzying outer limits of the genre they more or less created."

Robert's post-Zeppelin solo career grew out of his involvement with a group dubbed The Honeydrippers, basically a collection of local musicians who got together to play the blues. In early 1981, Robert made a number of low-key club appearances with the band, in a very real sense getting back to his roots. Before long, Plant had developed a close working relationship with guitarist Robbie Blunt, and eventually the pair decided to direct their energies towards a more serious venture. By September 1981, Robert & co. had started work on an album at Rockfield Studios in Wales.

In June of 1982, Robert Plant released his debut solo album, "PICTURES AT ELEVEN." It was an album of firsts. Foremost, it was the premiere full-scale recording of Robert Plant on his own, while marking his first studio work in three years. It was his first outing as a producer, as well as the first LP of Plant compositions to be performed outside Led Zeppelin. "PICTURES AT ELEVEN" also introduced Plant's new band: Robbie Blunt, bassist Paul Martinez, and keyboardist Jezz Woodroffe. Drumming support was provided primarily by star stickman Phil Collins (of Genesis and solo fame), with Cozy Powell also sitting in.

A worldwide success, "PICTURES AT ELEVEN" was a triumphant return to active duty from a master of the form. Quite understandably, many predicted that Plant's return to the stage was imminent. Robert, however, remained adamant that he wanted to make another album before going out on the road. For one thing, he felt it was absolutely essential that he have enough new material for a true solo Robert Plant concert. But beyond that, he also felt that his new music should continue to develop.

Precisely one year after the release of "PICTURES AT ELEVEN," Robert returned with his eagerly-anticipated second solo effort, "THE PRINCIPLE OF MOMENTS," the first album to be released on Plant's own Es Paranza label (distributed by Atlantic Records). As before, all the songs were penned by Robert in collaboration with the members of his band - Messrs. Blunt, Martinez & Woodroffe. Phil Collins was once again invited to handle the drum duties, with ex-Jethro Tull percussion ace Barriemore Barlow playing on two tracks. Very much an album of contrasts, "THE PRINCIPLE OF MOMENTS" brilliantly demonstrates Robert's continual exploration of new musical/lyrical ground, solidly confirming his success in establishing a fresh musical identity.

In late-August of 1983, Robert Plant embarked on his premiere concert tour as a solo artist, marking his eagerly-awaited return to stages

(cont'd)

around the world. The itinerary began with a triumphant six-week trek across North America, which garnered rave reviews from fans and critics alike. As the Chicago Sun Times noted of the tour's opening show, "From the high spirits throughout the crowd, it was obvious that Plant remains as much beloved on his own as he was with Zeppelin. No one I've seen on tour over the past year drew such a consistently excited response."

Just as Plant's solo albums have shown a steadfast refusal to re-hash the past, so his first solo tour further reveals new aspects of Robert's musical life. In fact, he holds firm to his decision not to perform any Zeppelin numbers, commenting: "I don't think it would be fair to anybody that I'm playing with now if they had to go through the motions of something that they hadn't been responsible for recording in the first place, and, more so, hadn't been responsible for writing." Meanwhile, "THE PRINCIPLE OF MOMENTS" has been topping charts around the world, offering further proof of Robert's full emergence as an artist in his own right.

It is remarkably refreshing, though not really surprising, that Robert has no intention of living off earlier glories. He has too much respect for the past, and much more interest in the present and the future. Plant's life has been a continual cycle of birth and re-birth. With two new albums under his belt, and his return to live performances, it is clear that an exciting new cycle has begun. As he says, "I'm finally coming to terms with a new role in a new game."

1183

robert plant

The Led Zep Scrapbook Volume One

robert plant

There is still such a thing as alternative Publishing

Robert Newton Calvert: Born 9 March 1945, Died 14 August 1988 after suffering a heart attack. Contributed poetry, lyrics and vocals to legendary space rock band Hawkwind intermittently on five of their most critically acclaimed albums, including Space Ritual (1973), Quark, Strangeness & Charm (1977) and Hawklords (1978). He also recorded a number of solo albums in the mid 1970s. CENTIGRADE 232 was Robert Calvert's first collection of poems.

Hype 'And now, for all you speeding street smarties out there, the one you've all been waiting for, the one that'll pierce your laid back ears, decoke your sinuses, cut clean thru the schlock rock, MOR/crossover, techno flash mind mush. It's the new Number One with a bullet ... with a bullet ... It's Tom, Supernova, Mahler with a pan galactic biggie ...' And the Hype goes on. And on. Hype, an amphetamine hit of a story by Hawkwind collaborator Robert Calvert. Who's been there and made it back again. The debriefing session starts here.

Rick Wakeman is the world's most unusual rock star, a genius who has pushed back the barriers of electronic rock. He has had some of the world's top orchestras perform his music, has owned eight Rolls Royces at one time, and has broken all the rules of composing and horrified his tutors at the Royal College of Music. Yet he has delighted his millions of fans. This frank book, authorised by Wakeman himself, tells the moving tale of his larger than life career.

There are nine Henrys, purported to be the world's first cloned cartoon character. They live in a strange lo fi domestic surrealist world peopled by talking rock buns and elephants on wobbly stilts.

They mooch around in their minimalist universe suffering from an existential crisis with some genetically modified humour thrown in.

Marty Wilde on Terry Dene: "Whatever happened to Terry becomes a great deal more comprehensible as you read of the callous way in which he was treated by people who should have known better many of whom, frankly, will never know better of the sad little shadows of the past who eased themselves into Terry's life, took everything they could get and, when it seemed that all was lost, quietly left him ... Dan Wooding's book tells it all."

Rick Wakeman: "There have always been certain 'careers' that have fascinated the public, newspapers, and the media in general. Such include musicians, actors, sportsmen, police, and not surprisingly, the people who give the police their employment: The criminal. For the man in the street, all these careers have one thing in common: they are seemingly beyond both his reach and, in many cases, understanding and as such, his only association can be through the media of newspapers or television. The police, however, will always require the services of the grass, the squealer, the snitch, (call him what you will), in order to assist in their investigations and arrests; and amazingly, this is the area that seldom gets written about."

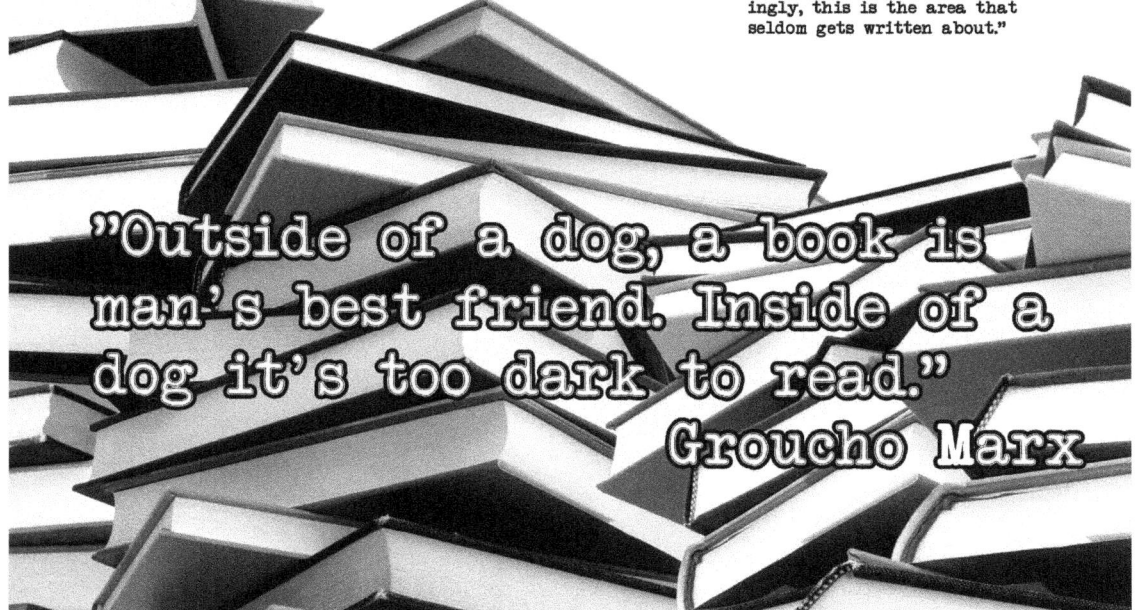

"Outside of a dog, a book is man's best friend. Inside of a dog it's too dark to read." Groucho Marx

Bill Harkleroad joined Captain Beefheart's Magic Band at a time when they were changing from a straight ahead blues band into something completely different. Through the vision of Don Van Vliet (Captain Beefheart) they created a new form of music which many at the time considered atonal and difficult, but which over the years has continued to exert a powerful influence. Beefheart rechristened Harkleroad as Zoot Horn Rollo, and they embarked on recording one of the classic rock albums of all time Trout Mask Replica - a work of unequalled daring and inventiveness.

Politics, paganism and .... Vlad the Impaler. Selected stories from CJ Stone from 2003 to the present. Meet Ivor Coles, a British Tommy killed in action in September 1915, lost, and then found again. Visit Mothers Club in Erdington, the best psychedelic music club in the UK in the '60s. Celebrate Robin Hood's Day and find out what a huckle duckle is. Travel to Stonehenge at the Summer Solstice and carouse with the hippies. Find out what a Ranter is, and why CJ Stone thinks that he's one. Take LSD with Dr Lilly, the psychedelic scientist. Meet a headless soldier or the ghost of Elvis Presley in Gabalfa, Cardiff. Journey to Whitstable, to New York, to Malta and to Transylvania, and to many other places, real and imagined, political and spiritual, transcendent and mundane. As The Independent says, Chris is "The best guide to the underground since Charon ferried dead souls across the Styx."

This is is the first in the highly acclaimed vampire novels of the late Mick Farren. Victor Renquist, a surprisingly urbane and likable leader of a colony of vampires which has existed for centuries in New York is faced with both administrative and emotional problems. And when you are a vampire, administration is not a thing which one takes lightly.

"The person, be it gentleman or lady, who has not pleasure in a good novel, must be intolerably stupid."

Jane Austen

Los Angeles City of Angels, city of dreams. But sometimes the dreams become nightmares. Having fled New York, Victor Renquist and his small group of Nosferatu are striving to re establish their colony. They have become a deeper, darker part of the city's nightlife. And Hollywood's glitterati are hot on the scent of a new thrill, one that outshines all others immortality. But someone, somewhere, is meddling with even darker powers, powers that even the Nosferatu fear. Someone is attempting to summon the entity of ancient evil known as Cthulhu. And Renquist must overcome dissent in his own colony, solve the riddle of the Darklost (a being brought part way along the Nosferatu path and then abandoned) and combat powerful enemies to save the world of humans!

Canadian born Corky Laing is probably best known as the drummer with Mountain. Corky joined the band shortly after Mountain played at the famous Woodstock Festival, although he did receive a gold disc for sales of the soundtrack album after over dubbing drums on Ten Years After's performance. Whilst with Mountain Corky Laing recorded three studio albums with them before the band split. Following the split Corky, along with Mountain guitarist Leslie West, formed a rock three piece with former Cream bassist Jack Bruce. West, Bruce and Laing recorded two studio albums and a live album before West and Laing re formed Mountain, along with Felix Pappalardi. Since 1974 Corky and Leslie have led Mountain through various line ups and recordings, and continue to record and perform today at numerous concerts across the world. In addition to his work with Mountain, Corky Laing has recorded one solo album and formed the band Cork with former Spin Doctors guitarist Eric Shenkman, and recorded a further two studio albums with the band, which has also featured former Jimi Hendrix bassist Noel Redding. The stories are told in an incredibly frank, engaging and amusing manner, and will appeal also to those people who may not necessarily be fans of

To me there's no difference between Mike Scott and The Waterboys; they both mean the same thing. They mean myself and whoever are my current travelling musical companions." Mike Scott Strange Boat charts the twisting and meandering journey of Mike Scott, describing the literary and spiritual references that inform his songwriting and exploring the multitude of locations and cultures in which The Waterboys have assembled and reflected in their recordings. From his early forays into the music scene in Scotland at the end of the 1970s, to his creation of a 'Big Music' that peaked with the hit single 'The Whole of the Moon' and onto the Irish adventure which spawned the classic Fisherman's Blues, his constantly restless creativity has led him through a myriad of changes. With his revolving cast of troubadours at his side, he's created some of the most era defining records of the 1980s, reeled and jigged across the Celtic heartlands, reinvented himself as an electric rocker in New York, and sought out personal renewal in the spiritual calm of Findhorn's Scottish highland retreat. Mike Scott's life has been a tale of continual musical exploration entwined with an ever evolving spirituality. "An intriguing portrait of a modern musician" (Record Collector).

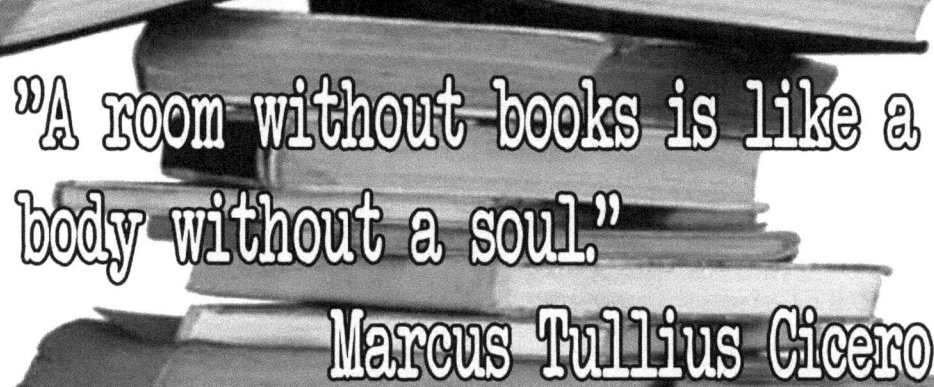

"A room without books is like a body without a soul."
Marcus Tullius Cicero

The OZ trial was the longest obscenity trial in history. It was also one of the worst reported. With minor exceptions, the Press chose to rewrite what had occurred, presumably to fit in with what seemed to them the acceptable prejudices of the times. Perhaps this was inevitable. The proceedings dragged on for nearly six weeks in the hot summer of 1971 when there were, no doubt, a great many other events more worthy of attention. Against the background of murder in Ulster, for example, the OZ affair probably fades into its proper insignificance. Even so, after the trial, when some newspapers realised that maybe something important had happened, it became more and more apparent that what was essential was for anyone who wished to be able to read what had actually been said. Trial and judgment by a badly informed press became the order of the day. This 40th Anniversary edition includes new material by all three of the original defendants, the prosecuting barrister, one of the OZ schoolkids, and even the daughters of the judge. There are also many illustrations including unseen material from Felix Dennis' own collection...

Merrell Fankhauser has led one of the most diverse and interesting careers in music. He was born in Louisville, Kentucky, and moved to California when he was 13 years old. Merrell went on to become one of the innovators of surf music and psychedelic folk rock. His travels from Hollywood to his 15 year jungle experience on the island of Maui have been documented in numerous music books and magazines in the United States and Europe. Merrell has gained legendary international status throughout the field of rock music; his credits include over 250 songs published and released. He is a multi talented singer/songwriter and unique guitar player whose sound has delighted listeners for over 35 years. This extraordinary book tells a unique story of one of the founding fathers of surf rock, who went on to play in a succession of progressive and psychedelic bands and to meet some of the greatest names in the business, including Captain Beefheart, Randy California, The Beach Boys, Jan and Dean... and there is even a run in with the notorious Manson family.

On September 19, 1985, Frank Zappa testified before the United States Senate Commerce, Technology, and Transportation committee, attacking the Parents Music Resource Center or PMRC, a music organization co founded by Tipper Gore, wife of then senator Al Gore. The PMRC consisted of many wives of politicians, including the wives of five members of the committee, and was founded to address the issue of song lyrics with sexual or satanic content. Zappa saw their activities as on a path towards censorship,and called their proposal for voluntary labelling of records with explicit content "extortion" of the music industry. This is what happened.

> "Good friends, good books, and a sleepy conscience: this is the ideal life."
> Mark Twain

An erudite catalogue of some of the most peculiar records ever made. We have lined up, described and put into context 500 "albums" in the expectation that those of you who can't help yourselves when it comes to finding and collecting music will benefit from these efforts in two ways. Firstly, you'll know you are not alone. Secondly, we hope that some of the work covering the following pages leads you to new discoveries, and makes your life slightly better as a result.

Roy Weard was born in Barking, then a part of Essex, in 1948. He spent most of the mid-sixties through to the mid seventies involved first in folk music and then in the psychedelic hippie scene. He toured with many bands in various capacities from T-Shirt seller to sound engineer, production manager and tour manager. He was involved in several bands of his own, played at many of the iconic free festivals, made three full length albums and two singles, wrote for music magazines, computer magazines and produced copious MySpace blogs. He has lived all over London, spent four years in Hamburg, Germany and finally settled in Brighton where he now resides. He still sings in a rock and roll band, promotes gigs, does a weekly radio show and steadfastly refuses to act his age. This is his story.

Michael Ronald Taylor (1938 - 1969) was a British jazz composer, pianist and co-songwriter for the band Cream.

Mike Taylor drowned in the River Thames near Leigh-on-Sea, Essex in January 1969, following years of heavy drug use (principally hashish and LSD). He had been homeless for three years, and his death was almost entirely unremarked. This is the first biography written about him.

www.ingramcontent.com/pod-product-compliance
Lightning Source LLC
Chambersburg PA
CBHW060923170426
43192CB00021B/2853